America's Religious History offers a comprehensive account of the history we must know in order to understand our present and pave a better way forward. The book is remarkable in its breadth and depth, in its precision and scholarship, and in its sheer readability. Thomas Kidd is a great gift to the contemporary American church, and this book demonstrates why.

—KAREN SWALLOW PRIOR, author of *On Reading Well* and *Fierce Convictions: The Extraordinary Life of Hannah More—Poet, Reformer, Abolitionist*

Thomas Kidd is an authoritative voice on American religion. Not only is he today's most prolific historian of American religious history, but he is an active commentator on social media who brings his expertise to bear on issues that matter. In this book, he joins his academic expertise with his acute insight into the present-day religious landscape. The result is an outstanding history of American religion that should be of interest to academics, ministers, and anyone else who wishes to understand the deeply significant influence of religion in the United States.

—JAMES P. BYRD, chair of the Graduate Department of Religion, associate professor of American religious history, Vanderbilt University

Kidd's learned entry into the crowded field of American religious textbooks offers a fresh perspective on a complex story. Ranging from European incursions into an already well-established Native civilization to the clashes that the Trump has engendered, his narrative shows the continual entwining of sacred and secular, calming and violent, dominant and resistant, private and public, and pious and irreligious. General readers will find an account as simple as it is lively, while specialists will find one marked by nuance and insight. And it is all executed with the graceful strokes of a master craftsman.

—GRANT WACKER, Gilbert T. Rowe Professor Emeritus of Christian History, Duke Divinity School, author of *One Soul at a Time: The Story of Billy Graham*

In this survey, Thomas Kidd provides a rich and complex survey of American Christianity, featuring a wonderful diversity of characters and actors, and he does so for both a general audience and for students. It is particularly strong for including sources on Latino Catholicism and Protestantism, a topic often ignored in textbooks. He incorporates the best of modern scholarship in a language accessible to all.

—PAUL HARVEY, professor and presidential teaching scholar, Department of History, University of Colorado

Thomas Kidd's brisk narrative of America's religious story brings together a variety of historical strands to create a highly readable, engaging introduction to the many traditions that constitute our contemporary landscape. Kidd's deep knowledge of his subject sharpens his eye for both underexamined but important episodes and significant historical trends. He has created a lively, rich account that will appeal to a wide audience. His excellent suggestions for further reading will satisfy readers wanting to dig more deeply.

—ANNE BLUE WILLS, professor of religious studies, Davidson College

AMERICA'S *RELIGIOUS* HISTORY

FAITH, POLITICS, AND THE
SHAPING *of a* NATION

THOMAS S. KIDD

ZONDERVAN
ACADEMIC

ZONDERVAN ACADEMIC

America's Religious History
Copyright © 2019 by Thomas S. Kidd

ISBN 978-0-310-58617-3 (hardcover)

ISBN 978-0-310-58620-3 (audio)

ISBN 978-0-310-58618-0 (ebook)

Requests for information should be addressed to:
Zondervan, *3900 Sparks Dr. SE, Grand Rapids, Michigan 49546*

Published in association with Giles Anderson and Anderson Literary Agency.

Cover design: Studio Gearbox
Cover image: William Vandivert / Getty Images
Interior design: Kait Lamphere

Printed in the United States of America

19 20 21 22 23 24 25 26 27 /LSC/ 15 14 13 12 11 10 9 8 7 6 5 4 3 2 1

To Barry Hankins

CONTENTS

Introduction 9

1. Religion in Early America 13
2. Reviving American Faith. 32
3. Religion and the American Revolution 51
4. The Era of the Second Great Awakening 70
5. Global and Domestic Missions 92
6. Slave Religion and Manifest Destiny. 111
7. The Slavery Controversy and the Civil War 130
8. Immigration and Religious Diversity. 150
9. Evolution, Biblical Criticism, and Fundamentalism. . .170
10. The Religious Challenges of the World Wars 188
11. Civil Religion and the Cold War 207
12. Civil Rights and Church-State Controversy 229
13. The Christian Right and the Changing Face
    of American Religion. 248
14. Immigration, Religious Diversity, and the
    Culture Wars. 268

Epilogue: American Religion in the Twenty-First Century. . 285
Index 297

INTRODUCTION

The story of American religion is a study in contrasts. Secular clashes with the sacred; demagoguery with devotion. Perhaps most conspicuously, religious vitality in America has existed alongside religious violence. To cite just one example, in 1782, during the latter years of the Revolutionary War, an American militia in the Ohio territory attacked Moravian mission stations in Native American communities along the Muskingum River. The Moravians were the first Protestant Christian group to establish mission stations throughout the broad Atlantic world. The Moravian Delaware Indians were pacifists, having embraced the German-background Moravian missionaries and their teachings about Jesus, the Prince of Peace. The interethnic mission station attracted unwanted attention from many of its neighbors. The Delaware converts sought to allay the suspicions of hostile forces surrounding them—including non-Christian Indians, American Patriots, and British authorities—by employing Christian charity and sharing what food they had with their neighbors, even in times of scarcity. American militiamen, however, were certain that the Moravian station at Gnadenhütten ("tents of grace") was a staging ground for Indian attacks on frontier settlers and that white war captives had at least passed through the village, if they weren't actually languishing there. Driven by genocidal rage against all Indians, Christians or otherwise, the white volunteers imprisoned and methodically murdered almost a hundred Moravian Delaware men, women, and children around Gnadenhütten, even as the doomed converts were reportedly "praying, singing, and kissing."

The stage was set for the Gnadenhütten massacre by a convergence of white Americans' hatred for Indians, the violence of the American Revolution, and the earnest missionary labors of the Moravians. Not all religious violence in American history has been as grotesque as that at Gnadenhütten. Sometimes the violence has taken rhetorical, legal, or other forms (what we would generically call religious "conflict"). We should not imagine that such religious fervor and viciousness is only part of a distant colonial American past. Indeed, episodes of religiously tinged mass murder have seemingly become more common in the years since the September 11, 2001, jihadist attacks in New York and Washington, DC. Mass shootings have become almost a routine feature of American life, and they often target places of worship. These include shootings at congregations such as the Sikh temple in Oak Creek, Wisconsin (2012), the First Baptist Church of Sutherland Springs, Texas (2017), and the Tree of Life Synagogue in Pittsburgh (2018). The shooting at the Emanuel African Methodist Episcopal Church in Charleston, South Carolina, in 2015 was unusual only in the sense that the congregation had endured a similar paroxysm of violence almost two centuries earlier when an alleged slave rebellion led by Denmark Vesey led to the execution of dozens of African American Charlestonians and the burning of the church building.

Religion has been a source of hope for many Americans and a focus of hate for others. The vitality of faith has endured, even in the face of murderous animosity, especially toward religious and ethnic minorities. Episodes of religious violence, from the Salem witchcraft controversy of 1692 to today's mass shootings, always receive disproportionate coverage from the media and from historians like me. What scholars call "lived religion"—the weekly rituals of prayer, reading of scripture, and going to services—rarely receives as much notice. We should not forget that it is in those habits of lived religion that most devout Americans find their reasons *to be religious*, as they pursue forgiveness, peace, guidance, and assurance for today and for the next life.

A book on American religious history can't give adequate coverage to all possible topics. Although I do touch briefly on Islam, Buddhism, and other religions, this book focuses on the history of Christianity in America. And while Catholics receive more coverage than adherents of non-Christian religions, the book is especially concerned with the fate of Protestantism in America. The Protestant way has been the most powerful religious strain in America since the founding of the British colonies beginning in the early 1600s. As we shall see, American Christianity has come under unprecedented pressure in recent decades, and that pressure has led to vitriolic controversies and major declines in some segments of Protestantism and Catholicism. Vitality is not a universal characteristic of American religion, of course. Yet forecasts of Christianity's doom in America seem premature, and the global future of Christianity seems bright indeed, at least in a numerical sense. In spite of the attention I give to Christianity, I attempt to make my narrative much more than a retelling of the careers of educated white male Protestant clergy and politicians. I seek to account for the remarkable diversity in American religion, a diversity that has only escalated since transformative changes in American immigration beginning in 1965. Vital commitment, ethnic diversity, and harsh conflict are the essential narrative threads in American religious history. They will surely be the primary stories in American religion in the coming decades too.

Chapter 1

RELIGION IN
EARLY AMERICA

Most of early America's colonizing powers wanted to bring the Christian gospel to the native peoples of North America. Sometimes they did so, but too often the colonizers' evangelistic overtures were paired with the threat of imperial coercion. The seal of the Massachusetts Bay Company featured a Native American man with a banner coming out of his mouth declaring "Come over and help us." This was a reference to Paul's vision of an imploring "man of Macedonia" in Acts 16:9, a verse that helped the founders of Massachusetts to see their colonizing enterprise as evangelistic to the core. Even before significant missionary work got under way, however, New Englanders were already fighting with Indians, most notably in the Pequot War of 1636–38, which saw the near extinction of the Pequot as a tribe. Far from a sign of salvation, the coming of Europeans seemed to many Native Americans to be an existential threat.

Once evangelistic work did begin in the colonies, some Native Americans under English, French, or Spanish rule committed themselves to Christian faith and to religious practice in a European style. Some internalized the precepts of Christian doctrine. On Martha's Vineyard off the Massachusetts coast, Wampanoag Indians peppered English missionaries with theological inquiries. "How many sorts of sinners are there in the world? . . . How many sorts of faith are there? . . . What are the keys of the kingdom of heaven?" The celebrated English missionary John Eliot helped to ordain a Wampanoag man named Hiacoomes as a pastor in 1670. Hiacoomes was the first ordained Indian pastor in colonial America, and one of a cadre of native leaders in the Indians' churches.

Not all was well between the colonizers and the Indians, however. Anger over killings, trade, and land claims in New England led to King Philip's War in 1675–76. Led by the Wampanoag sachem "King Philip" (Metacom), allied Indians destroyed more than a quarter of New England's settlements. New Englanders responded with retaliatory ravages against the Indians, including against many of the "praying Indians" whom they thought had converted to Christianity.

Mary Rowlandson, who chronicled the horrors of her captivity among the forces of King Philip, reserved special contempt for the praying Indians allied with Metacom. She claimed to have witnessed one turncoat Christian Indian, "so wicked and cruel, as to wear a string about his neck, strung with Christians' fingers." The early European colonies generally expressed godly ambitions for the new societies, but those ideals often crumbled as the realities of colonization set in. In early America, Indians, Europeans, and Africans (who typically came to the Americas as slaves) had different languages, cultures, and religious systems. Those differences, combined with the imperial aims of the Europeans, made violence likely in these early encounters. Conflict was more likely than any successful evangelization of colonized, conquered, and enslaved people. Nevertheless, Christianity took root among small groups of Christian Indians and African Americans, a development which would have enduring significance for the shape of American religion.

Christopher Columbus's voyages from Europe to the Americas signaled the beginning of clashes between Europeans, Africans, and Native

Americans. The result of these encounters was a distinctly Atlantic mix of cultures and religions. The exact religious beliefs and practices of early Native Americans and West Africans can be difficult to discern because of a relative lack of surviving sources documenting their faiths. Native Americans did leave archaeological evidence with traces of information about their religions. These remnants range from small stone artifacts to massive earthen mounds, often representing the shape of animals. Among the most impressive of these mounds is the earthen "bird mound," or pyramid, at Poverty Point in present-day northeastern Louisiana, in the Mississippi River floodplain. The bird mound was probably erected around 1400 BC. The uses of the bird mound are not entirely clear, but its scale is stunning. Though time and erosion have taken their toll on the mound, the seven-story hill is still a striking monument on the mostly flat landscape. It took about 238,000 cubic meters of soil to build, or about twenty-seven million large baskets of dirt. More surprisingly, excavations have suggested that the work at Poverty Point was completed in ninety days or less. This short time frame and prodigious size means that the mound builders must have used thousands of workers. It presumably went up for a specific purpose, likely ceremonial and spiritual. Some have suggested that the bird mound may have represented a red-tailed hawk. It may also have had connections to the solar calendar, as mounds elsewhere in America did.

Whatever the exact uses of the bird mound, it illustrates the way that the Native Americans' landscape was filled with spiritual significance. The particular beliefs of individual tribes varied considerably, and we should remember that there were perhaps five hundred different tribes living in the future United States when Columbus "discovered" America. However, indigenous American religions did share some common themes, such as the pervasive spirituality of their worldview. Most Native Americans saw no substantive difference between the spiritual and natural worlds. Medieval Europeans also saw the world as filled with spiritual powers, but their monotheistic convictions maintained a distinction between the things of God and the things of the world. For Indians, all living things had spiritual forces living within them, and the world of dreams was just as real as the waking world.

Most Native Americans believed that people should treat animals, including those they hunted, with respect. Europeans tended to believe that only humans had souls, but Indians saw animals as having spirits that they needed to handle with caution. The Micmacs of eastern Canada hunted beavers for fur and meat, but they had strict codes about how to treat the beavers. Menstruating women were not allowed to eat beavers, since the women were considered ceremonially unclean. When hunters butchered a trapped beaver, they tried not to spill any blood on the ground. If they mistreated the bones of a beaver, they believed that the "spirit of the bones . . . would promptly carry the news to the other beavers." This could bring bad fortune or cause the living beavers to flee the region in order to escape maltreatment.

Some Native American and African religions reserved a place for a supreme god. And there were other gods and lower spirits too. West African rituals focused on these spirits and on the people's ancestors, invoking both through special dances and music. To many Africans, lesser spirits were not necessarily good or evil, but disrespecting them invited trouble. In the Yoruba language of modern-day Nigeria, the spirits were "orishas." One way to protect against the power of the orishas was through the use of "gris-gris," or pouches containing items with magical or spiritual powers. These items could include amulets or verses of sacred scriptures, including those from the Qur'an. Some West African people in the era of the slave trade were familiar with Islam. Other West African slaves had been influenced by Catholic missionaries, prior to their forced transport to the Americas.

Medieval European Christians believed in a plethora of spiritual powers too. Yet Catholic and Protestant Christians from Europe had a clear sense of the overruling power of God the Father, and they felt that their faith compelled them to convert the non-Christians they encountered. The era of European colonization in the Americas began just a quarter-century before the Protestant Reformation started. The German monk Martin Luther inaugurated the Protestant movement in 1517, and soon tensions between Catholics and Protestants became constant themes in Europe and in the development of the American colonies. The wars of the Reformation in Europe gave extra urgency to the effort to evangelize the native people of the Caribbean (where Columbus landed) and of North and Central America. Protestants feared that the non-Christian people of the Americas would fall under Catholic sway, and vice versa. Spain and France brought thousands of Catholic priests in successive waves to the entire continent—from present-day Mexico to Canada—in order to evangelize Indians and to provide religious services for the European residents of the New World. Most of the priests were members of the Franciscan, Dominican, or Jesuit orders.

Some of these priests accepted the cruelty of colonization and even participated in it by using Indian slaves to work on plantations, but others became critics of European empire-building. Bartolomé de Las Casas was a Dominican priest who had witnessed the conquest of the islands of Hispaniola and Cuba in the early 1500s. Las Casas went on to own Indian and African slaves himself, but he soon became remorseful about the way that Spanish conquerors viciously treated the Caribbean natives. In his treatise *The Destruction of the Indies* (1552), Las Casas indicted Spanish colonizers for coming to the New World only to "dismember, slay, perturb, afflict, torment, and destroy the Indians." The writings of Las Casas and other dissident priests caught the eye of the pope and other Catholic authorities, who called for an end to the colonizers' worst abuses.

In spite of the harshness of many early encounters between the colonizers and native people, Christianity's influence did grow in the Americas. Arguably the most important development for the future of Hispanic Christianity was the reported appearance of the Virgin Mary to Juan Diego, an indigenous Mexican man, in 1531. Mary performed several miracles through Juan Diego in order to prove to a local Catholic bishop that she really had appeared. The shrine to Our Lady of Guadalupe in Mexico City became one of the most significant Catholic devotional sites in the world, and it receives millions of visits from Catholic pilgrims annually. Pope John Paul II would canonize Juan Diego as a saint in 2002. Devotional images of the Virgin of Guadalupe are ubiquitous in Mexican and Mexican-American culture today.

The Virgin of Guadalupe

The Spanish established footholds throughout New Mexico and Florida by the 1600s. In 1565 the Spanish founded Saint Augustine, the oldest permanent European settlement within the future United States. In 1607, they founded Santa Fé, New Mexico, in the northern reaches of Spain's American empire. Franciscans evangelized the Pueblo people of New Mexico. Many Pueblos affiliated with the missions, accepting Spanish protection, adopting farming, and attending Catholic services. Yet the Pueblo population of New Mexico dropped precipitously as they faced epidemic diseases, seasons of famine, and attacks from rival Indians. Pueblos who turned back to native religious practices faced retributive whippings and torture. So Pueblo resentment toward Spanish rule simmered below their apparent Catholic adherence.

The Spanish whipped one Pueblo religious leader named Popé for suspicion of sorcery in the mid-1670s. Popé retreated to Taos, New Mexico, where he said that he received revelations encouraging him to lead a revolt against the Spanish. The spirits told him that the god of the Spanish was nothing but "rotten wood" and that the traditional gods of the Pueblos would protect him. Popé became the leader of the Pueblo Revolt, the most successful Native American uprising against European colonial rule. The coordinated attacks on Spanish leaders began in August 1680. The religious character of the revolt was unmistakable, as the Pueblos killed dozens of priests and desecrated Catholic icons and chapels. At Popé's behest, his followers engaged in reverse baptisms, washing themselves in rivers with a native root to repudiate Christianity. The defeated Spanish evacuated New Mexico, only returning thirteen years later.

In the long story of Spanish colonization, Franciscan missions came fairly late to California. Father Junípero Serra was the key early leader of the California missions, establishing nine stations between 1769 and 1784. One of these was the mission at San Diego, California, in 1769. The arrival of the Spanish coincided with a devastating decline of population among California Indians, one even worse than what the Pueblos had experienced in New Mexico. Some of the dispersed California tribes simply ceased to exist, with survivors absorbed into neighboring tribes. Serra and other priests ruled over the mission Indians, sanctioning the use of harsh punishments when necessary to enforce discipline. Serra claimed that he "came here for the single purpose of doing [the Indians] good and for their eternal salvation." Many missionaries figured that the eternal rewards awaiting Indian converts would make up for whatever earthly suffering they endured. Pope Francis canonized Serra as a saint in 2015 despite protests from Native American groups who blamed him for the destruction of California's indigenous peoples.

NYPL, Public Domain

Father Junípero Serra

France had little success in establishing missions in their Caribbean colonies, among either the dwindling native populations or the legions of enslaved

Africans that came to island colonies such as Saint-Domingue (modern Haiti). French Catholic missionaries made more progress among the native peoples of Canada. Although Indian slavery in Canada was not uncommon, the French colonization of Quebec and Ontario was relatively less disruptive to native peoples than were British or Spanish colonies elsewhere. Fewer French people settled in Canada, so the colonizers were not as eager to seize native lands. Colonial Canada's economy was dominated by the fur trade. French hunters went deep into Indian territory in search of pelts and better hunting grounds. Jesuit missionaries would often accompany these fur traders and live among the Indians themselves. The Jesuits of New France made some of the most impressive efforts among the Europeans to learn native languages and study native cultures. Still, the Jesuits' incursions were fraught with danger. The Jesuits found some of their greatest successes among the Hurons of Ontario in the 1630s, but tribes affiliated with the Iroquois League overran the Huron missions in 1649. When decimating the Hurons, the Iroquois also captured several of the Jesuit missionaries and tortured them to death.

As with Juan Diego in Mexico, there were some signs of native internalization of the missionaries' message in Canada. In spite of Iroquois depredations against the Hurons and the French missionaries, by the 1660s Jesuits had founded mission stations among the five tribes comprising the Iroquois League. Among the Mohawks, the most famous convert to Catholicism was Catherine Tekakwitha. In 1676,

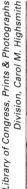

Library of Congress, Prints & Photographs Division, Carol M. Highsmith

Bronze statue of Saint Kateri Tekakwitha, Lily of the Mohawks, by artist Cynthia Hitschler, at the Shrine of Our Lady of Guadalupe in La Crosse, Wisconsin

Tekakwitha received Christian baptism from Jesuit missionaries in New York. She later relocated to a mission village in Quebec. Catherine helped organize a women's devotional group that practiced rigorous—some said harsh—forms of devotion, including ice baths and self-flagellation, as means to mortify their fleshly desires. When she died in 1680, she developed a following as a saint who could heal devotees. Tekakwitha also received formal recognition from Rome as a saint in 2012.

The English colonies in America were relative latecomers as compared to the Spanish ones in New Mexico and Florida. Some of the English colonies, such as Massachusetts and Pennsylvania, were founded for explicitly religious reasons. English people founded other colonies, such as Virginia and South Carolina, for business opportunity. Whatever the reasons for their inception, religious assumptions heavily influenced all the English colonies (as they influenced other European colonial ventures). England had broken away from the Roman Catholic Church in 1534, and Elizabeth I's long tenure as queen (1558–1603) had secured England for the Protestant cause for the foreseeable future. The English founded Virginia, their first permanent New World colony, in 1607 at Jamestown. The colonists built a church structure in 1608, which was likely the first Protestant house of worship in North America. An early Virginia leader declared that the colonists meant to tell the Indians of the "true God, and of the way to their salvation."

From the first, the Virginia colonists struggled to survive and to establish positive relations with the local Powhatan Indians. The desperate colonists imposed a system of martial law to bring order to the chaotic colony in 1611. Among the colony's regulations were threats to execute anyone who blasphemed. The Jamestown church was the scene of the marriage of John Rolfe and Pocahontas, the daughter of a Powhatan chief. Rolfe undoubtedly saw diplomatic value in the marriage, whatever his personal feelings for Pocahontas. Rolfe said that he was marrying her for the "glory of God . . . and for the converting to the true knowledge of God and Jesus Christ, an unbelieving creature, namely Pocahontas." If the marriage signaled hope for improved English-Powhatan relations, that hope collapsed in 1622. That year, the Powhatans rose up in a concerted attack to destroy the Virginia colony. After the Anglo-Powhatan War, Virginia colonists expressed doubt that the Indians could ever become real Christians.

Royal English authorities took over the colony after the Anglo-Powhatan War, and in the mid-1600s they worked to secure the Church of England's status as the one, official Protestant denomination of Virginia. The colony created a system of Anglican (Church of England) parishes, which supported churches and clergy and offered systems of poor relief for orphans and widows. One sign of the maturing Anglican culture of Virginia was the creation of the College of William and Mary in 1693, the only prerevolutionary college in the American South. The founders of William and Mary, like those of Harvard, Yale, and Princeton, envisioned the school as a "seminary of ministers of the gospel." The Church of England in the colonies was hamstrung, however, by the requirement that prospective ministers had to travel to England for ordination. The Church of England did have resident "commissaries" in the colonies to handle some affairs, but America did not receive its first resident Anglican bishop until 1784.

Because of their deep Protestant sensibilities, Virginians did not welcome the founding of Maryland, the neighbor to the north, in 1634. The proprietors of Maryland, the Calverts, were English Catholics who hoped that Maryland would become a haven for persecuted Catholics. Although Catholicism retained a significant influence on the colony, Maryland also attracted a number of Protestants. Maryland became marked by a religious diversity that would characterize many of the mid-Atlantic colonies. Maryland's fractious religious environment prompted its legislature to pass the 1649 "Act Concerning Religion," which enjoined the colonists to stop fighting with one another over spiritual matters. It also promised all Christians the "free exercise" of religion, a phrase that would reappear in the First Amendment to the United States Constitution. By the 1700s, however, Maryland had become a more conventional English colony with regard to religion—and a less friendly place for Catholics. The Calverts were only able to maintain their authority over the colony by converting to Anglicanism.

Maybe the most compelling and tragic religious story of the American colonial era unfolded in New England. The Separatists and Puritans who founded New England were animated by high religious ideals, and those vital ideals only made the failings of the colonies more conspicuous. The first wave of colonists came to Plymouth (which was later absorbed by Massachusetts) in 1620. These settlers were Separatists, but we often call them the "Pilgrims." English Separatists believed that England's legally established church was corrupt and irredeemable. They wanted to hold their own private church meetings instead of going to Church of England parishes, but it was not legal in England to start an independent congregation. Facing severe persecution, some English Separatists had already fled to the relatively freer climes of Holland.

Some of the Separatists in Holland worried about the corrupting effects of Dutch culture too. In 1620, just over a hundred people sailed to Plymouth on board the ship *Mayflower*. Upon arrival, the men of the colony signed the Mayflower Compact, committing themselves to the creation of a "civil body politic" that was devoted to "the glory of God, and advancement of the Christian faith, and honor of our king and country." While it is true that the Plymouth colonists held a special Thanksgiving celebration with local Indians around harvest time in 1621, they more likely ate eel than turkey.

In contrast to the Separatists, the Puritans believed that the Church of England needed reform, not abandonment. Yet events in the 1620s also convinced many Puritans that they could not remain in England and practice their faith in safety. Puritan pastors fell under persecution from

Anglican authorities, with some Puritan-leaning Anglican ministers losing their jobs. Puritan pastors and laypeople, including the lawyer John Winthrop, secured a charter for the Massachusetts Bay Company in 1629. At the outset of the "Great Migration" of Puritans in 1630, Winthrop delivered his speech "A Model of Christian Charity." In a phrase taken from the Gospel of Matthew, Winthrop told the Puritan colonists, "We shall be as a city upon a hill. The eyes of all people are upon us." The concept of the "city on a hill" would gain new life in American politics in the mid- to late twentieth century when the phrase was used by John F. Kennedy and Ronald Reagan, among others.

Few people have ever been more driven by theological conviction than the Puritans. The great Genevan reformer John Calvin was one of the most profound influences on the Puritans. But the preeminent shaper of Puritan thought was the Bible itself. Suspicious of church tradition and unbiblical practices, the Puritans studied the Scriptures in minute detail. They wanted their churches to implement all of the Bible's practices and doctrines. They wished to lay all man-made church customs aside. Following the guidance of Calvin and other Reformers, the Puritans saw the God of the Bible as unfathomably powerful and ruling over the salvation of individual men and women. Because all were sinners, the Puritans taught, all people were naturally inclined toward sin, which led to eternal separation from God in hell. Because of his mysterious grace, God chose a certain number of people for salvation. These were the "elect."

The Puritans of Massachusetts and Connecticut (founded in 1636) labored to maintain theological uniformity among all New Englanders. Like most Europeans in the early modern period, the Puritans were confident that the moral codes of the Bible could help them understand God's expectations for society. If Christian people allowed heretics or gross sinners to go unpunished, they were inviting God's judgment on their society. Thus the Puritans did not embrace a modern view of religious freedom. They came to New England to find religious freedom for themselves. However, they did not tolerate dissent from the Puritan way, even though it proved impossible to contain dissent altogether.

Roger Williams was one of the first major critics of the Puritans in New England. He had come to Massachusetts as a Puritan, but he gravitated toward Separatist convictions. Williams became convinced that while the government should enforce moral law, it could not rightly rule over people's consciences or force them into worshiping God. Williams also criticized Massachusetts for its unfair treatment of Native Americans. Massachusetts banned Williams from the colony in the mid-1630s, but he moved just to the south in New England and founded Providence, Rhode Island. Under Williams's guidance, Rhode Island would offer full religious liberty to its residents. Rhode Island's approach to religion made it a destination for a number of Christian sects. Jews also began arriving in Rhode Island as early as the 1650s. The mercurial Williams briefly embraced Baptist tenets following his expulsion from Massachusetts. Contrary to the common practice of the time, the Baptists (or "Anabaptists" to critics) believed that baptism was only for converted believers, not for infants. Williams helped to found the first Baptist congregation in America in Providence in 1638.

Another key dissenter from the Puritan way was Anne Hutchinson. Hutchinson, like Williams, had come to Massachusetts as a Puritan. She was a gifted teacher and began holding small-group meetings in her home to discuss sermons. As the meetings grew, Hutchinson began to indict most of Boston's pastors for teaching corrupt doctrine. Hutchinson advocated a staunch "free grace" position, arguing that there was nothing whatsoever that people could add to their salvation, nor could they make salvation more likely. Salvation was a work of God's grace alone, and she argued that only a couple of Boston ministers were staying true to that distinctive Protestant doctrine.

Boston authorities regarded Hutchinson and her supporters as "antinomians," or those who opposed the moral law of God. When she was brought up for trial in 1637, Hutchinson confessed to the court that she had received her views on grace from the Holy Spirit.

To the Puritan authorities, this smacked of gross radicalism. The court banished her from the colony. She told the judges, including Governor John Winthrop, "You have power over my body, but the Lord Jesus hath power over my body and soul."

Touro Synagogue, Newport, Rhode Island

Massachusetts routinely confronted threats from dissenters such as Williams and Hutchinson, as well as from Baptists, Quakers, and other prohibited Christian sects. A graver threat to the Puritan project was an apparent decline in piety in the second and third generations of Massachusetts colonists. Church membership rates were always relatively low there, as opposed to church attendance, which was mandatory. In order to join a church, people had to give a testimony of their conversion. It was not a given that church members would vote to accept the person into membership. If a person did join a Puritan church, it meant that they could take communion and have their children baptized. In the 1650s, fewer and fewer people in New England were joining churches, which caused concern among pastors about the growing number of unbaptized children in their midst.

This concern led to the "Halfway Covenant" of 1662, in which Massachusetts ministers agreed to allow people who had never joined a church to have their children baptized.

When King Philip's War, which pitted confederated Indian tribes against the English colonists, ravaged New England in the mid-1670s, colonists interpreted the war as a judgment for their spiritual half-heartedness. King Philip's War originated from decades of grievances over land claims and other issues. The Puritans saw it as a sign that New Englanders had done little to evangelize Native Americans, especially as compared to the work of French Catholic missionaries in Canada. In the 1670s and 1680s, the "jeremiad" became a signature sermon form among the Puritans. The name is derived from the bleak prophetic book of Jeremiah. The jeremiads lamented how far the Puritans had fallen from the godly passion of the founding generation. Historians have debated how literally to accept the jeremiads' narrative of New England's "declension." Sermons that look back nostalgically to a founding generation (of the New England colonies, or of the United States) and lament the failings of the current generation have carried great religious and political weight throughout American history. They do not always, however, reflect a literal pattern of decline.

The Puritan experiment in New England functionally came to an end in 1692. In the mid-1680s, England became frustrated with New England's relative independence in the empire. Authorities revoked Massachusetts's charter and placed it—as well as Connecticut, New York, and New Jersey—under the newly formed Dominion of New England. The Glorious Revolution of 1688–89 in England precipitated rebellions against the government of the Dominion of New England. Massachusetts hoped to get its old charter back; instead, the new English monarchs William and Mary gave Massachusetts a new charter in 1692. It restored some autonomy to Massachusetts but required that the Puritans tolerate the presence of other kinds of Protestants, such as Baptists and Anglicans. The inevitable diversity produced by this charter heralded the denouement of Puritanism.

Massachusetts's disappointment with the 1692 charter was compounded by the horrors of the Salem witchcraft controversy, which devastated northern New England that same year. Salem was unusual in its number of witchcraft suspects, although Europe had seen similar outbreaks from time to time. Scholars have endlessly debated why Salem became such a torrent of fear and allegations. Most of the accusations were by younger women or girls against older women. Nineteen accused witches were executed before Massachusetts officials stopped the trials, fearing that they depended too much on unconventional legal practices. Among the most criticized aspects of the trials was the acceptance of "spectral evidence," or testimony about seeing the spirits of the accused involved in malevolent activity. The shame of the trials left a lingering sense that New Englanders had turned their backs on God.

The story of New England Puritanism is the most linear religious story amid the European Christian diversity of colonial America. Massachusetts and Connecticut were founded as havens for the Puritans, who then faced the struggle to maintain their fervor and their relative independence from England. Rhode Island and the "Middle Colonies," including New York and Pennsylvania, featured more typical storylines of American religious history because of their striking vitality and diversity. South Carolina, with its mix of Anglicans, Puritans, Quakers, Scottish Covenanters, French Huguenots, devotees of African religions, and Jews, exhibited similar variety in a southern context. New York was originally founded as New Netherland, an outpost of the Dutch Empire. The Dutch Reformed Church was the official state church of that empire. In New Netherland, the Dutch Reformed tolerated other religious groups as long as they did not practice their faith openly or provocatively. A visiting Jesuit priest noted in the 1640s that, in spite of the official Dutch Reformed Church, New Netherland was full of other Christian groups, including "Calvinists, Catholics, English

Puritans, Lutherans, [and] Anabaptists." A small number of Jews also came to New Amsterdam (New York City) beginning in the 1650s.

The Quakers, among the most radical religious groups emerging from the ferment of the English Civil War in the mid-1600s, tested the patience of New Netherland authorities. Quakers started to appear in the colony in the late 1650s. They believed that the "Inward Light" of God lay within all people, which led them to adopt an egalitarian, or equality-focused, view of humanity. Quakers downplayed traditional differences between men and women and between people of different social classes and ethnicities. Quaker street preachers, who included both women and men, would pronounce the judgment of God on people, calling them to repent. In New Netherland, political and religious officials had Quakers arrested, imprisoned, and banished. When Dutch authorities mandated in 1657 that New Netherland residents report on any Quakers, the people of Vlissingen (Flushing) responded with a document that has become known as the Flushing Remonstrance. The remonstrance indicated that the people of Flushing did not wish to betray the Quakers but to welcome them in the spirit of Christian hospitality "as God shall persuade our consciences." The Flushing Remonstrance did not challenge the Dutch Reformed Church's authority, but it was an important symbol in the development of religious liberty. By the time of the American Revolution, increasing numbers of Americans believed that the government should not harass or persecute people for their religious beliefs or practices. The English would take over New Netherland in 1664, renaming it New York. Dutch cultural and religious influence endured in New York, however, as did the colony's religious diversity.

In the mid-1600s, Quakers found themselves persecuted both in England and America. Massachusetts even executed several Quakers between 1659 and 1661 after the colony had banished them and warned them not to return. West Jersey (which later united with East Jersey to form New Jersey) was dominated by Quaker refugees at its founding in 1664. The most famous refuge for the Quakers was the Pennsylvania colony, founded by William Penn. Penn came from an elite English family to whom the English government owed a significant debt, so King Charles II awarded Penn a charter for the Pennsylvania colony, which Penn founded in 1682. Having experienced persecution and imprisonment in England, Penn would allow Pennsylvania non-Quakers to practice their faith in freedom. Even in Pennsylvania, religious liberty had its limits, as the colony would not tolerate those who denied "the one Almighty and eternal God," used public profanity, or violated the Sabbath. Unlike in New England, the Quakers maintained relatively peaceful relations with local Native Americans for the first half-century of settlement in Pennsylvania.

European colonization was suffused with religious vitality and conflict. From the Franciscans who came in the first wave of Spanish colonization, to the Jesuits who traveled far into the Canadian interior, to the creation of English religious havens such as Massachusetts, Maryland, and Pennsylvania, religion was central to the story of the European conquest and settlement of North America. The dissenting nature of many of these European sects, combined with the spiritual practices of Native Americans and Africans in America, made early American religion remarkably diverse. Religious diversity played a part in fueling the violence that marked much of colonial America's history. In spite of the endemic conflicts, there were early signs that America could become not only a bastion of religious diversity but also a standard-bearer for what the Founding Fathers would call the "sacred rights of conscience."

WORKS CITED
AND FURTHER READING

Bremer, Francis J. *The Puritan Experiment: New England Society from Bradford to Edwards*. Hanover, NH: University Press of New England, 1995.

Demos, John. *A Little Commonwealth: Family Life in Plymouth Colony*. 2nd ed. New York: Oxford University Press, 1999.

Greer, Allan. *Mohawk Saint: Catherine Tekakwitha and the Jesuits*. New York: Oxford University Press, 2004.

Haefeli, Evan. *New Netherland and the Dutch Origins of American Religious Liberty*. Philadelphia: University of Pennsylvania Press, 2012.

Harper, Rob. "Looking the Other Way: The Gnadenhutten Massacre and the Contextual Interpretation of Violence." *William and Mary Quarterly*, 3rd ser., 64, no. 3 (July 2007): 621–44.

Horn, James. *A Land As God Made It: Jamestown and the Birth of America*. New York: Basic Books, 2005.

Kidd, Thomas S. *American Colonial History: Clashing Cultures and Faiths*. New Haven, CT: Yale University Press, 2016.

Las Casas, Bartolomé de. *An Account, Much Abbreviated, of the Destruction of the Indies*. Edited by Franklin W. Knight. Indianapolis: Hackett, 2003.

Martin, Calvin. *Keepers of the Game: Indian-Animal Relationships and the Fur Trade*. Berkeley: University of California Press, 1978.

Moorhead, James H. *Princeton Seminary in American Religion and Culture*. Grand Rapids: Eerdmans, 2012.

Nugent, Walter. *Into the West: The Story of Its People*. New York: Knopf, 1999.

Pestana, Carla Gardina. *Quakers and Baptists in Colonial Massachusetts*. New York: Cambridge University Press, 1991.

Rowlandson, Mary. *The Sovereignty and Goodness of God: With Related Documents*. Edited by Neal Salisbury. Boston: Bedford, 1997.

Sarna, Jonathan. *American Judaism: A History*. New Haven, CT: Yale University Press, 2004.

Silverman, David J. "Indians, Missionaries, and Religious Translation: Creating Wampanoag Christianity in Seventeenth-Century Martha's Vineyard." *William and Mary Quarterly* 3rd ser., 62, no. 2 (April 2005): 141–74.

Weber, David J. *The Spanish Frontier in North America*. New Haven, CT: Yale University Press, 1992.

Chapter 2

REVIVING AMERICAN FAITH

More than a century after the start of English colonization, the Great Awakening reshaped religion in British America. In the 1730s and '40s, thousands of people professed to have been born again, a reference to Jesus's words in the third chapter of the Gospel of John. Many colonists experienced conversion under the dazzling ministry of the Anglican revivalist George Whitefield, who became the most famous man in America. The revivals of the Great Awakening continued in regional expressions through the 1770s and '80s. The later stages of the awakening drew the American South into the fold of evangelical faith too. The southern colonies once had the lowest rates of church attendance, mostly because there were so few churches there. Now southern Christianity began to awaken.

Critics of the Great Awakening thought the revivals amounted to emotional chaos. The traveling Anglican minister Charles Woodmason was one of those critics. In 1767, Woodmason found backcountry South Carolina "eaten up by itinerant teachers, preachers, and impostors," including many Baptists, Presbyterians, and other evangelical missionaries who had come from the North. The backcountry settlers had so little experience with formal Christian religion that Woodmason believed it left them open to spiritual manipulation. Evangelical zealots tormented Woodmason too. They rioted outside his meetings and spread vicious rumors about him.

Woodmason claimed that even the Lord's Supper turned into a farce at evangelical meetings. During one sacramental assembly, an evangelical minister jumped onto a bench, waving the bread and hollering about the body of Christ. Another ran around with the cup, screaming about the blood of Christ. Chaos ruled, with "some howling—these ranting—those crying—others dancing, skipping, laughing and rejoicing." To radical evangelicals, such scenes evidenced the outpouring of the Holy Spirit for revival. To Woodmason, the disorder was utterly ungodly.

America's general pattern of spiritual vitality has often been paired with fears about an imminent spiritual downturn. Many pastors in America, especially in New England, had been worrying about the colonies' spiritual decline since at least the 1670s. By some measurements, however, the period from 1680 to 1740 was a time of growing religious strength. The number of Congregationalist churches, the traditional churches of the Puritans, had grown, with more than sixty new Congregationalist assemblies appearing in New England between 1680 and 1710. As the New England colonies expanded west and north, Congregationalist authorities made sure that new towns came with new meetinghouses.

Other denominations founded organizational hubs during the period. Many of them were in Philadelphia, which became America's most vital center for many Christian denominations. The establishment of the Quaker Yearly Meeting in Philadelphia in 1685 confirmed the city as the heartbeat of Quaker life. Presbyterians created the Philadelphia Presbytery in 1706, and then the Synod of Philadelphia (a group of presbyteries) in 1716. Even though Baptists emphasized congregational autonomy, in 1707 they founded the Philadelphia Baptist Association, which became the most influential Baptist organization in America in the 1700s. German Lutherans likewise formed the Lutheran Ministerium of Pennsylvania in 1748.

Anglican churches also continued to proliferate, especially in the South where the Church of England was established by law. Anglicans started almost ninety new colonial churches from 1680 to 1710. Although Anglican organization would suffer from the absence of resident bishops in the colonies, they also created the London-based Society for the Propagation of the Gospel in Foreign Parts (SPG) in 1701. The SPG was the most important agency of Anglican evangelization in the eighteenth century. The SPG aspired to bring more whites, blacks, and Native Americans into the Anglican fold. It would have the most numerical successes among whites. Some slave masters and other whites resented the SPG's overtures among Africans and Native Americans, believing that Christian ideals could foster insurrection among these oppressed groups. SPG officials assured plantation owners that their gospel would convey freedom from sin, not freedom from earthly slavery.

The work of SPG missionary Francis Le Jau near Charleston, South Carolina, confirmed that some slaves took the Christian message in unexpected directions. In 1710, Le Jau noted that the "best scholar of all the Negroes" in his parish was a sober and honest Christian. Le Jau worried, however, that this slave had embraced apocalyptic views. The minister feared that the slave's radical notions might sow "confusion" among the other slaves. Reading passages in the book of Revelation, Le Jau's student "told his master abruptly there would be a dismal time and the Moon would be turned into blood." Moreover, many in the slave community came to believe that an angel had given this man special revelations. Le Jau began to think it would have been better if the troubled man had "never seen a book."

The sense of religious decline that hovered over the late 1600s, even if some evidence painted a more positive picture, helped to fuel the

Great Awakening, especially in New England. The revivals also had deeper roots in European history. For decades, "pietist" groups had railed against nominal Christian commitment in Europe and argued that true Christianity entailed a vital personal relationship with the living God. Pietist movements complemented the Puritan reformers in the Church of England and similar Reformed impulses within Scottish and Scots-Irish Presbyterianism. When the Great Awakening came, it was a fully transatlantic Protestant movement. The revivals stirred Britain and the European continent, as well as the British colonies in America.

The "evangelical" Christians of the Great Awakening traced their movement back to the Bible and the early church revivals in the book of Acts. The term *evangelical* has, since 1980, become associated with a particular kind of Christian politics, namely white Christian support for the Republican Party. Yet we should not let today's political use of the term confuse its origins. At the outset, the word *evangelical* primarily related to spiritual reform and awakening. The term was used as an adjective, not a noun, as in "evangelical preaching" or an "evangelical book."

Early evangelicals prayed that God, by the power of the Holy Spirit, would awaken half-hearted Christians and bring non-Christians to faith. All people needed to experience the "new birth" of salvation, or to be born again. A recognition of one's sin and guilt, followed by acceptance of God's forgiveness through Christ, represented the moment of conversion. Ultimately, the revival preachers insisted, there was nothing that a man or woman could do to bring about conversion or revival. It was all a work of the Holy Spirit, the third person of the divine Trinity.

Earthly developments helped prepare colonial Americans for the Great Awakening too. In the early 1700s, some American pastors were concerned about the churches' apparent decline and liberal intellectual trends flowing in from Europe. By 1700, Harvard College had become a bastion of progressive Christian theology. Some of its professors criticized the traditional Calvinism of the Puritan founders. Yale College was founded in Connecticut in 1701 partly to offer a traditionalist counterweight to Harvard.

Colonists in these decades routinely faced war against Native Americans and Europe's Catholic powers, including France and Spain. In the 1720s, New Englanders fought a vicious war with Abenaki Indians in Maine. The French Catholic priest Sebastien Rale, a missionary among the Abenakis, had encouraged them to stand up against the land incursions of the English. Once again, competing Catholic and Protestant ambitions for Native American allegiances tragically led to violence. Massachusetts sent a war party to Rale's headquarters at Norridgewock, Maine, in 1724, and shot the Jesuit through the head. Overall, intellectual and military threats gave many colonists a sense that their traditional Protestant culture was in peril and in need of revival.

Pietist ministers began to lead revivals as early as the 1710s and 1720s. These pastors included the Scots-Irish Presbyterian preacher Gilbert Tennent and the Dutch Reformed Theodorus Frelinghuysen in New Jersey. Solomon Stoddard of Northampton, Massachusetts, the grandfather of the great preacher-theologian Jonathan Edwards, was an early Congregational revivalist. Stoddard had witnessed a number of "harvests" of souls during his long ministry. In 1727, New England also saw revivals in response to a major earthquake, which many interpreted as a sign of God's wrath.

Jonathan Edwards succeeded Stoddard at Northampton's Congregational church. In 1734 and 1735, Edwards led a remarkable revival that historians generally regard as the beginning of the Great Awakening. The Northampton awakening also inspired Edwards to write *A Faithful Narrative of the Surprising Work of God*, which was published in London, giving Anglo-American revival leaders a shared sense of the transatlantic nature of the revivals. In *A Faithful Narrative*, Edwards emphasized that he had used no novel tactics to get people to respond to his preaching. He saw the revival as a sovereign act of God. At its height, Edwards wrote, "There was scarcely a single person in the town, either old or young, that was left unconcerned about the great things of the eternal world. . . . And the work of conversion was carried on in a most astonishing manner, and increased more and more; souls did as it were come by flocks to Jesus Christ. From day to day, for many months together, might be seen evident instances of sinners brought out of darkness into marvelous light." *A Faithful Narrative* went on to become perhaps the best-known account of a revival in Christian history, outside of the book of Acts.

Edwards penned many influential writings, including his sermon "Sinners in the Hands of an Angry God," preached in 1741. He would make formidable defenses of Reformed theology, including the Calvinist view of the will and of original sin. Arguably Edwards's most enduring writings are those about revival, including *A Faithful Narrative.*

These writings emerged from the joys and the frustrations precipitated by the revivals. Perhaps Edwards's single most important composition was his 1746 *A Treatise Concerning Religious Affections.* In it, Edwards explained that while the revivals' emotionalism was controversial, the "affections" (or the "more vigorous and sensible exercises of the inclination and will of the soul") were essential to the Christian life. "True religion," he wrote, "consists in holy affections." When the Holy Spirit regenerates the heart of a believer,

Jonathan Edwards

"there is a new inward perception or sensation of their minds, entirely different in its nature and kind, from anything that ever their minds were the subjects of before." This "new spiritual sense" enables Christians to live in holiness. "To follow Christ in heart," Edwards concluded, "is to have a heart to follow him." Edwards's brilliance garnered an international following, even though he was eventually removed from his Northampton church due to conflict with powerful church members. Edwards then served at a mission among Stockbridge Indians in western Massachusetts before briefly assuming the presidency of the College of New Jersey (Princeton). He died from a smallpox inoculation gone wrong in 1758.

Edwards left the most profound theological legacy of the Great Awakening, but the most famous leader at the time was George Whitefield. Whitefield had a conversion experience while he was a student at the University of Oxford. He had a preternatural talent for preaching, and he had unwittingly cultivated his gift prior to his conversion by acting in plays. When he became an Anglican minister, Whitefield applied his talents to preaching. Soon he began drawing audiences that

George Whitefield

far exceeded the seating capacity of the churches. This prompted Whitefield to begin his "field preaching" ministry in which he spoke from a scaffold or field pulpit, often before tens of thousands. Whitefield's primary evangelistic targets were nominal Christians, whom he saw as unconverted and in danger of hell. "Repent," he told them, "and be converted that your sins may be blotted out. See that you have received the Holy Ghost before you [die]: For otherwise how can you escape the damnation of hell?" Note Whitefield's emphasis on conversion by the Holy Spirit, which was a distinctive theme of his preaching.

Whitefield proved to be a master of the new media of his time. He published fabulously successful sermons and travel journals, and he generated an enormous spike in the amount of printed materials and newspaper coverage of religion in the colonies. Whitefield was the first evangelical "celebrity pastor" and one of the first full-fledged celebrities of any kind in world history. Some have assumed that Whitefield was shallow and had no interest in theology, but this was not true. The itinerant routinely feuded with other evangelicals and pietist Christians over theological issues, such as Calvinist doctrine and the idea that God only chose the elect for salvation. Whitefield heartily embraced Calvinism and battled with evangelical colleagues, such as the Methodist John Wesley, who did not.

Whitefield's mastery of media helps to explain his longtime friendship with Benjamin Franklin, the evangelist's most important printer in America. Franklin had rejected the Calvinist faith of his Puritan parents, but he admired Whitefield's zeal and integrity. Franklin also saw an opportunity to make money from selling materials by Whitefield as well as publications by Whitefield's many antagonists. Franklin even sold engraved pictures of Whitefield. Franklin was initially skeptical about the reported crowd sizes at Whitefield's meetings, so when Whitefield came to Philadelphia, Franklin decided to make a calculation himself. The stunned Franklin estimated that more than thirty thousand people could hear Whitefield speaking at once. Of course, Whitefield was working in a preelectric age without amplification, making his vocal range all the more impressive.

Whitefield's ministry reached across boundaries of denominations. Many Anglican leaders criticized Whitefield because of the evangelist's cooperation with people of other Christian traditions. Whitefield told the indignant Anglican commissary in Boston that he "saw regenerate souls among the Baptists, among the Presbyterians, among the Independents, and among the Church [Anglican] folks,—all children of God, and yet all born again in a different way of worship." This kind of interdenominational spirit became a hallmark of evangelical Christianity, but it was highly unusual in Whitefield's time.

Whitefield also proselytized African Americans and Native Americans, even though many whites balked at telling those groups about the gospel or teaching them to read. Whitefield, Edwards, and other evangelical ministers made a point to converse with African American attendees and noted their conversions in accounts of the revivals. The white evangelicals' egalitarian impulse had limits when it came to slavery and slaveholding. Both Whitefield and Edwards at times expressed reservations about slavery and the slave trade. However, both owned slaves, and Whitefield even pushed for the legalization of slavery in colonial Georgia, where slavery was originally banned. Yet Whitefield's brand of faith still appealed to a number of African Americans, including some slaves. Phillis Wheatley, a Boston slave and the first African American woman to be published in America, devoted her first stand-alone published composition to Whitefield when the revivalist died in 1770. Wheatley received her freedom from slavery in 1773.

Historians have conventionally seen the Great Awakening as dividing colonists into "Old Lights" and "New Lights," or the opponents and supporters of the awakenings, respectively. While "Old Lights" certainly opposed the Great Awakening, the "New Lights" were profoundly divided among themselves. Moderate evangelicals supported the revivals, but they worried that their leveling effects might lead to chaos and could undermine the authority of ordained pastors. Radical evangelicals, conversely, saw the Great Awakening as a dramatic new outpouring of the Holy Spirit. The Spirit, they said, was working miracles and raising up common people—including women, slaves, children, and the poor—as religious leaders and "exhorters" in their own right. Some of the greatest controversies between moderate and radical evangelicals were spawned by the exhorters, people who were not ordained but who took on preaching roles in revival meetings. Moderate evangelicals were happy to see such people experience salvation, but they did not appreciate the radicals' "noisy" habits of worship and democratized approach to speaking in church meetings. Radicals welcomed the exhorters, even though they were people who would hardly ever address educated white men in any other public setting.

The ringleader of the New England radicals was James Davenport. Davenport's flamboyant ministry saw him leading crowds of supporters singing through the streets of New England and Long Island. Davenport was one of the main targets of a law restricting itinerants, or traveling preachers, passed in Connecticut in 1742. The preacher and his followers challenged the law, and a riot ensued in Hartford when colonial authorities banned Davenport from Connecticut. As a sheriff tried to lead Davenport away, the preacher began calling down the wrath of God. Officials summoned the colony's militia to help disperse Davenport's supporters. Davenport finally went too far in 1743 when he returned to Connecticut and held a book- and clothes-burning in New London. The burned books included some by moderate evangelical authors. As Davenport called on his followers to contribute their fancy clothes to the bonfire, he pulled off his own pants and cast them in the flames. A courageous woman snatched his pants out of the fire, threw them "into his face," and told Davenport that he was out of his mind. After this embarrassing scene, Davenport lost most of his followers and publicly apologized for his extreme tactics. Davenport was one of the best examples of how the intense vitality of the revivals could breed outrage, conflict, and even violent confrontations.

Some of the most influential preachers started off as radical-leaning evangelicals. Early in their careers, Whitefield and Gilbert Tennent of New Jersey both broached the provocative topic of unconverted ministers, a hallmark concern of the radicals. After his phenomenally successful preaching tour in New England in fall 1740, Whitefield indiscreetly opined that he thought the "generality of preachers" in the colonies "talk of an unknown, unfelt Christ." Likewise, in Tennent's infamous sermon "The Danger of an Unconverted Ministry" (1740), he warned that many colonial pastors were "Pharisee-Teachers" who had "no experience of a special work of the Holy Ghost." The truly converted should expect such ministers to "oppose the very work of God's Spirit upon the souls of men." In other words, the pastors who opposed the revivals did so because they were unconverted and possibly bound for hell. The pressure of criticism led both Whitefield and Tennent in a more moderate direction as the Great Awakening proceeded. When Whitefield visited Northampton, Jonathan Edwards personally cautioned the itinerant against denouncing ministers as unconverted and against depending too much upon spiritual impressions, such as verses and promptings received as direct words from the Spirit.

The radical impulse proved hard to contain. Legions of radical converts professed to have experienced dreams, visions, trances, and spirit journeys during the revivals. Typical was the diary record of the artisan Joseph Bean of Cambridge, Massachusetts, who wrote in 1742 that by "an eye of faith o methought I could see God and Christ at his right hand and the burning throne with millions of shining angels." Some visions were even more exotic, with people insisting they had witnessed angels or the Holy Spirit with their "bodily eyes." The most remarkable vision came in 1764 in Connecticut when one radical evangelical claimed that Jesus himself had physically appeared to his daughter. Moderate evangelicals scoffed at such "pretended" visions and worried that they would damage the movement.

Women experienced conversions and the intense spiritual phenomena of the Great Awakening as commonly as men. Women's roles in the revivals were complicated by a pervasive understanding that the Bible restricted women's leadership in churches. Women still became evangelical exemplars, however. Jonathan Edwards's wife, Sarah, spoke of encountering the "unspeakable joys of the upper world" during prayer and meditation. Sarah played a key if anonymous role in Edwards's treatise *Some Thoughts Concerning the Present Revival of Religion* (1742). Although Edwards was trending in a moderate direction by 1742, he could not deny the power of Sarah's spiritual transports. She would go into trance-like states for hours during which her "soul dwelt on high, and was lost in God." Edwards knew that this kind of experience drew charges of antinomianism and "enthusiasm" from critics. He also knew that her meditations were drawing Sarah into a deeper relationship with Christ. "If such things are enthusiasm and the fruits of a distempered brain," he wrote, "let my brain be evermore possessed of that happy distemper!"

However, Edwards drew a line at formal female authority in the church. When Bathsheba Kingsley of Westfield, Massachusetts, began preaching as an itinerant, Edwards called her a "brawling woman." A pastoral council including Edwards chastised Kingsley, telling her to limit her ministry to private influence. By taking on a public role, they said, Kingsley had "cast off that modesty, shamefacedness, and sobriety and meekness, diligence and submission, that becomes a Christian woman." Although some Baptist churches emerging from the awakenings appointed women as deaconesses, the Quakers remained the primary group in colonial America that permitted women preachers. Nevertheless, many women, such as Sarah Edwards and the prolific writer Sarah Osborn of Newport, Rhode Island, found ways as hosts, mentors, and influencers to become major revival leaders in their own right. In 1766–67, Osborn saw sometimes hundreds of people, both blacks and whites, assemble at her home for intense prayer meetings. Her pastor, Samuel Hopkins, wrote that Osborn was "greatly cautious, fearing to go beyond her line, as a woman, in endeavoring to promote their instruction and religious impressions." Concerning the revival, however, Osborn prayed, "The Lord command a blessing for Christ's sake. O for divine influence! O thou dove of heaven, descend. I am waiting for influence from heaven. Lord, except thou dost take the work into thine own hand, all will come to nothing."

The Great Awakening invigorated Christian commitment, but it badly divided American churches and denominations. The revivals' vitality bred conflict in law and in churches. Congregations split over how to respond to Whitefield and the other itinerants, and whether they should let the preachers speak in their churches' pulpits. Other churches saw prorevivalists leave the church and start their own

"Separate" meetings, especially in the New England colonies. Hundreds of Separate congregations opened during the mid-1700s, but many did not last long due to ineffective leadership or legal pressure from colonial authorities. In most of the colonies, churches and pastors were subject to licensing requirements. Colonial authorities would not permit people to start new churches on their own. Sometimes evangelicals abandoned churches led by antirevivalist pastors. Sometimes radical groups separated from churches pastored by moderate evangelicals. The latter scenario was the case with the Congregationalist church of Benjamin Lord of Norwich, Connecticut, in 1745 when thirteen members left and started a Separate congregation. They explained that the church was admitting unconverted people into the membership, and that Reverend Lord was insufficiently supportive of the revivals. One of the separating members, Mary Lathrop, simply stated that "I am not held here any longer than I am edified."

One of the most notable separations produced a new Narragansett Indian church in Westerly, Rhode Island, in 1750. The original white-led church had seen an influx of dozens of Native American converts in the early 1740s. These included Samuel Niles, who began to take on a pastoral role among his fellow Narragansetts. The church's white pastor worried about the disorder of separate "prayer and praise" meetings among the Indians and discouraged Niles from preaching to them. This tension finally led the evangelical Narragansetts to start their own small congregation. Niles's ethnicity and his radical religious practices worried a neighboring white pastor, who warned that Niles and the Narragansetts depended too much on "feelings, impressions, visions, appearances and directions of angels and of Christ himself in a visionary way."

One of the most influential white Separates, Isaac Backus, had separated from Benjamin Lord's Norwich, Connecticut, congregation in the mid-1740s. For Backus and many other Separates, church separation was the first step toward becoming Baptists. As we have seen, Baptists had already been present in the earliest British colonies. Many of the existing Baptist churches, including those associated with the Phila-delphia Baptist Association, were hesitant about the Great Awakening, if not outright opposed. Some Separate evangelicals, however, having already broken with religious tradition by starting new churches, began to look at the Bible's teaching on baptism with fresh eyes and thus to become Baptists.

Virtually all Christians in the 1740s practiced infant baptism, which they saw as introducing the child into the covenanted community of the church. (Quakers, emphasizing the spiritual nature of baptism, did not practice water baptism at all.) Some Separates, however, started to regard infant baptism as a remnant of corrupt Catholic practice. As the Separate Baptists read the New Testament, especially the book of Acts, they found no conclusive evidence of infant baptism. But they saw plenty of examples of baptism as an external confirmation of conversion and salvation. These Separates came to believe that infant baptism was the key reason why the membership of so many churches was mixed with unconverted people. Infant baptism put the cart of baptism before the horse of conversion.

In spite of his lack of college education, Isaac Backus had become a pastor over a Separate congregation in Massachusetts by 1747. Some of the Separate Baptists sought to convince Backus that infant baptism was unscriptural, and in 1751 Backus finally denied the validity of his own baptism as an infant and received baptism by immersion. After several years of trying to manage the tension between Separate Baptists and "paedobaptists," Backus founded a new Baptist church in 1756.

Separate Baptists, fueled with evangelistic zeal, began sending missionaries to the South by the mid-1750s. The lack of church infra-structure made the South an alluring target for Baptist missions. The most important Separate Baptist leader in the South was Shubal Stearns, originally of Connecticut. In 1755, Stearns and other family members founded the Sandy Creek Baptist Church in North Carolina. The Sandy Creek church and its affiliated association would become a center of Baptist growth and evangelization over the next several decades.

Separate Baptists like those of Stearns's church would help make the backcountry South into a hotbed of radical evangelical zeal, which the Anglican minister Charles Woodmason had witnessed, to his dismay.

While the Great Awakening split churches and spawned new ones, Protestant Americans were of one mind about the threat posed by Catholic imperial power. Since the Glorious Revolution of 1688–89, religious identity in America had centered on what colonists called the "Protestant Interest." This term referred to the international cohort of Protestants, headed by Britain, arrayed against the world forces of Catholicism, especially Rome, France, and Spain. In Britain, the Glorious Revolution spawned a century of wars or rumored wars against its European Catholic rivals. American colonists were particularly vulnerable to incursions by the Catholic powers, with New Englanders facing attacks from New France (Canada), and South Carolina and Georgia from Spanish Florida. American colonists framed their local military clashes as part of a global struggle between Catholics and the Protestant Interest.

In spite of their fights over the Great Awakening, New England's religious leaders could all support a 1745 expedition against the French fortress at Louisbourg in Canada at the entrance to the Gulf of Saint Lawrence. Massachusetts forces led the expedition, which was commanded by William Pepperrell, a friend and ally of George Whitefield. Pastors including Whitefield called for an outpouring of prayer to support the Louisbourg campaign. One published poem prayed "Destroy proud Antichrist, O Lord / And quite consume the Whore." "Scarlet whore" and "Antichrist" were common biblical epithets that Protestants assigned to the Catholic Church. When the British colonists defeated Louisbourg with relative ease, Jonathan Edwards exulted that the conquest was "a dispensation of providence, the most remarkable in its kind, that has been in many ages."

Tension between Catholic and Protestant powers in America finally exploded into the Seven Years' War in the 1750s and '60s. Historians often call the American theater of this conflict the French and Indian War. The war would decide the fate of eastern North America and the Caribbean. British colonists once again framed the war as a great struggle between Protestantism and Catholicism, along with the Catholics' Indian allies. Virginia evangelical pastor Samuel Davies insisted that the French and their Native American compatriots were animated by the spirit of "Popish slavery, tyranny, and massacre." Addressing Virginia militiamen, Davies cited Jeremiah 48:10 and its warning: "Cursed be he that keepeth back his sword from blood."

The Seven Years' War badly destabilized the traditional relationships between Native Americans and the European powers. In the Great Lakes region, many Native Americans had sided with the French because the French gave generous diplomatic gifts and did not have the same ambitions as the British to take their tribal lands. As the war turned against the French, some Native Americans turned to Indian prophets, who called for a renewal of native spirituality. One of the prophets, the Lenni Lenape (Delaware) leader Neolin, called on his followers to abandon European trade goods, including alcohol and firearms. Neolin said that the "Master of Life" had approached him in a vision and warned Indians to keep their distance from the British. "I do not love them at all," the Master of Life said of the British colonists. "They know me not, and are my enemies." Neolin and other prophets helped to inspire the mass Indian uprising against the British called Pontiac's Rebellion, which came in the mid-1760s on the heels of the Seven Years' War. Harsh retribution against the Indian rebels, and the resumption of a generous gift-giving policy by the British, helped to subdue the prophecy-fueled insurgency by 1765.

Britain triumphed in the Seven Years' War itself, marked by British conquest of the French at Quebec City in Canada in 1759 and the Spanish at Havana, Cuba, in 1762. British colonists, who had played a role in all the war's major American battles, were exultant. New Jersey governor William Franklin, the son of Benjamin Franklin, issued a proclamation for a day of prayer, anticipating that the war's outcome would result in the "happiness of the British Nation. These invaluable Blessings, and the effectual Security which is now given to the Protestant Interest" demanded that the people "prostrate themselves . . . before the Throne of Grace" and give heartfelt thanks to God. Victory in war demanded praise to the God of battles.

Salem, Massachusetts, pastor Thomas Barnard was perhaps the most effusive when he predicted that America would become "the late founded seat of peace and freedom. Here shall our indulgent Mother [Britain], who has most generously rescued and protected us, be served and honored by growing numbers, with all duty, love, and gratitude, till time shall be no more." Of course, there were problems between Britain and the American colonists simmering just under the surface. These problems would emerge almost immediately after the signing of the peace treaty ending the Seven Years' War in 1763. For the moment, however, the colonists luxuriated in the great victory for British power and Protestantism. William Franklin ended his 1763 prayer proclamation with the heartfelt petition "God Save the KING."

The twin forces of anti-Catholicism and revivalism had rejuvenated a vibrant and fractious Protestant culture in British America by the 1760s. But the tensions between London authorities and British Americans would make the future of the colonies far more tenuous than British officials could have imagined. When those tensions exploded over British sovereignty and taxes in America, the colonists often turned to religious concepts to make sense of the burgeoning crisis of empire.

WORKS CITED
AND FURTHER READING

Brekus, Catherine. *Sarah Osborn's World: The Rise of Evangelical Christianity in Early America.* New Haven, CT: Yale University Press, 2013.

Davies, Samuel. *Sermons by the Rev. Samuel Davies.* Philadelphia: Presbyterian Board of Publication, 1864.

Dowd, Gregory Evans. *War Under Heaven: Pontiac, the Indian Nations, and the British Empire.* Baltimore: Johns Hopkins University Press, 2002.

Fisher, Linford D. *The Indian Great Awakening: Religion and the Shaping of Native Cultures in Early America.* New York: Oxford University Press, 2012.

Gatiss, Lee, ed. *The Sermons of George Whitefield.* 2 vols. Wheaton, IL: Crossway, 2012.

Harvey, Paul. *Through the Storm, Through the Night: A History of African American Christianity.* Lanham, MD: Rowman & Littlefield, 2011.

Hatch, Nathan O. *The Sacred Cause of Liberty: Republican Thought and the Millennium in Revolutionary New England.* New Haven, CT: Yale University Press, 1977.

Hooker, Richard J., ed. *The Carolina Backcountry on the Eve of the Revolution: The Journal and Other Writings of Charles Woodmason, Anglican Itinerant.* Chapel Hill: University of North Carolina Press, 1969.

Hopkins, Samuel, ed. *Memoirs of the Life of Mrs. Sarah Osborn.* 2nd ed. Catskill, NY: Elliot, 1814.

Juster, Susan. *Disorderly Women: Sexual Politics and Evangelicalism in Revolutionary New England.* Ithaca, NY: Cornell University Press, 1994.

Kidd, Thomas S. *George Whitefield: America's Spiritual Founding Father.* New Haven, CT: Yale University Press, 2014.

———. *The Great Awakening: The Roots of Evangelical Christianity in Colonial America.* New Haven, CT: Yale University Press, 2007.

———. *The Protestant Interest: New England after Puritanism.* New Haven, CT: Yale University Press, 2004.

Klingberg, Frank J., ed. *The Carolina Chronicle of Dr. Francis Le Jau, 1706–1717.* Berkeley: University of California Press, 1956.

Nelson, William, ed. *Documents Relating to the Colonial History of the State of New Jersey*. Paterson, NJ: Call and Printing, 1902.

Smith, John E., Harry S. Stout, and Kenneth P. Minkema, eds. *A Jonathan Edwards Reader*. New Haven, CT: Yale University Press, 1995.

Taylor, Alan. *American Colonies: The Settling of North America*. New York: Penguin Books, 2002.

Chapter 3

RELIGION AND
THE AMERICAN
REVOLUTION

Alexander Hamilton had just begun his college career at King's College (later Columbia University) in New York City when he was swept up in the crisis between Britain and its American colonies. The furor over the Boston Tea Party and the resulting Intolerable Acts gripped him, but what worried Hamilton most was the Quebec Act, a British measure issued in 1774. Britain took control of Quebec during the Seven Years' War, so Britain needed to clarify how it would administer Quebec, a traditionally Catholic province. In 1774, the British announced that they would allow the open practice of Roman Catholicism there, while also extending Quebec's southern border to the Ohio River. It was one of the most poorly considered measures of the era. From Georgia to Massachusetts, colonists feared that the Quebec Act might be evidence of a Catholic conspiracy within the nominally Protestant British administration. Hamilton wrote some of his first newspaper pieces ever in response to the Quebec Act. "Arbitrary power, and its great engine the Popish Religion, are, to all intents and purposes, established in that province [Canada]," Hamilton warned. "What can speak in plainer language," he asked, of "the corruption of the British Parliament, than its act; which invests the King with absolute power over a little world . . . and makes such ample provision for the popish religion?"

Religion did not cause the American Revolution. Feuds over taxes and the British government's sovereignty did. Yet religion was omnipresent in the Revolution. Some religious issues, such as the Quebec Act, helped to precipitate American independence. More commonly, religious concepts and biblical rhetoric framed colonists' understanding of what was happening in the Revolution. The language of faith also undergirded the most powerful statement of human rights the world has ever seen: the Declaration of Independence. Members of the Continental Congress ran the gamut from the self-described "deist" Benjamin Franklin to the devout evangelical Roger Sherman of Connecticut, but they all knew they needed to frame the case for independence with reference to God their Creator. Most conspicuously, Thomas Jefferson and the Continental Congress proclaimed, "All men are created equal, [and] that they are endowed by their Creator with certain unalienable Rights, that among these are Life, Liberty and the pursuit of Happiness."

The successful conclusion of the Seven Years' War sent the colonists to the height of British patriotism. However, even before the war's end, political, cultural, and religious factors began to undermine Americans' attachment to Britain. Among the religious factors was a fear that the Anglican Church would impose a bishop on the colonies. A bishop could threaten the relative freedom enjoyed by American "dissenters," non-Anglicans such as Presbyterians and Congregationalists. Britain's religious and political authorities seemed oblivious to such concerns. In 1761, an Anglican leader working for the Society for the Propagation of the Gospel moved into a lavish mansion in Cambridge, Massachusetts, the home of Congregationalist-dominated Harvard. Bostonians reviled the new residence as the "bishop's palace." Critics warned that the Church of England was setting the stage for a bishop in America and an attack on dissenting churches.

"The Mitred Minuet" (1774)

Even in the southern colonies, which were officially aligned with the Anglican Church, there was widespread hostility to having an American bishop. The frustrated Anglican minister Charles Woodmason found that the dissenters had soured people in the backcountry Carolinas by "instilling democratical and commonwealth principles into their minds—embittering them against the very name of bishops." To Anglicans like Woodmason, "commonwealth principles" recalled Puritan Oliver Cromwell's rule in the 1650s when England had no king. "Commonwealth" writers criticized the power of the English church and crown. They trumpeted the citizens' rights to "life, liberty, and property," in political philosopher John Locke's phrase, against top-down religious and political power. Commonwealth principles especially resonated among dissenters. Such concepts also caught on among southern Anglicans in America who opposed the overweening control of London, whether in religious or political form.

Open hostility between Britain and the colonists ensued in 1765 with the passage of the Stamp Act. The act placed a tax on printed goods, including newspapers. Not surprisingly, newspaper editors led the charge against the "fatal STAMP." Many Americans viewed the controversy over the Stamp Act in religious terms. Protestors in Connecticut in 1766 rejoiced when news arrived of the Stamp Act's repeal, declaring that "victory was gained over the beast, and over his mark" (Revelation 13). "We can yet buy and sell without the mark," they rejoiced.

Some scholars cite this kind of talk as evidence of an American "civil religion." It is hard to find historic examples, though, where devotion to the American nation really morphed into a full-blown religion, as some have posited. Instead, the rhetoric of the Bible was so deeply ingrained in the colonies that Americans reflexively applied it to developments such as the Stamp Act. "Civil spirituality" is a better term for this kind of biblicist language. The fact that civil spirituality was not a formal religion per se does not deny its power in America. Civil spirituality has routinely justified movements such as the one that led to American independence.

The most popular speeches and tracts of the era appealed to religious concepts and biblical stories. Perhaps the most sensational pamphlet of the Revolutionary crisis prior to Tom Paine's *Common Sense* (1776) was the obscure Baptist preacher John Allen's *An Oration Upon the Beauties of Liberty* (1773). The Boston minister's pamphlet appeared in five editions and seven printings in just two years. Focusing on the prophet Micah, "a son of liberty," Allen showed that the biblical prophets stood both for rights and for righteousness. Allen challenged his fellow citizens that "if there be any vein, any nerve, any soul, any life or spirit of liberty in the sons of America, show your love for it; guard your freedom, prevent your chains; stand up as one man for your liberty."

Patrick Henry struck similar themes in his "Liberty or Death" oration of 1775, the most stirring speech of the Revolutionary era. Instead of Micah, Henry repeatedly referred to verses from the prophet Jeremiah. In his relatively short speech, Henry sought to convince

Virginia Patriots to prepare for war against the British. He repeatedly cited Jeremiah and other books of the Bible, though apparently without giving the chapter and verse. He probably assumed that the biblically literate audience would know the text when they heard it. Thus he warned that British promises of goodwill could "prove a snare to your feet" (Jeremiah 18:22). He feared that Virginians might become like those "who having eyes, see not, and having ears, hear not" (5:21). And he declared that "gentlemen may cry peace, peace—but there is no peace" (6:14). Appealing to the "holy cause of liberty" and the "God of hosts," Henry concluded his speech by raising his arms and proclaiming, "I know not what course others may take; but as for me, give me liberty, or give me death!"

Thomas Paine's inflammatory pamphlet *Common Sense* turned the focus of the Revolutionary crisis from resistance to declaring independence from Britain. Paine would eventually become the leading anti-Christian skeptic among the founders. That did not keep him from citing the Bible in perhaps the most important section of *Common Sense*, where he contended that monarchy contradicted the will of God. The original Hebraic "republic" had no king. "It was held sinful to acknowledge any being under that title but the Lord of Hosts," Paine observed. In 1 Samuel 8, however, the Israelites began clamoring for a king so they could be like the neighboring nations. In spite of God's warnings, they convinced the prophet Samuel to give them a king. "The Almighty hath here entered his protest against monarchical government is true, or the scripture is false," Paine argued. Paine added a dash of anti-Catholicism to clinch his argument, contending that "monarchy in every instance is the Popery of government." Both Catholicism and monarchy gave too much power to an individual, who tyrannically ruled in the spheres of religion and government, respectively.

Common and elite Americans made countless connections between religion and the Revolution. One of the most vivid but puzzling instances of such connections came in September 1775. Continental American army troops on their way to Quebec stopped on the Sabbath in Newburyport, Massachusetts. This was the final resting place of the evangelist George Whitefield, who had died in 1770. After a Sunday service at First Presbyterian Church, Newburyport, some of the Continental officers went down to the church's basement. There they opened Whitefield's tomb. The officers took pieces of Whitefield's clerical robes from the body, cut them up and distributed the fragments among the troops. What the officers had in mind was not entirely clear. Perhaps they hoped that these relics from the Protestant saint would help their cause. (Protestants were normally critical of relics as a species of Catholic superstition.) Although Whitefield had died five years before the Revolutionary War, many Americans assumed that Whitefield would have approved of independence.

Of course, many devout Americans did not support the American rebellion. Christian Loyalists had a variety of objections to the war. Some were pacifists. Others had suffered abuse from the colonial officials who were declaring independence. Many Christian African Americans believed that they would receive fairer treatment from British authorities than the Patriot leaders. Church of England leaders, especially in the northern colonies, felt that they could not accept an imperial breakup which would weaken their national church. Perhaps the most common Loyalist argument against the American Revolution was scriptural. They pointed to passages such as 1 Peter 2:17, which enjoined Christians to "fear God" and "honor the king." How could colonists obey this passage if they rejected the king's authority? Anglican minister Charles Inglis spoke for many when he denounced the rebellion as "one of the most causeless, unprovoked and unnatural that ever disgraced any country." The Christian Mohegan leader Samson Occom pled with Native Americans to stay out of the war too. "Peace never does any hurt," he cautioned. "Peace is from the God of peace and love. . . . Jesus Christ is the Prince of Peace."

The American Continental Congress during the war was ostensibly secular, but it sometimes issued proclamations for prayer, fasting, and thanksgiving that employed detailed theological language. Whereas the Declaration of Independence had used generic theistic language about the creator and "nature's God," a 1777 thanksgiving proclamation recommended that Americans confess their sins and pray that God, "through the merits of Jesus Christ," would forgive them. They further enjoined Americans to pray for the "enlargement of that kingdom which consisteth 'in righteousness, peace and joy in the Holy Ghost' [Romans 14:17]."

Some have argued that the Declaration of Independence illustrates the "secular character of the Revolution." The declaration was specific about the action of God in creation, however. A theistic basis for the equality of humankind was broadly shared by Americans in 1776. Like Paine, Thomas Jefferson did not let his own skepticism about Christian doctrine preclude the use of a theistic argument to persuade Americans. Jefferson was hardly an atheist, in any case. Like virtually all Americans, he assumed that God, in some way and at some time, had created the world and humankind.

The Virginia Declaration of Rights, which had been adopted just weeks before the Declaration of Independence, had spoken blandly of how "all men are by nature equally free and independent and have certain inherent rights." Drawing on the naturalistic theory of government crafted by John Locke, this first section of the Virginia Declaration made no explicit reference to God. When Jefferson and his drafting committee wrote the Declaration of Independence, however, they made the action of God in creation much clearer. "All men are created equal," and "they are endowed by their Creator," Jefferson wrote. The Declaration was not explicitly Christian, but its theism was intentional. This is not to say that the founding documents are uniformly theistic. The Constitution hardly referred to God at all, save for a paltry reference to the "Year of our Lord" 1787.

People in 1776 already understood that equality by creation made slavery and other American forms of inequality hypocritical. Many enslaved people in America realized that the Declaration was profoundly contradictory. If all men were created equal, they wondered, then why were we enslaved? A group of slaves in Massachusetts, which still had slavery at the time, reminded the state legislature in 1777 that they had "in common with all other men a natural and unalienable right to that freedom which the great Parent of the universe hath bestowed equally on all mankind."

Among the most powerful Christian critics of slavery at the time of the American founding was Lemuel Haynes, an African American soldier and pastor from Massachusetts. Haynes had been mentored by "New Divinity" pastors, the Revolutionary-era devotees of Jonathan Edwards's theology. The New Divinity was one of the most fruitful sources for antislavery thought. New Divinity theologians focused on the Christian obligation of service to the "least of these." Haynes wrote the remarkable document "Liberty Further Extended" as a response to the Declaration of Independence. Haynes affirmed the God-given principle of human equality, but he argued that it needed to be "further extended" to the most unfree of all, America's slaves. He built his argument on Acts 17:26, a favorite text of Christian antislavery writers. In the King James Version, this verse said that God "hath made of one blood all nations of men." Haynes concluded that "liberty is equally as precious to a black man, as it is to a white one, and bondage equally as intolerable to the one as it is to the other." Haynes and other New Divinity writers warned that Americans were courting the judgment

NYPL, Public Domain

Lemuel Haynes

of God with their hypocritical pleas for liberty for whites while they enslaved blacks.

Jefferson, a major slaveholder, could hardly disagree with such arguments against slavery. Later generations of southern slave masters would present slavery as a good. Jefferson's generation tended to portray slavery as a trap from which both whites and blacks could not extract themselves. "Can the liberties of a nation be thought secure when we have removed their only firm basis, a conviction in the minds of the people that these liberties are of the gift of God? That they are not to be violated but with his wrath?" Jefferson asked in *Notes on the State of Virginia* (1781). "Indeed I tremble for my country when I reflect that God is just: that his justice cannot sleep for ever." In spite of such sentiments, the hypocritical clash continued between the stated principles of the declaration and the reality of American slavery.

Slavery was one of two issues most frequently cited by critics regarding the hypocrisy of the Patriot movement. The other was religious liberty. As we have seen, many of England's American colonies were founded for religious reasons. Only Pennsylvania and Rhode Island offered religious freedom in anything like its modern meaning. The great religious diversity of many colonies caused conflict and elicited calls for religious liberty. These calls included Maryland's 1649 "Act Concerning Religion" and its promise of the "free exercise" of religion for all Christians. Into the Revolutionary era, however, many of the established churches still treated dissenters with contempt, if not outright violence.

The Great Awakening generated a new wave of activism for religious liberty. Especially in New England, where the Congregationalist Church was established, Separates and Baptists called on authorities to allow them to worship God in freedom. In Connecticut in 1748, a group of Separates petitioned the colonial legislature for religious liberty, calling freedom of conscience an "unalienable right" upon which the government should not intrude. Connecticut refused to act upon the Separates' plea, however.

Baptists were the most consistent advocates for religious liberty as the Revolution approached. As Separate Baptist churches and missionaries spread throughout the South, they fell under increasing persecution. In Virginia, where the Anglican Church was established, political and religious authorities took an especially harsh approach to dissenters. They put a number of legal requirements in place that made it difficult for dissenters to build churches and get preaching licenses. Many Baptists simply ignored these requirements. They suffered accordingly. Dozens of Baptist preachers were put in jail in Virginia in the 1760s and 1770s. One of them, James Ireland, was arrested for illegal preaching in Culpeper, Virginia, and was mercilessly hounded by anti-Baptist thugs. Ireland's supporters followed him to the jail, and Ireland tried to keep preaching to them through a window. Ireland's antagonists beat up his supporters, however, and some even urinated on him through the window as he attempted to keep speaking.

The plight of the Baptists drew the sympathy of nonevangelical leaders such as Thomas Jefferson and James Madison. Madison and Jefferson already believed in religious liberty as an intellectual precept. Theorists associated with the Enlightenment, such as England's John Locke, had argued for religious toleration for Protestant dissenters. The Enlightenment, as a catch-all term, can broadly refer to an emphasis on human rationality, scientific discovery, and naturalistic philosophy in the late 1600s and the 1700s. The abuse of Baptists and other dissenters hardened Madison and Jefferson's resolve to achieve disestablishment, or the end of state-supported religion. Madison deplored the persecution of dissenters. In a 1774 letter, he lamented the "diabolical hell conceived principle of persecution" then raging in Virginia. He asked his correspondent to "pray for Liberty of Conscience to revive among us."

The coming of the American Revolution was a turning point in the history of religious liberty in Virginia, and in America. Breaking away from Britain weakened the Anglican Church in the colonies, including in ones where the Anglican Church had been established. Dissenters made their support for the Revolution contingent upon an end to religious persecution. For example, Baptist leaders made clear that if their church members were going to serve in the Virginia state militia, they would require the appointment of Baptist chaplains, instead of just Anglican ones. The dissenters also bombarded the Virginia legislature with petitions calling for disestablishment and religious freedom. Jefferson recalled that the legislature was "crowded with petitions to abolish this spiritual tyranny [of the established church]. These brought on the severest contests in which I have ever been engaged."

The crusade for religious liberty won a significant victory in the 1776 Virginia Declaration of Rights. Patriot leader George Mason, the primary author of the Declaration of Rights, initially spoke of guaranteeing the "fullest toleration" of dissenters, employing terminology from John Locke. Madison wanted to go further, successfully arguing for a promise of "free exercise of religion." Tolerance implied forbearance granted by the government. Free exercise, to Madison, suggested that religious practice was a fundamental right upon which government should not encroach. Free exercise was a foundational concept that would reappear in the First Amendment to the US Constitution, which Madison would help to frame fifteen years later.

The Virginia Declaration of Rights guaranteed religious liberty, but it seemed not to touch the established Anglican Church. This was unsatisfactory to the militant dissenters. In October 1776 they produced a "Ten Thousand Name" petition calling for full religious freedom. "Your petitioners," it said, "having long groaned under the burden of an ecclesiastical establishment beg leave to move your honourable House that this as well as every other yoke may be broken and that the oppressed may go free" (Isaiah 58:6). The phenomenal ten-thousand name list probably totaled more than 10 percent of the entire white male population of Virginia. The campaign for religious liberty was generating mass popular support.

The Anglican Church in Virginia wobbled at the outset of the

Revolution, but full disestablishment had to wait another decade. The Virginia legislature suspended the "tithes," or obligatory religious taxes, supporting the church during the Revolutionary War. Once the war was over, the debate over establishment resumed. Some, like the popular Patrick Henry, argued that state funding for Christian churches should continue. Henry appreciated the growing power of the dissenters, however, so he proposed a "general assessment" for religion, under which citizens had to pay to support religion, but they could designate the church that would receive their support. Supporters of the general assessment believed that they could both honor religious liberty, and keep bolstering religion with state support.

The dissenters did not believe that the general assessment entailed real religious liberty. Total disestablishment was their goal. Madison and Jefferson once again partnered with Baptists and other non-Anglicans against the general assessment. Madison's 1785 *Memorial and Remonstrance* made a powerful case against any form of establishment. "The Religion then of every man must be left to the conviction and conscience of every man," Madison wrote. "It is the right of every man to exercise it as these may dictate. This right is in its nature an unalienable right." Dissenters showered the legislature with petitions against the general assessment. Ultimately the Virginia legislature tabled Henry's plan.

The defeat of the general assessment bill opened the door for Virginia to re-consider Jefferson's Bill for Establishing Religious Freedom, which he had originally proposed in 1779. Jefferson was away in Paris in the mid-1780s, so Madison took charge of the religious freedom bill. Jefferson employed a rationalist Christian argument to promote religious liberty. "Almighty God hath created the mind free," the bill declared. "All attempts to influence it by temporal punishments, or burthens, or by civil incapacitations, tend only to beget habits of hypocrisy and meanness, and are a departure from the plan of the holy author of our religion, who being lord both of body and mind, yet chose not to propagate it by coercions on either, as was in his Almighty power to do, *but to extend it by its influence on reason alone.*" The bill guaranteed full religious freedom to all Virginians: "no man shall be compelled to frequent or support any religious worship, place, or ministry whatsoever . . . but that all men shall be free to profess, and by argument to maintain, their opinions in matters of religion." The bill's adoption in early 1786 signaled the end of religious establishment in Virginia.

Most other states joined the trend toward disestablishment, though few took such a decisive step as Virginia did. Most states continued to have some form of a religious test for officeholders, such as requiring them to affirm a belief in God and the Bible. States also honored specifically Judeo-Christian morality in law, through statutes against Sabbath breaking or similar offenses. Several New England states continued to maintain state establishments of religion well into the 1800s. Federalists, the supporters of the Constitution, had originally contended that the Constitution did not need a Bill of Rights, but pressure from Anti-Federalist critics forced James Madison and other Federalists to support having one, including the First Amendment's religion clauses.

The fact that the religion clauses appear first in the First Amendment illustrates the primacy that the founders attached to religious liberty. To them, it was arguably the foundational freedom. The First Amendment stipulated, "Congress shall make no law respecting an establishment of religion, or prohibiting the free exercise thereof." The restrictions on establishment-making originally applied only to the national government, but during the twentieth century, the Supreme Court "incorporated" the First Amendment's protections in order to place religious restrictions on the states, as well. In 1791, the framers understood an "establishment of religion" to mean a national denomination. The First Amendment was prohibiting Congress from creating a national church or doing anything to inhibit the free exercise of religious practice. Article VI of the Constitution also prohibited religious tests for national officeholders. This prohibition, along with the First Amendment, won widespread approval from Baptists and other champions of religious liberty.

As the first president, George Washington wished to convey the protections of religious liberty to traditional "outsider" groups such as Catholics and Jews. In 1790, Moses Seixas, warden of the Touro Synagogue in Newport, Rhode Island, congratulated Washington on his election as president. Seixas insisted that the canopy of religious liberty should cover Jews in America. America embraced "a Government, which to bigotry gives no sanction, to persecution no assistance—but generously affording to All liberty of conscience, and immunities of Citizenship," he wrote. Washington replied warmly, echoing Seixas's phrases about the government giving "bigotry no sanction, to persecution no assistance." Washington prayed that the "Children of the Stock of Abraham, who dwell in this land, continue to merit and enjoy the good will of the other inhabitants, while every one shall sit in safety under his own vine and fig tree, and there shall be none to make him afraid." "Vine and fig tree" alluded to Micah 4:4, one of Washington's favorite Bible verses. References to the vine and fig tree appeared dozens of times in Washington's writings.

Madison and the Baptists had predicted that disestablishment would lead to purer, more vital religion in America. Whether religious liberty caused it or not, disestablishment was indeed followed by perhaps the greatest era of religious growth in American history. Glimmers of that growth began to appear during the Revolution itself. In 1780, legions of people crowded the churches of New England in response to the "Dark Day," when smoke from forest fires plunged the region into eerie darkness. Many saw the blanket of gloom as a warning from God. The Dark Day proved to be the inauguration of a major series of revivals known as the New Light Stir, lasting from 1780–82.

Immediately following the Revolutionary War, Methodist preachers began to swarm through the new American states. Founded by John and Charles Wesley in England, the Methodist movement was initially a reform effort within the Anglican Church. John Wesley had vociferously opposed the American rebellion, which put the Methodist work in America on hold during the war. Then in 1784, the Methodists granted autonomy to the American Methodist Episcopal Church. John Wesley appointed Francis Asbury, a master religious organizer, as one of America's Methodist co-superintendents in 1784. Breaking down traditional racial barriers, Asbury and other Methodist leaders encouraged some African American men to become leaders too. One was the dynamic preacher Harry Hosier, a former slave who had become a Methodist circuit preacher by the early 1780s. Thomas Coke, Asbury's co-superintendent, regarded Hosier as one of the "best preachers in the world, there is such an amazing power attends his preaching." There were limits to white Methodists' racial egalitarianism, however. Hosier apparently never received ordination, probably because of white reluctance to give a black man such authority.

Asbury did eventually ordain Richard Allen as a deacon in the Methodist church, despite Allen's status as a former slave. Allen was also a powerful preacher whose sermons drew crowds of both blacks and whites. An incident at a Philadelphia Methodist church convinced Allen that the city's blacks needed a separate church, however. Allen's pastoral colleague Absalom Jones was forcibly removed from a white section of the sanctuary where he had tried to kneel and pray. Jones, fed up with such discriminatory treatment, founded the African Episcopal Church of St. Thomas, while Allen in 1794 established the Bethel Methodist Church. Both of these congregations became key centers for Christian African Americans in Philadelphia.

The early national period saw an even greater flowering of religious diversity in America. The freedom afforded by disestablishment and the growing array of ethnic groups settling in America bolstered many new movements and churches. Among the most extraordinary sects were those led by Jemima Wilkinson, the "Public Universal Friend," and Ann Lee, the founder of the Shakers. The Dark Day of 1780 was a turning point in the ministries of Wilkinson and Lee, as both took it as a providential sign of approval on their unusual callings. Wilkinson was a preacher in Rhode Island who claimed to be the genderless vessel of the Holy Spirit and a prophet of the coming millennium, or thousand-year reign of Christ on earth. Like many sects tied to an individual, Wilkinson's movement did not create an enduring institutional legacy.

Jemima Wilkinson

Lee's ministry had begun in England before she moved to America. The Shakers, known for their exuberant, charismatic worship, believed that true Christians must practice celibacy. Celibacy always restricted the number of Shaker adherents, but in the 1780s they recruited hundreds of converts away from mainstream evangelical churches in New England and New York. Lee died in 1784, but the Shakers would reach the height of their popularity in antebellum America. By the early twenty-first century, the sect had become vanishingly small.

Shaker dancing

Increasing German immigration bolstered the Lutheran and Jewish presence in America during the eighteenth century. In 1795, Jews founded the first Ashkenazi synagogue in America, Philadelphia's Congregation Rodeph Shalom. Philadelphia's original synagogue, Mikveh Israel, was Sephardic, meaning that it observed rites associated with Spanish or Portuguese Jews. Ashkenazi Judaism was associated with Central and Eastern European Jews. The founders of Congregation Rodeph Shalom explained that they felt more comfortable worshiping "according to the German and Dutch rules." Congregation Mikveh Israel was apparently content to allow the Ashkenazi congregation to meet separately from them.

Far across the continent, Catholic missions continued to spread into the northern reaches of Spain's American empire as the Revolutionary War proceeded. Franciscans and Spanish workers began construction on a mission station and fort at the new settlement of San Francisco, California, in 1776. The work began just months after the Declaration of Independence was issued in Philadelphia, although the independence of Britain's east coast colonies and the founding of San Francisco had no causal connection to one another. In a celebration of the opening of the San Francisco mission, a priest "sang the mass with the ministers, and at its conclusion a procession was formed, in which an image of Our Seraphic Father San Francisco, patron of the port, presidio, and mission, was carried on a frame." The priest describing the festivities wrote that the "only ones who did not enjoy this happy day were the heathen." This comment suggested much about the California missions and the impossible situation into which they placed many Indians. The missions recruited great numbers of Indian proselytes. As we saw in chapter 1, California Indians suffered from high mortality rates after the coming of the missions, and the priests were constantly at risk of revolt from Native Americans, who often found the conditions in the missions abusive and intolerable.

As with so much of American history, the remarkable diversity of American religion at the time of the nation's independence makes it difficult to contain within a single narrative thread. This is especially the case if you extend the focus beyond the thirteen British colonies declaring independence to non-Anglo settlements such as the new one in San Francisco. The Revolution itself was no war of religion, but religious categories framed and inspired it. Developing alongside the major themes of American independence was a dizzying host of visionary prophets, founders of immigrant congregations, and clashing Europeans and Indians. Still, the era of the American Revolution ushered in an unprecedented era of religious liberty, with cascading effects for the vitality and conflict in American religion.

WORKS CITED
AND FURTHER READING

Brekus, Catherine A. *Strangers and Pilgrims: Female Preaching in America, 1740–1845*. Chapel Hill: University of North Carolina Press, 1998.

Byrd, James P. *Sacred Scripture, Sacred War: The Bible and the American Revolution*. New York: Oxford University Press, 2013.

Cohen, Charles L. "The 'Liberty or Death' Speech: A Note on Religion and Revolutionary Rhetoric." *William and Mary Quarterly*, 3rd ser., 38, no. 4 (Oct. 1981): 702–17.

Dreisbach, Daniel L. *Reading the Bible with the Founding Fathers*. New York: Oxford University Press, 2016.

Dreisbach, Daniel L., and Mark David Hall, eds. *The Sacred Rights of Conscience*. Indianapolis: Liberty Fund, 2009.

Haas, Lisbeth. *Saints and Citizens: Indigenous Histories of Colonial Missions and Mexican California*. Berkeley: University of California Press, 2013.

Harris, Matthew L., and Thomas S. Kidd, eds. *The Founding Fathers and the Debate Over Religion in Revolutionary America*. New York: Oxford University Press, 2011.

Hooker, Richard J., ed., *The Carolina Backcountry on the Eve of the Revolution: The Journal and Other Writings of Charles Woodmason, Anglican Itinerant*. Chapel Hill: University of North Carolina Press, 1969.

Hutson, James H. *Church and State in America: The First Two Centuries.* New York: Cambridge University Press, 2007.

Kidd, Thomas S. *God of Liberty: A Religious History of the American Revolution.* New York: Basic Books, 2010.

Morrison, Jeffry H. *John Witherspoon and the Founding of the American Republic.* Notre Dame, IN: University of Notre Dame Press, 2005.

Noll, Mark A. *America's God: From Jonathan Edwards to Abraham Lincoln.* New York: Oxford University Press, 2002.

Saillant, John. *Black Puritan, Black Republican: The Life and Thought of Lemuel Haynes, 1753–1833.* New York: Oxford University Press, 2002.

Sandoz, Ellis, ed. *Political Sermons of the American Founding Era, 1730–1805.* 2 vols. Indianapolis: Liberty Fund, 1998.

Chapter 4

THE ERA OF THE SECOND GREAT AWAKENING

By the year 1800, American Christianity, in tandem with the nation's population, entered a new phase of westward growth and organization. The nation's progress into the West displaced many Native Americans and precipitated the monumental Louisiana Purchase of 1803, by which the United States roughly doubled in size. Even before the Louisiana Purchase, white settlers surged into the Ohio River Valley region and the Deep South. By the 1840s, westward settlement spread out to California and the Oregon Territory, with people seeking gold and more farmland. Churches and itinerant pastors kept up with and even surpassed the pace of settlement, and they sometimes sought to address the plight of displaced Native Americans. Led by the Methodists and Baptists, churches socially organized the West on the ground level.

The Second Great Awakening was punctuated by massive revivals. These included its seminal event, the Cane Ridge Revival in Kentucky in 1801. Revivals often resulted in significant seasons of church growth. More than a series of revivals, the Second Great Awakening was also a process by which millions of Americans came into the fold of Christian congregations. Sometimes attending a revival was a critical part of the process for those who became devout church members. Just as important over the long term were the quieter labors of hard-working ministers who spread through the Midwest, Southwest, and ultimately the Far West. Town by town, family by family, they gave frontier people a message of gospel hope. They also provided them with a local church, which often represented the only regular social outlet that frontier families had.

Countless preachers and Christian laypeople participated in the frontier expansion of Christianity. For example, Joseph Willis was a former slave turned Baptist pastor, who may have delivered the first Protestant (or at least Baptist) sermon west of the Mississippi River. Willis received his freedom in 1787, the year of the Constitutional Convention in Philadelphia. Willis went from South Carolina into the Mississippi Territory and then into Louisiana. Napoleon Bonaparte of France acquired the vast Louisiana Territory, which included the future state of Louisiana, from Spain in 1800. Willis arrived in Louisiana around the time that President Jefferson arranged to procure the territory from France.

Willis helped to found Calvary Baptist Church near Alexandria in 1812, not long after Louisiana achieved statehood. He endured prejudice and threats of physical harm, partly because he was an African American man exercising religious leadership, and partly because he was a Protestant in a heavily Catholic region. (This Catholic heritage was due to the Spanish and French colonial influence in the area.) Nevertheless, Willis became a key Baptist organizer in Louisiana, working to establish several other Baptist churches. Fellow Baptists selected him as the first moderator of the Louisiana Baptist Association. African Americans would rarely find such opportunities to lead in white-dominated denominations. Willis's experience did illustrate the egalitarian potential in evangelical churches, and the relative social fluidity of the frontier. Willis likely would not have found such opportunities for leadership had he remained in South Carolina. Instead, he became one of a legion of traveling pastors who heralded the religious and social organization of the American frontier during the long era of the Second Great Awakening.

At the time of the American Revolution, church affiliation and membership rates remained surprisingly low. Some of the reasons for the low rates are easy to understand. White Christian overtures toward African Americans and Native Americans remained limited and accordingly bore few converts. Even among whites, however, church infrastructure was weak in rural areas, where most Americans lived. The Revolutionary era had only seen the beginnings of Methodist and Baptist evangelism. Those zealous groups would take the lead among Protestant adherents in the antebellum period. Still, a gap also remained between church attendance and church membership. Some of the most faithful attendees worried whether they showed satisfactory evidence of conversion, a prerequisite to membership in many Baptist, Congregationalist, and other churches.

In the immediate aftermath of the Revolution, Protestant churches entered a vital season of growth. The Methodists emerged from their self-imposed exile, which had resulted from John Wesley's opposition to the Revolution. The Methodists' highly managed "circuit" system brought regular preaching and church fellowship to thousands of Americans who previously had little access to them. In 1784, the Methodists counted about 15,000 adherents in America. By 1790, that number had quadrupled to 60,000. In 1810, Methodist adherents had more than doubled again to 150,000 members.

Baptists were committed to congregational autonomy and were not as centrally managed as the Methodist circuits were. They saw remarkable successes over the same period, though, led by bold preachers such as Louisiana's Joseph Willis. From about 35,000 American adherents in 1784, Baptists jumped to 65,000 by 1790, and more than

170,000 in 1810. Most Baptists in this era were Calvinists who affirmed the divine election of believers to salvation. The Revolutionary era also saw the rise of Freewill Baptist churches in New England. The Freewill Baptists quarreled with their Calvinist brethren over whether every person possessed the ability to receive Christ's offer of salvation. Freewillers insisted that instead of just dying for the sins of the elect, Christ had "tasted death for every man."

In the last quarter of the eighteenth century, much of the Baptist growth in America transpired in New York and on the northern frontier of New England. Baptists of the region's Shaftsbury Association prayed in 1790 that God would "pour down his Holy Spirit in the land, and revive pure and undefiled religion among us." That prayer was met with a stunning expansion of the association's member congregations. In 1791, the Shaftsbury Association had 26 churches with about 1,700 members total; by 1800 it had reached 46 churches and 4,100 members.

Evangelical churches began to reach African Americans in greater numbers as well, even before the formal beginning of the Second Great Awakening. Again, Methodists and Baptists led the way. White leaders among the Methodists and Baptists consciously reached out to African Americans. In some cases they supported black leaders as preachers and local church officers. We have already seen this inclusive tendency in cases such as the Methodists Richard Allen and Harry Hosier and the Baptist pastor Joseph Willis. The origins of evangelical growth among African Americans went back to the eve of the Revolution. In 1773, African American Baptists led by the former slave David George founded the Silver Bluff Church in western South Carolina, probably the first lasting African American church in American history. Like many African Americans, George sided with the British in the American Revolution, eventually finding his way to British-controlled Nova Scotia in 1782. A decade later, George and much of his Canadian Baptist congregation moved across the Atlantic to Sierra Leone, which had become a refuge for many former slaves in the British Empire.

Prior to the Civil War, Christian African Americans commonly attended white-pastored churches. Slavery remained a thorny issue in churches and not simply because of the question of slaveholding itself. Churches routinely confronted moral dilemmas created by chattel slavery, in which slaves were treated as pieces of transferable property. One of the most frequent issues was how to deal with slave marriages broken up by the sale of a spouse. Could a slave who had been forcibly removed from his or her spouse get remarried? Church members who owned slaves sometimes faced probing inquiries about the way that they disciplined their slaves. Whites widely accepted the idea that masters must use physical punishments. How much was too much? In 1772, one Baptist church in Virginia prohibited the punishment of slaves by "burning." Hardly a theoretical issue, this question had been prompted by the cruel actions of Brother Charles Cook toward one of his slaves. The church members suspended Cook, but he won reinstatement the next month following an apology given before white and black members.

Patterns of periodic growth had preceded the Second Great Awakening by a decade or more. A major season of revival began in the early 1800s, with its epicenter in Kentucky. The Presbyterian preacher James McGready was the key initiator of the fresh revivals. This fiery itinerant covenanted with three Kentucky congregations he oversaw to pray for "the outpouring of [the Holy Spirit], that his people may be quickened and comforted, and that our children, and sinners generally, may be converted." Starting in 1800, McGready wrote, the Lord "answered their prayers far beyond their highest expectations." McGready and other Presbyterians led weekend-long sacramental assemblies centered on the outdoor celebration of communion. Presbyterians from Northern Ireland and Scotland had known of these kinds of "solemnities" for centuries. Now what critics called "Holy Fairs" were exported to the American frontier.

Presbyterian minister Barton Stone, a future founder of the "Christian" movement (or the Churches of Christ), knew of McGready's revival work and began planning a mass meeting at Cane Ridge, near Lexington, Kentucky, for August 1801. The Cane Ridge meeting was advertised for weeks in advance and drew approximately twenty thousand people over the course of the weekend. At that time, Lexington itself only had two thousand residents. Many attendees at Cane Ridge and similar revivals planned to camp in wagons for the weekend, giving the assemblies the name "camp meetings."

Cane Ridge had a small meetinghouse, and it could hardly contain the throngs who came to the assembly. Dozens of ministers took turns preaching at sites surrounding the meetinghouse. This was a Presbyterian revival at heart, but Baptist and Methodist pastors were also involved. The round-the-clock services were intense, especially at night. Attendees saw and heard "sinners falling, and shrieks and cries for mercy awakened in the mind a lively apprehension of that scene, when the awful sound will be heard, 'arise ye dead and come to Judgment.'"

Cane Ridge Meetinghouse

Some participants, overcome with emotion and the travails of conversion, cried or danced uncontrollably. Others fell into trances that lasted up to twenty-four hours. Such experiences were not unusual among the radical evangelicals of the First Great Awakening. In the Second Great Awakening, however, they became more widespread, especially at the frontier revivals.

The question of conversion was a life-and-death issue for evangelicals. They believed heaven and hell were at stake in a person's faith in Christ, or lack thereof. Some conversions happened quickly, over the course of a single revival meeting. Others took longer. One Kentucky slave named Letty experienced conversion through the influence of her brother Asa, who labored as a Baptist exhorter. Neither Asa nor Letty were entirely convinced that her faith was sincere. The despondent Letty, fearing she could never be saved, considered drowning herself in the waters of the nearby Ohio River. As she threw herself headlong toward the river, though, a verse from the Gospel of Matthew sprung into her mind: "Come, ye blessed of my Father, inherit the kingdom prepared for you from the foundation of the world." She finally found her faith secured and confirmed. Soon she gave her testimony of faith before a Baptist church, which voted to admit Letty to believer's baptism and church membership.

Letty was just one of untold numbers of people in Kentucky and elsewhere experiencing conversion in 1800–1801. The rural churches of the Elkhorn Association of Baptists in Kentucky baptized thousands of new converts during those two years. The total membership of the churches grew threefold from 1,642 to 4,853. Between August and December 1801 alone, Kentucky Baptists may have baptized almost 2,500 people, or more than 1 percent of Kentucky's population. In the years following Cane Ridge, the Presbyterians saw debilitating infighting over theological issues such as those that led to the formation to Stone's "Christian movement." Stone and other Presbyterian ministers had developed concerns about Calvinist doctrine and the churches requiring subscription to the Westminster Confession of Faith. The Baptists and

Methodists, conversely, were on a pattern of long-term growth. The Methodists' numbers in Kentucky expanded tenfold from 1800 to 1820, during a time when the population of Kentucky grew by about 150 percent. That demographic increase was significant, but it was outpaced by the religious growth.

Charles Finney of New York became the most influential revivalist of the later stages of the Second Great Awakening. Finney trained as a lawyer until a dramatic conversion experience in 1821 convinced him to take up preaching. His family background was Presbyterian, but Finney gravitated away from the Calvinist emphases of the Presbyterian tradition. In particular, he taught that all people had free will to accept Christ's offer of forgiveness. Like Methodists and Freewill Baptists, Finney insisted that saving faith was not available only to God's elect. Finney also rejected the older notion that revivals were mysterious, unpredictable works of the Spirit. "Religion is the work of man," Finney wrote in his controversial *Lectures on Revivals of Religion* (1835). "It is something for man to do. It consists in obeying God." Of course, Finney conceded, Christians needed God to influence the work of revival. But God had given the church the means to induce revival. Primarily these means were gospel preaching and prayer.

If the church faithfully executed its responsibility, God would send revival every time. Finney sneered at those who said the timing of revival was up to God. Finney imagined that his critics would say, "It is very wrong for you to attempt to get up a revival, just because you think a revival is needed." Finney scoffed that "this is just such preaching as the devil wants." A belief in God's sovereignty should never preclude revivals, he insisted.

Finney saw his greatest preaching successes in the growing cities of upstate New York, such as Rochester and Utica. He introduced a series of "new measures," or techniques that sparked his revivals and led to greater numbers of conversions. The most famous of these was the "anxious bench." This was a pew at the front of the church or assembly hall where those in the travails of conversion could receive prayer and encouragement.

Finney also adopted other theological emphases that were more akin to Methodism than his native Presbyterianism. Most notably, Finney taught that Christians could achieve a high level of holiness called "perfection." This was not entire sinlessness, but a consecrated state in which a believer would seek to please God in all aspects of life. Finney also believed that Christians should exercise godly influence on society. He urged followers to avoid alcohol and dancing, and he stood against Christians owning slaves. Finney also gave women a prominent role in his meetings, allowing some to take on quasi-preaching roles as exhorters.

A number of women worked as itinerant preachers during the first half of the nineteenth century. Some of them, such as the politically connected Harriet Livermore, even appeared before special sessions of Congress. Women, as was typical in American church history, formed the majority of attendees in the ascendant evangelical denominations. Few of those denominations granted women speakers formal ordination, being mindful of biblical injunctions such as those in 1 Corinthians 14 against women speaking in churches. But some women argued that God *did* intend for women to preach. The African Methodist preacher Jarena Lee, for example, reasoned that "if the man may preach, because the Saviour died for him, why not the woman? Seeing he died for her also. Is he not a whole Saviour, instead of a half one?"

The Methodist leader Phoebe Palmer became a key advocate of the early "Holiness" movement. Inspired by Finney's type of emphasis on perfection, the Holiness movement made a deep impression on Methodism and other denominations, including the Wesleyan Church and the Church of the Nazarene. A popular speaker, Palmer became the first female Methodist class leader in New York City. Class meetings were Methodist small groups devoted to accountability and mentoring.

Influenced by her sister Sarah Lankford, Palmer experienced "entire sanctification" in 1837. She wrote that she could conceive of no "higher ambition, than to be endued with the unction of the Holy One, and then permitted, by the power of the Spirit, to say to every lover of Jesus, 'This is the will of God, even your sanctification' [1 Thessalonians 4:3]." As suggested by Finney, those who experienced entire sanctification lost all desire to sin. For Palmer, the invitation for Christians to experience sanctification became as much of a fixture of revival meetings as the appeal to sinners to accept salvation. The quest for holiness became a signature mark of vital Christianity in America.

The early decades of the 1800s saw huge religious growth, diversification, and conflict. The period of disestablishment also afforded a more prominent role for religious skeptics. Surging Christian commitment actually fed the skeptical backlash. Of course, the story of doubt about traditional faith was a much older one. In the colonial era, some Americans expressed serious questions about traditional Christian theology, especially about Calvinism. Some of the earliest skeptical views, especially universalism, emerged *from* Calvinism. Universalists espoused the notion that God would eventually save all people through Christ. If God chose some (the elect) for salvation, why would he not choose everyone? Charles Chauncy, Jonathan Edwards's key adversary during the First Great Awakening, became one of America's first universalists. Chauncy secretly cultivated universalist views for years before finally going public in the 1780s. He even coined a code term for universalism ("the pudding") because it was so controversial. Chauncy posited that since God was preeminently benevolent, he would not "bring mankind into existence, unless he intended to make them finally happy." Chauncy's brand of universalism still assumed that God was sovereign over the salvation of sinners, yet his emphasis on God's overruling beneficence led Chauncy to believe that God would choose to save all.

Deism was less an outgrowth of Calvinism than a rejection of it. We can see this most obviously in the case of Benjamin Franklin, who by his teen years had come to doubt his Puritan parents' faith. His father gave antideistic tracts to the bright boy, but Franklin found the deists' arguments more convincing than traditional Christians' arguments against deism. Thus, as Franklin wrote in his wildly popular *Autobiography*, he became a "thorough deist." To Franklin, deism meant downplaying doctrine and focusing on virtue and benevolent service as the essence of Christianity. He also doubted the divinity of Christ and the reliability of the Bible.

Deism was fashionable among educated men in the American Revolutionary era. Thus deism was overrepresented among the Founding Fathers. Thomas Jefferson was a more strident deist than Franklin, though Jefferson mostly kept his skepticism quiet until his political career had ended. Jefferson did consider himself a Christian, but he only revered Jesus as a moral teacher, not the Son of God. He wrote in 1803 that "to the corruptions of Christianity, I am indeed opposed; but not to the genuine precepts of Jesus himself. I am a Christian, in the only sense in which he wished any one to be; sincerely attached to his doctrines, in preference to all others; ascribing to himself every human excellence, and believing he never claimed any other."

Jefferson was convinced that Jesus's followers had imposed the claims of divinity on him after he died. This accounts for the so-called Jefferson Bible, which was Jefferson's multilanguage edition of the Gospels. Jefferson used a penknife to literally cut out sections of the Gospels that he found implausible, especially a number of the miracles attributed to Jesus. In the final verse of the Jefferson Bible, Jesus's disciples "rolled a great stone to the door of the sepulchre, and departed." There was no resurrection in his account. The Jefferson Bible was not published until the early twentieth century, but it illustrates the deistic image of Jesus as a great moral teacher and nothing more.

In letters to John Adams and others, Jefferson scoffed at Christian doctrines such as the virgin birth and the Trinity. He found the doctrine of the Trinity utterly unreasonable, and looked forward to the time "when we shall have done away the incomprehensible jargon of the Trinitarian arithmetic, that three are one, and one is three." Such criticism of the Trinity gave rise to the Unitarian movement, which emphasized the unity of God. Jefferson was quite sanguine about the prospects for Unitarianism, writing in 1822 that "I trust that there is not a *young man* now living in the United States who will not die an Unitarian." Numerically, the former president was wildly wrong. Unitarianism would never compete with groups like Baptists or Methodists for adherents. Unitarian thought did become culturally influential, drawing in proponents such as Jefferson, John Adams, and other elite Americans.

Unitarianism's foremost theological defender was William Ellery Channing, a Boston minister and social reformer. His definitive sermon on "Unitarian Christianity" came in 1819. Channing emphasized that Unitarians focused on the New Testament as God's supreme revelation to humankind. Nevertheless, he said, the whole Bible was a "book written for men, in the language of men." It was to be interpreted like other books, and it demanded the use of reason because "its style nowhere affects the precision of science." As for the movement's defining belief, Channing proclaimed that "we object to the doctrine of the Trinity, that, whilst acknowledging in words, it subverts in effect, the unity of God." He rejected the idea that God existed eternally in three coequal persons: Father, Son, and Holy Spirit. To the contrary, he argued, "There is one God, and . . . Jesus Christ is a being distinct from, and inferior to God."

The Unitarian movement gained an institutional focus with the founding of the American Unitarian Association in 1825. In 1961, that association merged with the Universalist Church to create the Unitarian Universalist Association. The denomination continues to have about one thousand affiliated congregations in America as of the 2010s. There was a strong anti-institutional bent within Unitarianism, however, as exemplified by the teachings of Ralph Waldo Emerson.

Walt Whitman

Emerson started off as a Unitarian pastor in Boston, but he resigned his pastorate in 1832 to devote himself to full-time speaking and writing on the radically anti-institutional, individual-focused transcendentalist movement. Emerson downplayed the value of formal religion, which he saw as almost invariably corrupt. "I am not engaged to Christianity by decent forms, or saving ordinances," Emerson said. "What I revere and obey in it is its reality, its boundless charity, its deep interior life" and "the perfect accord it makes with my reason through all its representation of God. . . . Freedom is the essence of this faith." The unfettered spirituality of the individual became the touchstone of Emerson's transcendentalist movement.

The deistic-Unitarian-transcendentalist trajectory in American thought may have reached its expressive height in the poetry of Walt Whitman, who had come out of a Quaker background before embracing transcendentalism. Whitman believed that no religion had the market cornered on spiritual veracity. Advocating a "Religious Democracy," Whitman asserted that each individual must find truth for himself or herself. "The ripeness of religion," he wrote in 1871, "is doubtless to be looked for in this field of individuality, and is a result that no organization or church can ever achieve."

Thomas Jefferson, Ralph Waldo Emerson, and many other religious commentators in the period from 1800 to 1860 shared a desire to bring

Christianity back to its original purity. But Americans could not agree upon what that original purity entailed. Liberal critics saw the Bible, and hidebound interpretations of it, as barriers to untainted faith. Conservatives saw the Bible alone as the guide to pristine, "restored" Christianity. Barton Stone and Alexander Campbell, early leaders of the Churches of Christ movement, believed that God wanted to elevate true Christians above the bickering denominations and to build a simple "Christian" movement based just on the Bible. Christian unity based on the Bible alone, Campbell predicted, would bring about the wholesale conversion of the nations to Christianity.

The Churches of Christ were a product of the frontier revivals of the Second Great Awakening. Though they started small, they grew quickly like the more prominent Baptists and Methodists. By 1900, there were more than a half a million adherents of the Churches of Christ. Yet vitality and conflict marked the history of the Churches of Christ too. Infighting over issues such as the use of musical instruments in worship led to a division between the Churches of Christ and the Christian Church (Disciples of Christ) in the late nineteenth century. The split was formalized in 1906. (We should not confuse the Churches of Christ with the United Church of Christ (UCC), a mainline Protestant denomination formed in 1957 as a merger of previous Congregationalist and Reformed churches.)

While the primitivism of the Churches of Christ looked backward to the original form of Christianity, many Christians across denominations equally looked forward to the end of all things. Since the Revolutionary era, America had seen the rise of millennial sects, such as the Shakers, who focused on the return of Christ to earth, or the establishment of the thousand-year reign of Christ. Many evangelicals operated with a sense that revivals and the worldwide spread of the gospel would result in Christ's return and/or the beginning of the millennium. American Bible interpreters also spun elaborate theories about the precise sequence of events leading up to Christ's return. Using numbers from apocalyptic books such as Daniel and Revelation, some commentators developed novel interpretations of Bible prophecy about what would happen in the last days.

The most influential such interpreter in the Second Great Awakening was New York's William Miller. Miller, a Baptist, had dabbled in deism prior to a dramatic conversion experience. His conversion led him to dive into Bible study, with special attention to the apocalyptic books.

Anti-Millerite cartoon

Some Christians were predicting that the millennium would actually precede Christ's return, but Miller did not see that sequence forecast in Scripture. Instead, based on a calculation derived from Daniel 8:14, Miller concluded that Christ was going to return to earth sometime between March 1843 and March 1844. Though many sneered at Miller's specificity, he had the courage to predict a date at which he would still be alive. "If I have erred," he said, all would soon know it. When Christ failed to physically appear at the predicted time, Miller recalculated his prediction to October 22, 1844. When Christ still tarried, Miller's legions of followers scattered. Some rejected Miller's eschatology (or theology of the last days) altogether. Others argued that 1844 did represent a critical turning point in redemptive history, just not the one that Miller had anticipated.

The chief institutional legacy of the Millerite movement was the Seventh-day Adventist Church, led by Ellen White. White and her followers still emphasized belief in prophecy and Christ's second coming, but they became convinced that Christ's church needed further purification before his return. They especially emphasized that Christians should observe the Jewish Saturday Sabbath (thus "Seventh-day") and adopt pure practices of eating and drinking. White claimed to have received hundreds of revelations from God to guide her ministry. With regard to health and eating, she insisted that "our bodies are Christ's purchased possession, and we are not at liberty to do with them as we please. . . . Therefore the question with us is not, 'What is the world's practice?' but, 'How shall I as an individual treat the habitation that God has given me?'" Adventists came to believe in vegetarianism, and their dietary views eventually became part of the American culinary mainstream. The corn flakes cereal of Adventist doctor John Harvey Kellogg started to become a staple of many Americans' breakfasts in the 1910s. Indeed, the Adventists remain one of the most enduring examples of the connections in American religion between the body, health, and faith. In contemporary America, medical researchers routinely study Adventists because of their remarkable longevity.

Most Americans rejected the details of William Miller's eschatology. They did not discard his fascination with the end times and the fulfillment of biblical prophecies, however. Starting in the mid-nineteenth century, "dispensational" theology became prominent in Britain and America. Dispensationalism illustrated the enduring Christian concern with future prophecy fulfillment. First systematized by the Anglo-Irish minister John Nelson Darby, dispensationalism broke redemptive human history up into a number of chronological "dispensations," such as the dispensations of law and of grace. Dispensationalists placed a great deal of emphasis on the future "rapture" of the church, when believers would be supernaturally taken from the earth prior to Christ's final return. Although dispensationalists have disagreed on details, the rapture generally coincided with the rise of the Antichrist and his forces' military assault on a restored Israel. This scenario culminated in the Battle of Armageddon, the return of Christ, and the inauguration of the millennium. The popularity of Darby's type of theology also helped to formalize a reaction against it. Thus "postmillennial" theology became more concrete by the mid-nineteenth century. Postmillennial theologians were those who expected Christ's return to happen *after* the millennium's thousand years of peace and righteousness. Commenters today often use "pre-" and "postmillennial" to describe earlier figures in church history, such as Jonathan Edwards, but this distinction is anachronistic prior to the rise of dispensational theology in the mid-1800s. Key American evangelists from Dwight Moody to Billy Graham were influenced by premillennial dispensationalism. The most important text popularizing dispensationalism was the Scofield Reference Bible, first published in 1909 by Oxford University Press. This work became the most influential study Bible of the twentieth century.

Mormonism, or the Church of Jesus Christ of Latter-day Saints, may be the most uniquely American religion. Although it transgressed the bounds of Christian orthodoxy, the Mormon faith was also a product of the ferment caused by the Second Great Awakening, democratized religion, and the openness of the frontier. Mormonism's founder, Joseph Smith, came of age in upstate New York, in a region that some have called the "Burned-Over District" because it was swept by so many revivals. His parents drifted both economically and spiritually. Smith professed to be disturbed by the bickering sects of the Second Great

Awakening era, not knowing where to turn for truth. Just before he turned fifteen, Smith was praying in the woods when he experienced his first vision. "I was seized by some power which entirely overcame me. . . . Thick darkness gathered around me, and it seemed to me for a time as if I were doomed to sudden destruction." God the Father and Jesus appeared to Smith, however, and told him that he must join no existing church, "for they were all wrong."

Then in 1823, Smith said that he received a visit from an angel named Moroni. Unlike angels such as Gabriel, Moroni was not an angel identified in the Bible or elsewhere in the Christian tradition. Moroni directed Smith to golden tablets that he found hidden at a nearby hill. By using a seer stone he had discovered while digging a well, Smith translated the plates, which he said were written in a forgotten language called Reformed Egyptian. In 1830, Smith published the translation as the Book of Mormon. Smith's book presented an epic, Old Testament–style narrative about the ancient struggles in the Americas between Hebrew tribes called the Nephites and Lamanites. Jesus himself had appeared to these tribes after his resurrection. In a cataclysmic battle, the Lamanites finally destroyed all of the Nephites except for Mormon and his son Moroni, who hid the plates on which Mormon had recorded the history of the tribes. After he died, Moroni transformed into an angel, who began appearing to Smith in the 1820s.

While traditional Christians reject the Book of Mormon, it is by any standard a remarkable production, especially from a person of little formal education such as Smith. Mormons cite this quality of Smith's work as one of the best evidences for the Book of Mormon's authenticity. While the Bible is silent about America having any special role in redemptive history, the Book of Mormon and Smith's revelations put America at center stage in the restoration of God's true church. The Mormons' opponents mercilessly harassed them, and Smith sometimes egged his persecutors on. In such a Bible-saturated culture, it was unacceptable to critics that Smith claimed access to new information about Jesus and divine history that other Christians had not known.

Placing the Book of Mormon and Smith's other revelations at the same level of the Bible contradicted centuries of Christian theology and tradition. The Mormons also embraced specific doctrines that Trinitarian Christians found unacceptable. For instance, Mormons taught that the Father, Son, and Holy Spirit do not represent the three persons of one God, but that "each member of the Godhead is a separate being."

More socially provocative was the Mormon endorsement of polygamy. In an 1843 revelation, Smith said that just as the Old Testament patriarchs had many wives, so also could Mormon men have multiple wives in the restored church. Smith recorded that God told him that "Abraham received concubines, and they bare him children, and it was accounted unto him for righteousness, because they were given unto him, and he abode in my law." Such controversial views forced the Mormons to flee from persecution multiple times during Smith's tenure as Mormon leader. The Mormon community went to Ohio and Missouri before Smith and his followers settled in Nauvoo, Illinois, in the late 1830s. There Smith continued to adopt more controversial stances. He set up a Mormon militia and declared himself a candidate for president in the 1844 US election. Illinois authorities finally put Smith and his brother Hyrum in jail in mid-1844. That June, a lynch mob broke into the jail and murdered the Smith brothers.

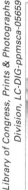
Library of Congress, Prints & Photographs Division, LC-DIG-ppmsca-05659

The Nauvoo Temple

Unlike many sects with a visionary leader, the Mormons did not collapse after Smith's death. His successor Brigham Young was, in a sense, an even more important leader in the history of Mormonism than Smith. Young took a large contingent of Mormons into the Mountain West in 1846–47. They settled at the Great Salt Lake in Utah, which they originally called Deseret. Over time, Mormon settlement spread from Utah throughout the West, north into Idaho and west into Nevada and California. Utah became a unique American territory and state, inextricably identified with the Church of Jesus Christ of Latter-day Saints.

Hostility toward the Mormons followed them to Utah, however. In the 1860s the federal government banned bigamy, or marrying someone when you are already legally married to another person. Mormon leaders challenged this law in the Supreme Court case of *Reynolds v. United States* (1879), which represented the first major religious liberty case in American history. In it, the court cited Thomas Jefferson's celebrated 1802 letter to the Danbury Baptists of Connecticut, in which he asserted that the First Amendment's religion clauses had built "a wall of separation between church and state." Although Jefferson was not directly involved in the framing of the First Amendment, the court asserted that this letter was an "authoritative declaration" of the amendment's intent.

The court concluded that under the First Amendment "Congress was deprived of all legislative power over mere [religious] opinion, but was left free to reach actions which were in violation of social duties or subversive of good order." Thus, it decided that the First Amendment's promise of "free exercise" of religion did not permit people to disobey valid laws in the name of religion. If they could, it would "make the professed doctrines of religious belief superior to the law of the land, and, in effect, to permit every citizen to become a law unto himself," the court ruled. Under continuous pressure, the Mormon Church finally agreed in 1890 to prohibit marital practices that contradicted the law of the land. Not coincidentally, Utah achieved statehood in 1896.

A remarkable cadre of revivalists and religious organizers had successfully exploited the new American nation's religious free market by the eve of the Civil War. Particularly across the frontier regions of the Ohio River and Mississippi River Valleys, restless and relentless leaders forged a new infrastructure for American religion. Fueled by bursts of revival, the pastors of the Methodists, Baptists, and many smaller denominations went from town to town starting new churches that would become the social and spiritual sinews of a growing nation. For lack of a better term, we call this sprawling organizational and revivalist process the Second Great Awakening. The leaders of that awakening were hardly satisfied with just building churches. They wanted to transform American society and evangelize the world.

WORKS CITED
AND FURTHER READING

Aron, Stephen. *How the West Was Lost: The Transformation of Kentucky from Daniel Boone to Henry Clay.* Baltimore: Johns Hopkins University Press, 1996.

Atkinson, Brooks, ed. *The Essential Writings of Ralph Waldo Emerson.* New York: Modern Library, 2000.

Boles, John B. *The Great Revival: Beginnings of the Bible Belt.* Rev. ed. Lexington: University Press of Kentucky, 1996.

Bowman, Matthew. *The Mormon People: The Making of an American Faith.* New York: Random House, 2012.

Channing, William E. *The Works of William E. Channing.* Boston: American Unitarian Association, 1888.

Conkin, Paul Keith. *Cane Ridge: America's Pentecost.* Madison: University of Wisconsin Press, 1990.

Hatch, Nathan O. *The Democratization of American Christianity.* New Haven, CT: Yale University Press, 1989.

Kidd, Thomas S. *Benjamin Franklin: The Religious Life of a Founding Father.* New Haven, CT: Yale University Press, 2017.

Kidd, Thomas S., and Barry Hankins. *Baptists in America: A History.* New York: Oxford University Press, 2015.

Lacorne, Denis. *Religion in America: A Political History*. Translated by George Holoch. New York: Columbia University Press, 2011.

Lee, Jarena. *Religious Experience and Journal of Mrs. Jarena Lee*. Philadelphia: Printed for the Author, 1849.

Mathews, Donald G. "The Second Great Awakening as an Organizing Process, 1780–1830: An Hypothesis." *American Quarterly* 21, no. 1 (Spring 1969): 23–43.

McLoughlin, William G., ed. *Lectures on Revivals of Religion, by Charles Grandison Finney*. Cambridge, MA: Harvard University Press, 1960.

Oden, Thomas C., ed. *Phoebe Palmer: Selected Writings*. New York: Paulist, 1988.

Sandeen, Ernest. *The Roots of Fundamentalism: British and American Millenarianism, 1800–1930*. Chicago: University of Chicago Press, 1970.

Schlereth, Eric R. *An Age of Infidels: The Politics of Religious Controversy in the Early United States*. Philadelphia: University of Pennsylvania Press, 2013.

Schmidt, Leigh Eric. *Holy Fairs: Scottish Communions and American Revivals in the Early Modern Period*. Princeton, NJ: Princeton University Press, 1989.

Stanley, Susie C. *Holy Boldness: Women Preachers' Autobiographies and the Sanctified Self*. Knoxville: University of Tennessee Press, 2002.

White, Ellen G. *The Ministry of Healing*. Washington, DC: Review and Herald, 1905.

Whitman, Walt. *Complete Prose Works*. New York: Appleton, 1910.

Chapter 5

GLOBAL AND
DOMESTIC MISSIONS

The early nineteenth century saw a great flowering of Protestant missions and social reform movements. As churches grew in influence, many leaders began to call on Christians to transform America's cities, the American West, and even the "heathen" world with the gospel. The global aims of missionary leaders were nearly boundless. Yale College president Timothy Dwight addressed the American Board of Commissioners for Foreign Missions in 1813 and envisioned American missionaries dismantling the worldwide infrastructure of competing religions, including Catholicism. He envisioned a day when "the Romish cathedral, the mosque, and the pagoda, shall not have one stone left upon another . . . when the Popish, Mohammedan, Hindoo, and Chinesian worlds shall be created anew."

Missions and social reform were hardly new concepts in American history. The founders of the seventeenth-century colonies often cited evangelism of Native Americans as one of their goals. And the Spanish and French Catholic colonists often did more to evangelize Indians than the Protestant colonies. New England's Puritans wished to reform society according to Christian principles, including the ideals of charity and relief for the poor. Even the deist Benjamin Franklin took an interest in Christian social reform, making an explicitly religious case for the founding of Philadelphia's charity hospital in the early 1750s.

But the level of effort in missions, evangelism, and reform ballooned after 1810. The evangelists and reformers turned their eyes to the American West, America's cities, and the wider world, and they saw great needs. Congregationalist missionaries Samuel Mills and Daniel Smith spoke for many when in 1815 they described the burgeoning American frontier, "from Lake Erie to the Gulf of Mexico," as "the valley of the Shadow of Death. Darkness rests upon it. Only here and there, a few rays of Gospel light pierce through the awful gloom." Baptist and Methodist evangelists might have painted a bit brighter picture, of course. Congregationalist agencies and other northeast-led forces of "national evangelism," as historian Sam Haselby has labeled them, typically overlooked the work of the Baptist and Methodist "frontier revivalists."

Mills and Smith were especially bothered by the absence of Bibles in the West. Hundreds of thousands of Bibles were required to make up the deficit nationally. This concern for placing Bibles in people's hands was the result of the Protestant conviction of *sola Scriptura*. Scripture alone was the inspired Word of God, a unique gateway to salvation. Evangelicals believed that if they put the Word of God in people's hands, many would be saved. To many Americans, even nonevangelicals, the Bible also represented a pillar of civilization. John Adams, a Unitarian, called the Bible the "best book in the world." He explained that the "Bible contains the most profound philosophy, the most perfect morality, and the most refined policy, that ever was conceived upon earth. It is the most republican book in the world." Adams was less interested in the Bible's saving message than its power for ethical and cultural refinement. To Mills and Smith, the absence of Bibles in so many homes was a "foul blot on our national character. Christian America must arise and wipe it away." Responding to such calls, evangelical reformers founded national Bible and Christian educational societies, such as the American Bible Society (1816). They sought to bolster evangelism and American civilization by making Bible ownership in America ubiquitous.

Evangelicals also contemplated the possibilities of going "into all the world" and preaching "the gospel to every creature," as Christ had commanded in Mark 16. Following the example of British evangelicals, Americans initiated systematic efforts at missions in the early 1800s, highlighted by the creation of the American Board of Commissioners for Foreign Missions (ABCFM) in 1810. The ABCFM would establish missions among Native Americans, as well as in China, India, the Middle East, Africa, and elsewhere around the globe.

Aside from the West and the world, the other focus of evangelism and social reform in this era was the urban poor. The situation in cities raised correlated concerns such as temperance (antialcohol) movements and the evangelization of Catholic immigrants. Many Protestant pastors and social reformers realized that reaching the cities required new methods. One Congregationalist minister in Boston illustrated the reformist concern when he proclaimed in 1843 that the "removal of human wretchedness, and the elevation of degraded man is the business of life."

As we saw in the previous chapter, the Louisiana Purchase of 1803 brought the vast territory between the Mississippi River and the Rocky Mountains into the nation, giving a revitalized western focus to immigration and ministry. Congregationalist minister Lyman Beecher illustrated the western-oriented mindset. Beecher was one of the greatest proponents of revivalism in New England during the Second Great Awakening. The opportunities and threats posed by western expansion led him to relocate to Cincinnati in 1832. In his landmark sermon "A Plea for the West" (1835), Beecher explained that salvation and civilization were both at stake in the evangelization of the frontier. "The religious and political destiny of our nation is to be decided in the

West," he declared. Beecher was horrified by the prospect that Catholics might beat out Protestants for western adherents. He anticipated a "conflict of institutions for the education of her sons, for purposes of superstition, or evangelical light; of despotism, or liberty." As the United States claimed more territory in the mid-1800s—by annexing Texas, asserting American sovereignty over the Oregon Territory, and seizing northern Mexico in the Mexican War—such concerns about the West increasingly animated Protestant observers.

While Congregationalists and Presbyterians thought in terms of establishing national organizations to reach the West, Baptists, Methodists, and the Churches of Christ tended to act locally. Thus these three populist denominations formed innumerable congregations in the West before the Civil War, many of them before Beecher made his famous plea. Methodist "circuit riders" took the gospel through the vast stretches of the frontier. One of them, James Gilruth, worked in the Detroit District of the Ohio Methodist Conference. He spent his days combining mundane frontier chores with the proclamation of salvation through Christ. Gilruth's journal showed him working from sunup to sundown in the 1830s, hauling wood and hay and chasing racoons out of storehouses. When Gilruth would preach at camp meetings, though, he would forget his humble setting and rejoice in the power of the Lord and the "comfort of the Spirit."

Beecher's fears about Catholicism in the West were overwrought. Nevertheless, Catholic organization and outreach did grow in the late 1700s and early 1800s. John Carroll was appointed Bishop of Baltimore in 1789, becoming America's first Catholic bishop. Also in the Baltimore area, Elizabeth Ann Seton (an adult convert to Catholicism) started the Sisters of Charity community, which worked with orphans and hosted a girls' school. In 1975, Seton would become the first native-born American to be named a Catholic saint. A steady flow of immigrants from Ireland and Germany made the Catholic Church the largest single Christian group in America by 1850, a position that no one Protestant group would ever overtake. Catholics would become an even more formidable numerical presence in America's great cities by the mid- to late-nineteenth century.

As illustrated by Beecher's plea, Catholicism in antebellum America came under assault from many Protestant quarters for being dangerous and un-American. The growing vitality of both Catholicism and Protestantism made conflict a certainty. The suspicion of Catholics occasionally resulted in violence, such as when a mob in Massachusetts destroyed an Ursuline convent in 1834. One of the most popular and salacious anti-Catholic publications of the era was *Awful Disclosures by Maria Monk of the Hotel Dieu Nunnery* (1836), which made graphic accusations about physical and sexual abuse at a convent in Montreal. The book was perhaps the greatest bestseller in antebellum America prior to *Uncle Tom's Cabin* (1852), by Harriet Beecher Stowe, the daughter of Lyman Beecher.

Catholicism found articulate defenders in America too. The most influential Catholic apologist in the nineteenth century was the former transcendentalist Orestes Brownson. Brownson argued that the authority of Catholicism was the ideal antidote to the fractious individualism of America. To Brownson, Catholicism was the perfect complement to American freedom: Catholicism "is necessary to sustain popular liberty, because popular liberty can be sustained only by a religion free from popular control." Catholicism was "made not by the people, but for them," Brownson wrote.

Catholics gave much attention to the West as well. They preceded Protestants there in the colonial era in the future states of New Mexico, Texas, Louisiana, California, and Michigan. Many Maryland Catholics relocated to Kentucky beginning in the early national period. French priests of the Sulpician order, some of whom had fled the French Revolution in the 1790s, supplied a number of resident priests in Kentucky. By 1815 there were approximately ten thousand Catholics living in Kentucky. Catholics founded five women's communities in the United States between 1790 and 1820, including the Sisters of Loretto and the Sisters of Charity of Nazareth, both in Kentucky. Catholics had also founded fourteen colleges by 1830. Most of them did not endure, but some did, including the 1819 Catholic college that was the forerunner to St. Louis University.

American Catholics sometimes borrowed a revivalistic spirit from their Protestant neighbors. In the 1820s, one Sulpician priest in the Diocese of Bardstown, Kentucky, wrote of meetings marked by "vividness of sorrow" and "abundance of tears, which accompanied the confession of [the people's] sins." Many congregants "gave extraordinary evidence of repentance," the priest wrote, "and showed a firm resolution to lead for the future, lives more Christian, or more perfect." Priests routinely warned that drunks, the sexually profligate, and other sinners risked God's wrath in hell, and that parishioners needed to surrender their lives to God and to the church's devotional rituals.

Some Jews also shared in the revivalistic impulse and the expansion into the West. The key figure in this process—and arguably the key American Jewish figure before the Civil War—was Isaac Leeser. The prolific Leeser was hired as a hazan, or leader of Jewish liturgy, at Philadelphia's venerable Congregation Mikveh Israel in 1829. Sermons were not traditionally central to Jewish services, but Leeser pioneered the delivery of English-language homilies focused on the theme of "regeneration." This was a distinctively Protestant term, but Leeser applied it to the American Jewish context. "The whole regeneration of Israel," Leeser warned, "rests on the basis of the precepts and commandments which we have received as the will of our Father in heaven." Leeser also contended that the Jewish tradition, especially the Hebrew Bible (what Christians conventionally call the

Isaac Leeser

Library of Congress, Prints & Photographs Division, LC-US262-5827

Old Testament), was essential to the American cultural tradition. The Bible, Leeser proclaimed, was "the book more venerable than all books, the parent of pure belief, the foundation of true human happiness, of religion without bigotry, of liberty without licentiousness."

Leeser was especially passionate about Jewish education. He wrote, translated, and edited more than a hundred books, including the first Jewish translation of the Hebrew Bible into English in 1853. The tireless Leeser traveled broadly in America and Canada, trying to rejuvenate Jewish communities which often had little leadership or resources. In 1851–52, Leeser took a remarkable journey through the Midwest and South, noting that he visited "at least twenty-five settlements or congregations of Israelites, from the shores of Lake Erie to the Gulf of Mexico." He once even traveled to California to bolster the Jewish community there.

As Protestant leaders and organizations turned their eyes westward, one of their animating concerns remained the evangelizing of Native Americans. For both Catholics and Protestants, this concern dated back to the colonial era. Serving as a missionary among Native Americans had come to be seen by evangelicals as a hallmark of spiritual commitment during the Great Awakening. In 1749, Jonathan Edwards published a phenomenally popular biography of David Brainerd, his protégé and a missionary to the Indians. Edwards's *Life of David Brainerd* was likely the most widely read publication Edwards ever wrote. Many later American missionaries were said to have taken two books with them: the Bible and Edwards's Brainerd biography.

The revivals of the Second Great Awakening in New England, as well as the spread of "New Divinity" theology, fueled a new passion for missions. Edwards had commended Brainerd's missionary work to his evangelical audiences. However, Edwards's broader philosophy of ethics struck some of his disciples as nebulous since Edwards had spoken of true virtue as "benevolence to being in general." New Divinity theologians such as Samuel Hopkins helped to concretize an ethic of "disinterested benevolence" that fostered charitable and evangelistic endeavors. One of the most conspicuous of these endeavors was missionary work. New Divinity leaders founded the Connecticut Missionary Society and the Massachusetts Missionary Society at the end of the eighteenth century.

The episode that advocates memorialized as the birth of American missions was the 1806 "Haystack Prayer Meeting" at Williams College in Massachusetts. Five Williams students who had gathered to pray were sent scurrying under a haystack by a sudden summer storm. Undaunted, the students prayed more fervently and dedicated themselves to the cause of missions. In 1810, New Divinity students at Andover Theological Seminary helped to found the ABCFM. The ABCFM was formally nondenominational, but it was led primarily by New England Congregationalists. Despite its "foreign" appellation, half of the ABCFM's efforts in its first decade went toward the evangelization of Native Americans. Over time the ABCFM tended to see more opportunity with "heathens" around the globe who were somewhat more "civilized" and seemed more likely to convert to Christianity than American Indians.

The ABCFM's first mission stations among the Cherokees and Choctaws were named for David Brainerd and John Eliot (the Puritan missionary to Indians), respectively. They also established stations among the Chickasaws, Creeks, and Osages. The ABCFM's strategy was to establish schools, believing that civilization and education were predicates to evangelization, and the US government was happy to support the civilizational aspect of the ABCFM ministry. Congress appropriated ten thousand dollars a year—a significant sum at the time—to assist the ABCFM and other missions organizations in the 1820s.

One of the most prominent Cherokee converts to Christianity was Galagina, who took the English moniker Elias Boudinot, the name of one of America's Founding Fathers and a president of the American Bible

Society. Galagina studied New Divinity theology at schools including Andover Theological Seminary. In 1823, Galagina returned to Cherokee territory in Georgia. He helped translate the New Testament using the new Cherokee syllabary developed by his fellow tribesman Sequoya. Galagina also worked in 1828 with the ABCFM printer and missionary Samuel Worcester to establish the *Cherokee Phoenix*, the first newspaper printed partly in a Native American language.

The discovery of gold in north Georgia, as well as the inauguration of Andrew Jackson as president in 1829, did not bode well for the Cherokees or the missionaries' work among them. As US authorities sought to remove the Cherokees from their lands, Cherokee leaders and some missionaries tried to resist. The imprisonment of ABCFM missionary Samuel Worcester ultimately led to the Supreme Court case of *Worcester v. Georgia* (1832), in which the court affirmed that the Cherokee nation was not subject to Georgia state laws. Nevertheless, Georgia authorities and President Jackson ignored the ruling. ABCFM officials came to believe that removal was inevitable. With Worcester's encouragement, Galagina took a controversial step in 1835 when he signed away Cherokee tribal lands in a treaty that only had the blessing of a minority of Cherokee leaders. This Cherokee minority agreed with the white missionaries that further resistance was futile. Worcester and Galagina relocated to Oklahoma with the Cherokees prior to the infamous "Trail of Tears," which transpired in 1838. Cherokee rivals assassinated Galagina in 1839 for his role in signing away their lands.

The ABCFM sent missionaries around the world, to places including the Middle East, the Indian subcontinent, Micronesia, and the Sandwich (or Hawaiian) Islands. Hawaii had for years served as a stopover in British and American voyages across the Pacific Ocean. The ABCFM sent its first missionary contingent to Hawaii in 1819. One of the most intriguing missionaries in Hawaii was Betsey Stockton, who once had been a slave to a president of the College of New Jersey (Princeton). Stockton formally went to Hawaii as a servant to the ABCFM missionaries, but she also worked as a missionary and educator in her own right. This made Stockton one of the earliest female missionaries to go out from the United States.

A few years after the arrival of ABCFM missionaries, they began to see converts among Hawaiian leaders, including Chiefess Kapiolani. In 1824, the zealous convert Kapiolani challenged the authority of the traditional Hawaiian fire goddess Pele. In a dramatic confrontation, Kapiolani entered an active volcano and declared her newfound faith in Christ in the cauldron of the fire goddess. By 1837, some ninety ABCFM workers were laboring in Hawaii, backed by hundreds of native Hawaiian assistants. That year, the islands saw the start of a phenomenal revival. Eventually tens of thousands of Hawaiians, a sizeable percentage of the islands' population, were affiliated with Christianity and the message of the missionaries.

In spite of these successes, ABCFM missionaries struggled to avoid political controversies in Hawaii. ABCFM agents routinely meddled in government controversies and sometimes took material advantage of converts. Although the ABCFM tried to crack down on abuses, critics routinely raised charges of exploitation. The American novelist Herman Melville, for example, scoffed that the Hawaiian "natives [have] been civilized into draught horses, and evangelized into beasts of burden." Evangelical missionaries were not the only American religious option, either. Mormons began to arrive in Hawaii in 1850, eventually turning the islands into one of Mormonism's centers of greatest strength outside of Utah.

Protestant missionaries eventually made their way to the Pacific Northwest too, as explorers and traders opened areas such as the Oregon Territory. The ABCFM sent missionaries Marcus and Narcissa Whitman to present-day Washington state in 1836. There they labored among white settlers and the Walla Walla and Cayuse Indians. Like most of the ABCFM missionaries, the Whitmans saw themselves as being on a mission of charity and salvation. Narcissa wrote of their desire to "save the Indian-the hunted, despised and unprotected Indian-from entire extinction." They also wanted to save the Indians from the overtures of Jesuit missionaries, who had set up Catholic stations in the region. Increasing numbers of American arrivals came to the Northwest via the "Oregon Trail." More white settlers meant more land pressure and new bouts of epidemic disease among the Walla Wallas and Cayuses. Marcus was a doctor, but he had little success at preventing measles and other diseases among the Indians. Resentful Cayuses killed the Whitmans in 1847, believing that they were to blame for the disasters their tribe had experienced over the past decade.

While the ABCFM was the most prominent of the missions-sending agencies, it was hardly the only one going into the West or around the globe. Early Baptist missionaries were, like many Congregationalists, influenced by the New Divinity theology of Jonathan Edwards's successors. Baptists and Congregationalists partnered in the founding of the Female Society for Missionary Purposes in Boston. One of the key leaders of this society was the Baptist Mary Webb, who had been a paraplegic since her childhood. Webb had grown up as a Congregationalist (and thus had been baptized as an infant), but she received baptism as a believer in 1798. Inspired by the teaching of New Divinity theologian Nathanael Emmons, Webb and a number of other Boston-area women founded the Female Society for Missionary Purposes in 1800, which encouraged the distribution of Bibles and other Christian literature "by missionaries in destitute places."

Adoniram Judson, the most influential Baptist missionary of the era, started out as a Congregationalist missionary with the ABCFM. Judson, his wife Ann Hasseltine, and his father, a Congregationalist pastor, were all influenced by New Divinity principles. Judson had a conversion experience while studying at Andover Theological Seminary and was instrumental in founding the ABCFM. In 1812, the Judsons left the United States to work as ABCFM missionaries in India. As an early biographer noted, Judson and the first ABCFM missionaries to the East had become "convinced that Asia, with its idolatrous myriads, was the most important field on earth for missionary effort." News of the successful ministry of British missionaries, as well as the protective infrastructure of the British Empire in India, also made the Indian subcontinent an attractive destination.

One of the most celebrated English missionaries working in India was the Baptist William Carey, whose book *Enquiry into the Obligations of Christians, to Use Means for the Conversion of Heathens* (1792) marked the advent of the modern missions movement. Carey helped to found the English Baptist Missionary Society. American and British missionaries often operated in a symbiotic relationship, especially on the Indian subcontinent, in spite of tensions between their two nations created by the American Revolution and the War of 1812. As he sailed to India, Judson studied the theology of baptism so that he would be prepared should the British Baptist missionaries challenge his belief in paedobaptism. Instead of bolstering his commitment to the baptism of infants, Judson's study led him to accept Baptist principles too. Ann and Adoniram eventually received believer's baptism by immersion in Calcutta. They resigned from the ABCFM and started a Baptist mission in Burma in 1813. Their mission prompted the formation of the Baptists' Triennial Convention in 1814, the first national Baptist organization. African American Baptists led by Lott Cary of Richmond, Virginia, also created the African Baptist Missionary Society in 1815. In 1821 Cary himself went to Liberia in West Africa as a missionary.

Baptists also sent missionaries among Native American groups. One of the most important early Baptist missionaries in the Midwest was Isaac McCoy, who had experienced conversion and received baptism during the high season of revivals in Kentucky in 1801. The Triennial Convention appointed him as a missionary in 1817. McCoy established stations among Native Americans in Indiana and Michigan, working among the Ottawa Indians in Michigan and trying to shield them from French Catholics and the exploits of white whiskey traders. McCoy was so dismayed by the harmful effects of alcohol among the Indians that he became a proponent of relocating Native Americans west of the Mississippi River. He thought doing so would help the Indians avoid being swept into the "vortex of ruin by whiskey sellers."

McCoy saw relatively few Indian converts under his ministry. More successful was the Baptist work among the Cherokees, primarily because the white Baptists in western North Carolina and north Georgia gave Cherokees significant leadership responsibilities. The most influential white Baptist missionary among the Cherokees was Evan Jones. Jones began work in western North Carolina in the early 1820s. He encouraged native leadership among the Cherokees, including that of Tastheghetehee, whose Anglicized name was Jesse Bushyhead. Bushyhead had experienced conversion at an ABCFM school, but by the late 1820s he had come to believe in Baptist views. Evan Jones helped Tastheghetehee secure ordination as a Baptist missionary. By the early 1830s, Jones, Tastheghetehee, and other Cherokee Baptists began to see dozens of Cherokee conversions. The Cherokee missionaries were able to convince some non-English speaking Cherokees to embrace Christianity too. Overall, however, the conversion of non-Anglicized Native Americans was quite rare during this era.

The white and Cherokee Baptist missionaries also ran afoul of Andrew Jackson's Indian removal campaign in the 1830s. Unlike Isaac McCoy, Evan Jones opposed the removal of Indians into the West. Jones also denounced the treaty signed by Cherokee Galagina (Elias Boudinot) as "unjust and unauthorized." Tastheghetehee and Jones remained with the Cherokee Christians even as American soldiers began rounding them up for the forced march to Oklahoma. They baptized dozens of converts on the eve of the Trail of Tears. Jones estimated that 175 new church members were added as the Cherokees languished in detention camps. Jones, Tastheghetehee, and other Baptist missionaries finally helped detachments of Cherokees make the grueling march into the West, during which thousands of Cherokees would perish. Jones and Tastheghetehee's groups crossed an icy Mississippi River in late 1838 and finally arrived in the Indian Territory in Oklahoma in early 1839.

Baptist and Congregationalist missionary efforts were impressive, but the Methodists were probably the most mission-oriented of all Protestant denominations. Many of their preachers and circuit riders *were* missionaries. Itinerant Methodists visited people from home to home in the vast stretches of the frontier. The Methodist *Book of Discipline*, the denomination's guide to doctrine and practice, said that God had raised up Methodist clergy in order to "reform the continent, and to spread Scriptural holiness over the land." Probably the first Methodist to target Native Americans for evangelization was the free African American minister John Stewart. Stewart had experienced conversion at a Methodist camp meeting in Ohio and felt called to begin working among the Wyandots of north-central Ohio. First licensed as an exhorter, Stewart eventually became a Methodist minister in 1819. Stewart's pioneering work among the Wyandots inspired the creation of the Methodist Missionary Society in 1819.

Some Protestants did question the validity of the missionary movement. Why did Christians need any organizations besides churches to do the work of the kingdom? Such critics, including

Methodist Missionary Society membership form

members of the Churches of Christ and "Primitive" Baptists, said that God had ordained no extra-churchly organizations to perform evangelism. The critics had a populist bent and were suspicious of New England–dominated missions organizations like the ABCFM. Antimissions critics noted that the missionaries always seemed to be asking for money and that they drained resources from churches. Primitive Baptists also had a hyper-Calvinist streak, which inclined them to think that God would gather the elect without the assistance of missionary societies. Primitive Baptist critiques of the national societies began to emerge in the 1810s. By the 1820s and '30s, Primitive Baptists dominated Baptist life in parts of the South and Midwest. By 1844, some sixteen hundred Baptist churches had broken away from the pro-mission Baptists of the Triennial Convention. It was the most crippling split among Baptists until the formation of the Southern Baptist Convention in 1845.

Besides the global cause of missions, evangelical Christians also fostered an enormous campaign for religious literacy, education, and moral reform. Religious groups founded some six hundred magazines between 1790 and 1830. Agencies like the American Bible Society and the American Tract Society (1825) seized upon technological advances in publishing to make inexpensive Bibles and other religious literature widely available. These groups drew prominent supporters to the cause. For example, the Episcopalian John Jay, who was one of the authors of the *Federalist Papers* and the first chief justice of the Supreme Court, served as president of the American Bible Society (ABS) in the 1820s. These societies became engines of evangelistic print, with the ABS alone producing more than a million copies of the Scriptures between 1829 and 1831.

During that period, the ABS engaged in a feverish campaign to place a Bible in every American home. The effort was a great success in settled areas of the East, but it struggled in rural areas of the South and Midwest. As we have seen, northeastern evangelicals worried about the irreligion and Catholic competition in the West, so the ABS labored tirelessly to suffuse the frontier with the Scriptures. During this "Bible in every home" campaign, one anonymous ABS agent rode some two thousand miles across the trans-Mississippi frontier in just six months, preaching, raising money, and encouraging local ABS affiliates. By the end of the campaign, the ABS had not succeeded in getting Bibles into many homes in the Gulf Coast region or Mississippi River Valley. The attempt, however, had made the Bible more pervasive than ever before in America.

Religious reformers also led the way in educating children and teenagers. Until the 1830s, education in most areas was still based in churches. College education remained rare and, until the 1830s, was exclusively for men. In the late 1700s, Sunday schools began to appear as a way to bring literacy and religious education to children. These Sunday schools flourished especially in cities. They originally tended toward a "republican" model of education, seeking to inculcate values of good citizens. By the time of the formation of the American Sunday School Union in Philadelphia in 1824, Sunday schools focused more on the need for students and teachers to experience evangelical conversion. In time, most major denominations would establish their own Sunday schools and fold them into their churches. The American Sunday School Union remained a powerful interdenominational force, founding some seventy thousand Sunday schools during the 1800s.

Protestants also remained dominant in college education, in spite of a small number of "secular" schools, such as Thomas Jefferson's University of Virginia (1819). Even the University of Virginia assumed that students would learn the biblical precepts "on which all sects agree." Concern for the frontier West led to the founding of colleges there, as well as in more established areas of the East. Between 1815 and 1848, the number of colleges and universities in America jumped from 33 to 113. Among the new schools dotting the frontier were Charles Finney's Oberlin College, founded in Ohio in 1833; the Catholic college Notre Dame, founded by the Congregation of the Holy Cross in Indiana in 1842; and the Baptists' Baylor University, chartered by the Republic of Texas in 1845. The early 1800s also saw the advent of stand-alone divinity schools designed for graduate study for ministry after a student's degree from an undergraduate institution. Andover Seminary, established in 1808 as a counterweight to Unitarian-dominated Harvard, was the first such divinity school. Presbyterians also established a separate divinity school at Princeton in 1812. Princeton Theological Seminary would exercise enormous influence on American Presbyterianism in the nineteenth century, with such faculty scholars as Charles Hodge, who probably taught more graduate students than any other professor in America during the era.

The cities, teeming with new immigrants, also seemed like a new frontier to antebellum Protestants. Evangelical leaders such as Phoebe Palmer, the Methodist pioneer of the Holiness movement, applied their reformist faith in benevolent ministry to city dwellers. Palmer founded the "Five Points" mission in New York City in 1850, one of the first Christian missions in a tenement district in America. The Five Points mission was originally focused on evangelism and religious education, but it soon broadened to include vocational training and safer housing. The competing aims of the mission sometimes caused conflict between leaders, and Palmer herself tended to prefer straightforward evangelism to social relief. The Five Points mission nevertheless impressed observers with its ministry to the destitute. One guidebook recommended that visitors see a Thanksgiving or Christmas program there, with hundreds of mission children "singing charmingly, exhibiting great proficiency in education and a wonderful knowledge of the Bible, sitting down to a well-laid table." Evangelical reformers longed to see such scenes multiply among the destitute of America's cities.

One of the direst concerns that evangelical reformers had about city life was pervasive alcohol abuse. Lyman Beecher spoke for many when he argued that drunkenness was not only sinful for an individual, but that it undermined the "national conscience or moral principle." In 1826, Beecher helped to establish the American Temperance Society (ATS). Alcohol abuse was a major social problem in antebellum America, and the temperance movement attracted more than a million members to local affiliates of the ATS. Women took prominent roles in temperance. Many Americans assumed that women played a critical role in upholding moral standards for wayward fathers, brothers, and sons. *Temperance* as a term did not necessarily mean entire abstinence, but in the mid-1800s it became increasingly common for Protestants to believe that an obedient Christian should never take a drink. The movement helped attach a new social stigma to drunkenness, and America's per capita rate of alcohol consumption dropped significantly between the 1830s and 1850s.

By the mid-1800s, Americans had made significant advances in spreading the Christian gospel, and the Bible itself, throughout America and around the world. They had also opened significant new fronts in battles against poverty, drunkenness, and lack of education. In the 1830s, the abolitionist movement—perhaps the most celebrated reform effort of the era—was just beginning. Many white northern Christians would also come to denounce slavery, but many other white Americans in the South and North saw the Bible as endorsing slavery. Most African American Christians, of course, had no doubt about the institution's immorality and did whatever they could to undermine it. In time, this moral debate would feed the acrimony that finally led to the Civil War.

WORKS CITED
AND FURTHER READING

Beecher, Lyman. *A Plea for the West.* 2nd ed. Cincinnati: Truman & Smith, 1835.

Brownson, Orestes. *Essays and Reviews Chiefly on Theology, Politics, and Socialism.* New York: Sadlier, 1887.

Conroy-Krutz, Emily. *Christian Imperialism: Converting the World in the Early American Republic.* Ithaca, NY: Cornell University Press, 2015.

Dreisbach, Daniel L. *Reading the Bible with the Founding Fathers.* New York: Oxford University Press, 2016.

Fea, John. *The Bible Cause: A History of the American Bible Society*. New York: Oxford University Press, 2016.

Franchot, Jenny. *Roads to Rome: The Antebellum Protestant Encounter with Catholicism*. Berkeley: University of California Press, 1994.

Guthman, Joshua. *Strangers Below: Primitive Baptists and American Culture*. Chapel Hill: University of North Carolina Press, 2015.

Haselby, Sam. *The Origins of American Religious Nationalism*. New York: Oxford University Press, 2015.

Jeffrey, Julie Roy. *Converting the West: A Biography of Narcissa Whitman*. Norman: University of Oklahoma Press, 1991.

Kling, David W. "The New Divinity and the Origins of the American Board of Commissioners for Foreign Missions." *Church History* 72, no. 4 (Dec. 2003): 791–819.

Leal, Elise. "'All Our Children May be Taught of God': Sunday Schools and the Roles of Childhood and Youth in Creating Evangelical Benevolence." *Church History* 87, no. 4 (December 2018): 1056–90.

Long, Kathryn. *The Revival of 1857–1858: Interpreting an American Religious Awakening*. New York: Oxford University Press, 1998.

McLoughlin, William G. *Cherokees and Missionaries, 1789–1839*. New Haven, CT: Yale University Press, 1984.

Mintz, Steven. *Moralists and Modernizers: America's Pre–Civil War Reformers*. Baltimore: Johns Hopkins University Press, 1995.

Phillips, Clifton J. *Protestant America and the Pagan World: The First Half Century of the American Board of Commissioners for Foreign Missions*. Cambridge, MA: Harvard University Press, 1969.

Richards, Thomas C. *Samuel J. Mills: Missionary Pathfinder, Pioneer and Promoter*. Boston: Pilgrim Press, 1906.

Smith, Timothy L. *Revivalism and Social Reform: American Protestantism on the Eve of the Civil War*. Rev. ed. Baltimore: Johns Hopkins University Press, 1980.

Spalding, Martin John. *Sketches of the Early Catholic Missions of Kentucky*. Louisville: B. J. Webb & Brother, 1844.

Sussman, Lance J. *Isaac Leeser and the Making of American Judaism*. Detroit: Wayne State University Press, 1995.

Wayland, Francis. *A Memoir of the Life and Labors of the Rev. Adoniram Judson*. 2 vols. Boston: Phillips, Sampson, and Company, 1853.

Chapter 6

SLAVE RELIGION AND MANIFEST DESTINY

Most African slaves arrived in America with little to no background in Christianity, and white Christians made only slow evangelistic progress among African Americans before the American Revolution. By the 1830s, however, the mass conversion of much of the African American population to some form of Christianity had begun. Baptists and Methodists made major inroads among African Americans, sometimes appointing African American men as pastors, exhorters, or elders. These black leaders, including the African Methodist Episcopal pastor Richard Allen and the Baptist pastor David George, were typically more effective than whites were at reaching African Americans. The specter of black conversions and black religious leadership was still frightening to some whites. The vitality of black Christianity set the stage for some of the worst outbreaks of racial violence in the antebellum era.

White critics had worried that Christianizing African Americans, especially slaves, was dangerous. Doing so might give slaves notions about their rights as Christians and about God's deliverance for those in bondage. Whites routinely saw religious factors behind slave uprisings. The 1822 Denmark Vesey rebellion was ostensibly centered in

Charleston, South Carolina, at the popular African Methodist Episcopal Church, which the carpenter Vesey had helped to found in the late 1810s. Some historians today question whether there was an actual plot among Charleston's African Americans or whether white instigators fabricated the charges. In 2015, this historic church also became the scene of the murder of nine congregants by a white supremacist shooter. African American churches have long been a focus of white concern and sometimes of white violence.

The most notorious slave uprising of the antebellum era was not a figment of whites' imaginations. Nat Turner's rebellion in southern Virginia in 1831 also had religious origins. Turner was a visionary and a lay Baptist preacher, who was inspired by apocalyptic passages in the Bible. He saw apparitions in the sky and blood in the fields, making him believe that Judgment Day was imminent. In 1828, he received a revelation that the satanic "Serpent was loosened, and Christ had laid down the yoke he had borne for the sins of men, and that I should take it on and fight against the Serpent." For Turner, white slave-owning families represented the power of the Serpent. As he observed successive eclipses, he believed that God was instructing him to make war against slavery. In August 1831, Turner and dozens of his followers rose up and killed about sixty whites, using axes, clubs, and their bare hands. Turner evaded capture for weeks, but white authorities cracked down on the neighboring black community. They arrested, lynched, and summarily executed several dozen African Americans in retaliation.

"Horrid Massacre in Virginia" (1831)

Turner himself was finally captured in October 1831. When someone asked Turner if he stood by his murderous acts, Turner responded, "Was not Christ crucified?" Virginia authorities executed Turner by hanging and then skinned and dismembered his body.

Nat Turner was hardly a representative African American Christian leader. Suffering under slavery and oppression were nevertheless common experiences of African Americans. Many black Christians—especially slaves—attended white-led congregations, sometimes with the master's family. It is difficult to know if individual slaves found such churches satisfying or whether the specter of white supremacy was a constant offense to them. Most white church leaders were happy to have blacks attend their churches, seeing them as individuals in need of salvation regardless of their social standing. Whites also believed that Christianity, when rightly understood, would foster obedience and hard work among slaves. Therefore, white Christians tended to see Nat Turner as holding aberrant beliefs, although some antievangelical critics saw his uprising as a natural result of the Christianization of slaves. One observer argued that Turner's revolt was a by-product of evangelical preachers' "ranting cant about equality." Some whites demanded that the churches stop evangelizing slaves and teaching them to read.

Free African Americans attended a range of congregations: some independent black churches, some white-led churches where they were in the majority, and some white churches where they were in the minority. In some, they sat amongst white congregants during services. In churches with larger sanctuaries, blacks would sit in a balcony, while whites sat in pews on the main floor. The South had fewer independent black churches during the antebellum era than did the northern states. Yet it was not unusual for southern white churches to allow blacks to form auxiliary congregations with semiautonomous status.

White leaders delicately balanced their desire for black Christianization and blacks' desire for religious autonomy. For example, First Baptist Church of Richmond, Virginia, licensed black preachers to minister to the city's African Americans, but the church revoked a dozen of those licenses when Turner's revolt happened. Five years after the rebellion, the church remained primarily African American: some

2,000 of 2,400 church members were black. In 1841, the white congregation authorized the founding of the First African Baptist Church to allow for the "peculiar instruction" that slaves and free blacks were believed to require. This hesitant trend toward allowing independent black churches would become an avalanche in the immediate aftermath of the Civil War.

Many African American Christians, especially slaves, met in informal religious services during the antebellum period. In the slave quarters and brush arbors (sometimes called "hush harbors" because of their secrecy), slaves voiced their own songs, prayers, and sermons. These meetings quietly marked the advent of an African American Christian tradition. In unguarded moments, Christian slaves would contrast the preaching they heard in the white-pastored churches with that in the brush arbors. Many white pastors would simply lecture them about honesty and hard work. A former slave named Lucretia Anderson recalled one white pastor who would badger the enslaved people about their duties: "Serve your masters. Don't steal your master's turkey. Don't steal your master's chickens. . . . Do whatsoever your master tells you to do." Her father was an enslaved preacher who would hold meetings in the quarters, with "some real preachin'. . . . They used to sing their songs in a whisper and pray in a whisper." One slave who escaped from a Virginia plantation lamented that the "white clergymen don't preach the whole gospel." If caught for holding illicit religious services, the slaves could get into serious trouble. Floggings for attending slave services were routine.

Christian slaves longed to read the Bible, and antebellum slave religion was deeply biblicist. On this point, the slaves' faith connected to the white-led evangelical tradition. Slave interpretations of the Bible contrasted sharply with those of the slave masters, however, at least on the topics of slavery and freedom. Many masters still did not want their slaves to learn to read, fearing it would make them unruly. One former slave recalled (in colloquial dialect as recorded by interviewers) that they were "never allowed to learn anything. All the readin' they ever hear was when they was carried through the big Bible. The massa say that keep the slaves in they place." Even so, slaves who remained illiterate could gather biblical knowledge through the repetition of sermons, catechisms, and spirituals (hymns). One missionary among slaves observed that "to those who are ignorant of letters, their memory is their book."

"Prays' Meetin'," Lillian Richter Reynolds, ca. 1935–43

Slave spirituals were perhaps the most significant African American biblical repository. Hymns had been a key part of the evangelical movement since the First Great Awakening. Slaves also introduced their own words and tunes, drawing on African traditional music, dance, and worship. The spirituals employed biblical narratives such as triumph in Christ, liberation from sin, and Israel's exodus from Egyptian slavery. "Ride on King Jesus" emphasized Jesus's victory over earthly powers:

Ride on, King Jesus,
No man can a-hinder me . . .
King Jesus rides on a milk white horse [Revelation 19]
No man can a-hinder me.
The River Jordan did he cross,
No man can a-hinder me.

The primary significance of these songs was the worship of God. They had this-worldly implications too. As the great abolitionist and former slave Frederick Douglass wrote, the frequently sung refrain "I am bound for the land of Canaan" represented "something more than a hope of reaching heaven. We meant to reach the *North.*"

It was not hard to see the temporal meaning of certain spirituals. For example, at the outset of the Civil War a group of South Carolina slaves were detained for singing these lines:

We'll soon be free,
We'll soon be free,
We'll soon be free,
    When the Lord will call us home.
My brudder, how long,
My brudder, how long,
My brudder, how long,
        'Fore we done sufferin' here?

The African American educator Booker T. Washington recalled that as emancipation approached, "there was more singing in the slave quarters than usual. It was bolder, had more ring, and lasted later into the night." By the Civil War's end, slaves had less reason to sing quietly or to mask the double meanings of the spirituals.

Like their white counterparts, black male Christians in the nineteenth century were typically reluctant about giving women formal pastoral roles. Women still took a more vocal role in the brush arbors than white women usually did in their churches. In general, more expressive forms of worship in the United States have also made more space for women's voices, and that seems to have been the case in the slaves' meetings. One Scottish observer of a meeting of freed people after the Civil War said that "the pious negroes delight in prayer; and the women, at some of their religious meetings, are as free to lead as the men. Their prayers are full of fire." One woman named Nancy Brooks prayed in the meeting: "O Father Almighty, O Sweet Jesus, most gloriful King, will you be so pleased as to come dis way and put your eye on dese yere mourners?" Not all was comforting in Brooks's prayer, as she asked that God would remind the attendees of the reality of judgment. "Won't you be pleased to shake dese yere souls over hell, and not let 'em fall in?"

African American Christians such as Brooks believed that hell was a threat for all sinners. Conversion, and the acceptance of Christ's forgiveness, was central to many slaves' religious experience. As with biblicism, conversionism connected slave religion to the broader trends of the Second Great Awakening. Anthony Burns, who would later become the focus of one of the most controversial runaway slave cases in American history, converted amid William Miller's apocalyptic predictions in 1843. Miller's predictions, in addition to a scarlet fever epidemic and the appearance of a comet, made the young Burns concerned for the fate of his soul. He asked his master in Virginia for permission to be baptized, but his master initially refused. The master, who was not a church member, feared that Burns would use getting baptized and joining the church as a pretext to become disobedient. Later his master agreed, and Anthony Burns received believer's baptism and joined the Falmouth Baptist Church. In that church, white and black members sat in sections set apart by pine boards. Burns could barely read, but he soon became a Baptist exhorter and evangelist in "hush harbor" meetings.

Many African American Christians adopted the technique of the "anxious bench" from the Finneyite revivals, where penitents would go forward for special prayers to help them convert. However, African

Americans experienced conversion in many ways. Large numbers seem to have had visionary experiences in their travails. Visions were also common in white evangelical experience, but some whites dismissed visions as unreliable or overly enthusiastic. Often the visions of black converts followed images taken straight from the Bible. Sometimes the transcendent experiences were also quite tactile. One black convert recalled being able to "feel the darkness [of hell] with my hands." Of whatever ethnicity, converts tended to report that they went through a season of despair over their sinfulness. This season might culminate in a vision or sermon that made damnation and hell real to them. Then the convert would come to believe that Jesus could save them from damnation. Accepting spiritual rescue, the convert would bask in their newly reconciled status. They often testified of feeling that they had a new life and the ability to see spiritual realities. Conversion, especially for slave preachers, was typically recalled as the pivot point of their lives.

Not all slaves became Christians, of course. And not all Christian slaves became Protestants. At the Civil War's end, there may have been about 100,000 African American Catholics, concentrated in historically Catholic areas of the South, including Louisiana and Maryland. Catholics in America tended not to practice as segregated a religion as did Protestants. In the nineteenth century, immigrant Catholics often felt that they were cultural "outsiders" in a sea of Protestants. Thus the need for white-black separation may not have seemed as pressing, as white Catholics were outsiders of another kind. It was more difficult for individual black Catholics to receive formal recognition in the Catholic Church, especially as priests, than it was for blacks to become Baptist or Methodist pastors. The first black priest to minister in the United States was the former slave Augustus Tolton, who received ordination in Rome in 1888. Anecdotal evidence would suggest that some African Americans did not resonate with the formal liturgies of the Catholic Church, or its Latin readings. Elizabeth Ross Hite recalled that her master's family wanted the slaves to be Catholics, but the slaves preferred their secret meetings. "You see, the Catholic preachers from

France wouldn't let us shout, and the Lawd done said you gotta shout if you want to be saved. That's in the Bible," Hite said.

African Americans had longstanding traditions of magic, "conjure," "hoodoo," and other forms of folk religion. Whites too had a deep heritage of magic, witchcraft, and divination that had roots in the medieval European past. Yet African Americans' occult spiritual practices had origins in older West African cultures. These folk traditions stood in some tension with the rising tide of Christian commitment among African Americans. Some Christians—especially clergy—saw serious conflict between sanctioned Christian authorities and folk religion's practitioners. Other Christians saw no contradiction and still went to fortune-tellers or sought herbal remedies. Formal doctoring in the 1800s was typically inaccessible to poorer people and often unhelpful to those who did receive treatment. So many Americans sought herbal or magical aid. Conjuring folk routinely employed medicine bags containing talismanic materials like human hair, fingernails, or snakes' rattles or teeth. The bags, which resembled the older African "gris-gris," could be used to protect or curse people, depending on the contents.

One of Catholicism's greatest areas of strength was in the Southwest, which remained outside of US control until the 1840s. The United States would become the dominant power in the Southwest when it annexed Texas and conquered much of northern Mexico in the Mexican War of 1846–48. In colonial times, European Franciscan missionaries had led religious efforts in the Southwest. Starting in the late 1700s, however, Hispanics born in Mexico came to the fore as priests in New Mexico. By the time of the Mexican War, the Franciscan presence in New Mexico had ended, and native-born parish priests became the norm. Father Ramón Ortiz was an example of these new priests. He was born in Santa Fe, New Mexico, trained for the priesthood in Mexico, and served for decades in the El Paso district and in Ciudad Juárez, south of the Rio Grande River. Ortiz futilely tried to rally resistance to the US occupation of the El Paso region in the 1840s and '50s.

Church and plaza at Ciudad Juarez, 1857

The US takeover of much of the Southwest meant that Mexico lost its control of territory in future American states from Texas to California. Annexation also ended the formal establishment of Catholicism in those areas, though Catholicism continued to exert a strong influence. The advent of US sovereignty was paralleled by the increasing employment again of European-born immigrants as Catholic priests and nuns in the Southwest. Catholics expanded their administrative presence, creating new dioceses—administrative districts led by individual bishops—in places such as Galveston (1847), Santa Fe (1853), and San Francisco (1853). Bishops and clergy tended to be arranged by ethnic groups: French priests in Texas, New Mexico, and Arizona; Irish priests in northern California; and Spanish priests in southern California.

Protestant leaders expected that America's supposed "manifest destiny" of God-ordained territorial expansion to the Pacific would also lead to the downfall of Hispanic Catholicism. One minister thought the conquest of northern Mexico heralded the "beginning of the downfall of Antichrist, and the spread of the Savior's power of the gospel." The US takeover of northern Mexico was, indeed, damaging to the formal structures of Catholicism there. The northern reaches of Mexico had long been neglected by Spanish and Mexican church officials anyway. In 1851, Jean Baptiste Lamy, the first bishop of Santa Fe, New Mexico, found that there were only twelve priests ministering to tens of thousands of Catholics spread over a vast area. Lamy would put his imprint on New Mexico Catholicism, initiating in 1869 the construction of Santa Fe's St. Francis of Assisi Cathedral. It was conspicuously designed in the pattern of the Romanesque Revival, an architectural style then fashionable in Europe. Outside of major towns, many southwestern Catholics received only occasional visits from itinerant priests, who performed baptisms, marriages, and other rites. One itinerant priest in southern Texas recalled riding from ranch to ranch on horseback, offering the Mass, catechism, and church rituals to farm workers and cowboys, before moving on the next day to another settlement.

Yet the isolation and weakness of southwestern Catholicism in the mid-1800s can be overstated. In the late 1840s, José de la Guerra y Noriega, a prominent Spanish-born Catholic in California, assured Bishop John Hughes of New York that the Mexican War had not left California destitute of pastoral care. Sixteen Mexican priests remained in the territory despite the war. This would hardly be enough to confront the population explosion that California would see in the era of the Gold Rush of the 1850s. Still, Catholic infrastructure continued to expand. In 1856, the Daughters of Charity of St. Vincent de Paul founded a school and orphanage in Los Angeles. Most of these Catholic sisters were Irish, but some were of Hispanic background, including some from Los Angeles itself. Italian-background Jesuits also continued to evangelize the western states and territories. In 1873, an Italian Jesuit founded a publishing house in Albuquerque, New Mexico, which in 1875 began publishing *Revista Católica*, the first Spanish-language Catholic newspaper published in the United States. In 1877 Italian

Jesuits founded a Catholic college in New Mexico that eventually moved to Denver and took the name Regis University.

Everyday Catholicism in the United States, including in the Southwest and West, was often punctuated more by seasonal devotions and celebrations than by weekly Mass attendance. For Mexican Catholics, no devotional celebration meant more than the Feast of Our Lady of Guadalupe, marked annually in December. A Catholic observer recorded a Guadalupe celebration in Colorado in 1873, noting that hundreds paraded with a statue of Our Lady of Guadalupe. The parade ended at the town church, where the priest gave a sermon and said High Mass. The observer wrote, "The attendance was extremely good and everyone was happy with how splendid the fiesta turned out to be. . . . Glory to Mary Most Holy who chose to favor us in such a manner."

Our Lady of Guadalupe Church, Peralta, New Mexico

While Hispanic Catholics had deep historical roots across what would become the southwest United States and Florida, English Catholics had a significant presence in Maryland and Kentucky, as did French Catholics in the Great Lakes and in Louisiana. East of the Mississippi River, the ethnic composition of American Catholicism shifted dramatically starting in the 1820s due to waves of Irish and

German immigration. Troubles in Ireland's agrarian economy sent many desperately impoverished Irish people in search of food and work. Millions of Irish people would come to the United States during the antebellum period. An especially large surge happened in the late 1840s when in just six years a million Irish people fled their country due to famine conditions. Most of those immigrants were Catholics. Many were truly destitute, straining the resources of cities and churches to accommodate them.

The immigration ships often arrived in perilous circumstances. For example, ships appeared in 1847 outside of Quebec City in Canada, many with epidemic disease onboard. Priests tried to minister to the dying, as passengers died on the chilly shores of the Saint Lawrence River. A young Irish priest was assigned as chaplain to the quarantined immigrants. He moved from ship to ship carrying "the consolations of religion to the dying. Amidst shrieks, and groans, and wild ravings . . . he pursued his holy task," a historian of Irish Catholics wrote. The priest himself became ill after a month of service. By summer 1847, hundreds of immigrants at the quarantine station were dying every day. Scenes like this were repeated up and down the east coast of North America in the late 1840s. Nevertheless, the Irish created large ethnic and religious enclaves in America. In cities such as Boston and New York, leading Irish figures in church and government would create political machines that endured well into the twentieth century.

Germany supplied the other great wave of European immigration prior to the Civil War. Germans were more divided religiously than the overwhelmingly Catholic Irish. Nevertheless, millions of German Catholics eventually immigrated to the United States. A high point for German Catholic immigration came during the 1870s *Kulturkampf*, when Catholics faced intense persecution in Germany. The antebellum phase of German immigration was also due to pressures on farmers in Germany, and changes brought by Europe's Industrial Revolution. However, most German immigrants were more financially stable than the Irish, with typical Germans coming as part of middle-class families.

Some Germans settled on the East Coast, but they were more likely than Irish settlers to land in midwestern centers such as St. Louis or Cincinnati.

German Lutherans and other immigrant Protestants fought long-standing battles over whether to assimilate into dominant English-speaking culture in America, or whether to maintain ethnic separation in church and social life. The association of Lutheran Churches that became the Lutheran Church—Missouri Synod was founded in 1847 by a dozen German pastors. The Missouri Synod was, from the outset, committed to cultural and theological conservatism. They also con-sciously focused on ministering to new German arrivals to America. By the beginning of the twentieth century, this denomination was approaching 700,000 members.

By contrast, the General Synod of Lutheran Churches was the key organization among Lutherans advocating for Americanization and the practice of revivalism. The synod's prominent leader in the antebellum period was Samuel Schmucker. Schmucker, a graduate of Princeton Seminary, championed interdenominational causes such as the American Sunday School Union. Schmucker was no liberal, but he did downplay some of the Lutherans' more distinctive beliefs, such as the idea that the real presence of Christ's body inhered within the Lord's Supper. By mid-century, the number of American Lutherans of all stripes was growing quickly, with total Lutheran congregations more than doubling from about 1,200 to 2,800 churches between 1850 and 1870. Sectional schism rent the Lutheran General Synod during the Civil War, and the northern branch also suffered a schism over adherence to Lutheran confessions in 1866, leaving Lutheran denominations in disarray until a significant reunification transpired in 1918. This reunion created the denominational predecessor to the Evangelical Lutheran Church in America (ELCA). Despite its declining membership and controversies over issues such as homosexuality, the ELCA remains the largest American Lutheran denomination today.

If Schmucker was one of the great champions of revivalist Christianity among Lutherans, German Reformed theologians at Mercersburg Seminary in Pennsylvania were among revivalism's most articulate opponents. Mercersburg's John Williamson Nevin attacked Charles Finney's new measures in *The Anxious Bench* (1843). In an era when many Protestants and even some Catholics were revivalistic, Nevin highlighted the risks of evangelical techniques and emotionalism. "Spurious revivals are common, and as the fruit of them, false conversions lamentably abound," Nevin wrote. "An anxious bench may be crowded, where no divine influence whatever is felt. . . . Hundreds may be carried through the process of anxious bench conversion, and yet their last state may be worse than the first." Nevin and his colleague Philip Schaff developed "Mercersburg Theology" as an alternative to regnant evangelical piety. They emphasized the person of Christ, the Lord's Supper, and a respect for Christian history, including the pre-Reformation Catholic heritage. Nevin, Schaff, and Mercersburg Seminary's influence was slight during their own era, but the Mercersburg Theology retained an outsized popularity in the decades since the Civil War. It especially appealed to Protestants who wished to find a third way between the poles of fundamentalism and liberal modernism.

The era of Nat Turner's rebellion saw the emergence of a more militant abolitionist movement in America as well. Christian critics had been raising moral questions about the slave trade and chattel slavery since the American colonial period. Slaves knew firsthand of slavery's horrors, but they typically did not have public platforms from which to safely air their grievances. The Revolutionary era had featured a few African American public figures, such as the pastor Lemuel Haynes and the poetess and former slave Phillis Wheatley, who registered pointed attacks against slavery, and growing numbers of black and white evangelical Christians in that time proclaimed that chattel slavery violated human dignity and the laws of God.

Upstart evangelical denominations, especially the Baptists and Methodists, showed fleeting signs of commitment to abolitionism in the 1780s. Some of that sentiment even appeared among white pastors in the South. Virginia Baptists in 1789 passed a resolution contending that slavery was "a violent deprivation of the rights of nature, and inconsistent with a republican government, and therefore recommend it to our brethren, to make use of every legal measure to extirpate this horrid evil from the land." By the 1790s, such direct political attacks on slavery waned in the white South. Paternalist ideology became the norm among white southern defenders of slavery. Citing the Bible's seeming acceptance of slavery in the ancient world, the paternalists argued that Christians could own slaves but that they needed to treat slaves kindly, as people would treat their own children.

The early 1800s saw a massive expansion of slavery into new lands from Georgia to Texas. With the advent of the cotton gin in the 1790s, cotton quickly became the centerpiece of the southern economy, and the key export for the whole nation. Northerners might not be growing cotton, but many of them were weaving southern cotton into textiles, and shipping cotton out to England. Nat Turner's revolt in 1831 forced Americans into more radical pro- or antislavery positions. Some argued that slavery needed to be defended at all costs, while others contended that if Americans did not abolish this evil institution, they could expect to reap more violence. The intensity of Christians' pro- and antislavery views, as well as both sides' incessant claims that the Bible supported their position, made a violent outcome to the national crisis over slavery more likely.

Even before Nat Turner's revolt, a radical abolitionist movement had begun to develop, signaled by the publication of David Walker's *Appeal* (1829). Walker was a free African American from North Carolina who resettled in Boston. As part of the African Methodist Episcopal Church, Walker took a fierce stance against slavery, arguing that slaves should rise up against their masters. Walker exposed the hypocrisy of Christian masters who ruthlessly suppressed the "brush arbor" meetings. As soon

as the slaves began singing and praying, the slave patrols would burst
in upon the believers "and drag them out and commence beating them
as they would rattle-snakes. . . . Have not the Americans the Bible in
their hands? Do they believe it? Surely they do not. . . . Unless you
speedily alter your course, you and your country are gone!!!!! For God
Almighty will tear up the very face of the earth!!!" Such retributive
rhetoric terrified white defenders of the slave system.

The year 1831 saw the launch of William Lloyd Garrison's abolitionist newspaper, *The Liberator.* White southerners worried that the
circulation of Garrison's newspaper and Walker's *Appeal* played a role
in Turner's revolt and other rumored slave plots. Many of the most
prominent abolitionists, such as Theodore Dwight Weld (a disciple of
Charles Finney), were evangelicals. The Quaker-background Garrison
was a religious skeptic who, in his writings against slavery, nevertheless
employed the moral zeal of an evangelical preacher. Citing Isaiah 28,
Garrison called the US Constitution
a "covenant with death, and an agree-
ment with hell," because it did not ban
slavery in America.

Frederick Douglass

One of the most compelling
advocates of abolition was the former
slave Frederick Douglass. Douglass
had become literate partly through
learning to read the Bible. His 1845
autobiography denounced the supposedly Christian white South, where
the most pious believers could also be
the most vicious abusers of slaves.
One could easily get the impression
that Douglass's narrative was hostile to Christianity, but he denied
that this was his intent. He denounced the "slaveholding religion of
this land," not the "Christianity of Christ," he said. "I love the pure,
peaceable, and impartial Christianity of Christ: I therefore hate the

corrupt, slaveholding, women-whipping, cradle-plundering, partial and hypocritical Christianity of this land."

Southern defenders of slavery admitted there were some abusive slave masters, but argued this hardly meant that slavery in general, or slavery "in the abstract," was unbiblical. Antislavery advocates pointed to the spirit of Christ's teachings, such as the "golden rule" ("Do unto others as you would have them do unto you"), as evidence that the Bible was against slavery. Proslavery advocates pointed to the letter of the Bible, which never explicitly prohibited slavery and included many passages that accepted the existence of ancient Hebrew and Roman slavery. They denied that owning slaves necessarily made a person a "mansealer," the biblical term for people who captured, kidnapped, and enslaved others. In the Revolutionary era, a number of southern founders, such as Thomas Jefferson, had admitted that slavery was immoral, even if they did little to encourage emancipation. By the early 1800s, white slave masters and many white pastors began to argue that slavery was a God-ordained good. Baptist pastor Thornton Stringfellow wrote, "The Old Testament and the New, sanction slavery, [and] under no circumstances enjoin its abolition, even among saints. . . . If pure religion, therefore, did not require its abolition under the law of Moses, nor in the church of Christ—we may safely infer, that our political, moral and social relations do not require it in a state." Strident pro- and antislavery advocates could hardly engage in reasoned conversation, so confident as they were that they had God on their side.

In the aftermath of Nat Turner's revolt, slavery was on its way to becoming the most divisive issue in America. In such a deeply biblicist culture, any such moral debate had religious implications. The Bible did not yield simple answers regarding slavery, however. The lack of a biblical consensus on slavery would divide the Protestant denominations and eventually sunder the nation itself.

WORKS CITED
AND FURTHER READING

Brekus, Catherine A. *Strangers and Pilgrims: Female Preaching in America, 1740–1845.* Chapel Hill: University of North Carolina Press, 1998.

Dolan, Jay P. *The American Catholic Experience: A History from Colonial Times to the Present.* Reprint, Notre Dame, IN: University of Notre Dame Press, 1992.

Fox-Genovese, Elizabeth, and Eugene D. Genovese. *The Mind of the Master Class: History and Faith in the Southern Slaveholder's Worldview.* New York: Cambridge University Press, 2005.

Harvey, Paul. *Through the Storm, Through the Night: A History of African American Christianity.* Lanham, MD: Rowman & Littlefield, 2011.

Hinks, Peter P., ed. *David Walker's Appeal to the Coloured Citizens of the World.* University Park, PA: Penn State University Press, 2000.

Johnson, Clifton H., ed. *God Struck Me Dead: Voices of Ex-Slaves.* Updated ed. Cleveland: Pilgrim, 1993.

Kapp, Friedrich. *Immigration and the Commissioners of Emigration of the State of New York.* New York: Nation, 1870.

Littlejohn, W. Bradford. *The Mercersburg Theology and the Quest for Reformed Catholicity.* Eugene, OR: Pickwick, 2009.

Matovina, Timothy. *Latino Catholicism: Transformation in America's Largest Church.* Princeton, NJ: Princeton University Press, 2012.

Najar, Monica. *Evangelizing the South: A Social History of Church and State in Early America.* New York: Oxford University Press, 2008.

Nevin, J. W. *The Anxious Bench.* Chambersburg, PA: Weekly Messenger, 1843.

Raboteau, Albert J. *Slave Religion: The "Invisible Institution" in the Antebellum South.* Updated ed. New York: Oxford University Press, 2004.

Scully, Randolph Ferguson. *Religion and the Making of Nat Turner's Virginia: Baptist Community and Conflict, 1740–1840.* Charlottesville: University of Virginia Press, 2008.

Stringfellow, Thornton. *Scriptural and Statistical Views in Favor of Slavery.* 4th ed. Richmond, VA: Randolph, 1856.

Chapter 7

THE SLAVERY CONTROVERSY AND THE CIVIL WAR

Abraham Lincoln, the skeptical son of Calvinist parents, used religious rhetoric to greater effect than any other American president. His Second Inaugural Address is teeming with biblical references. Perhaps his most intriguing religious allusion came in the Gettysburg Address (1863). In it, he anticipated that because of the Civil War "this nation under God shall have a new birth of freedom." The concept of a nation "under God" may seem familiar, but what did a "new birth of freedom" mean? Lincoln was alluding to the new birth of conversion, or the experience of being "born again." The term *new birth* was not quoted directly from the Bible but from evangelical sermons, such as George Whitefield's "The Nature and Necessity of the New Birth." Lincoln was positing that the carnage of the war represented America's conversion experience. It was as if a nation, like a person, could be born again. The nation's old self of slavery was dying; America was being born again into freedom.

Like the American Revolution, the Civil War was not a war of religion. More than most American wars, however, the Civil War was framed by religious belief. The intensity of Americans' religious commitments made the debates over slavery more intractable and the war more relentless. Religious conviction spurred many of the most influential figures in the leadup to the war, including rebel slave Nat Turner, novelist Harriet Beecher Stowe, and would-be revolutionary John Brown. Enslaved and free black Christians knew that slavery was wrong. White Christians could not agree on the morality of enslaving human beings, and they tore the nation apart over slavery's future in America.

The debate over slavery's morality had troubled American churches and denominations since before the American Revolution. Critics of slavery, such as African American pastor Lemuel Haynes, had pointed out the tension between Christianity's ethic of human dignity and the shameful practices of American chattel slavery. During the Revolutionary era, the ideal of equality by creation (as articulated in the Declaration of Independence) inspired some denominations to condemn slave owning. Even in the white South, glimmers of Christian antislavery sentiment appeared from time to time. Methodists met in Baltimore in 1784 and denounced slavery, calling on Methodist church members to free their slaves, though they retracted that call under pressure from proslavery members. As we have seen, Virginia Baptists called slavery a "violent deprivation of the rights of nature." And in 1818, the Presbyterian General Assembly indicted slavery as "a gross violation of the most precious and sacred rights of human nature."

Like most white-led Christian groups, the Baptists and Presbyterians failed to go beyond rhetoric to take action against slavery or slave owners in their midst. There was too much economic and political pressure to look the other way. The invention of the cotton gin in 1793 led to a monumental expansion of slavery and cotton growing in the interior of the South, especially in places like the Mississippi Delta. By the time of the Missouri Compromise in 1820, every congressional controversy over

US expansion into the West became tied to the expansion of slavery. As it spread from Georgia to Texas, chattel slavery became ever-more integral to the southern and national economy. Much of the slave-grown cotton in the South ended up in northern ports, where bankers and traders arranged for the bulk of the crop's shipment to England. As the cotton trade went, so went the American economy. Thus even many white northerners had a vested interest in preserving slavery.

Nonetheless, the abolitionist movement, led by advocates such as William Lloyd Garrison and Frederick Douglass, continued to grow in the North. Independent black churches were the most consistent voices of antislavery sentiment in the pre–Civil War era. African Americans and white abolitionists made the first of August an annual celebration, marking the date of British emancipation of Caribbean slaves in 1834. For example, in 1848 African Americans rallied on August 1 at the Ford Street Baptist Church in Rochester, New York. They marched in procession to a city square waving banners with slogans such as "Ethiopia Stretches Forth Her Hands to God" (a reference to Psalm 68:31). Frederick Douglass addressed the throng and commended the legacy of Nat Turner, a "man of noble courage" who was inspired by "a God of justice."

Boston emerged in the 1830s as a hotbed of abolitionist sentiment, led by figures such as Garrison and the Unitarian minister William Ellery Channing. Channing refuted the common proslavery argument that abusive masters alone were the problem with slavery. "An institution so founded in wrong, so imbued with injustice, cannot be made a good," he wrote. He insisted that slavery itself was "radically, essentially evil." Channing began as a gradualist antislavery moderate in the mid-1830s but within several years became convinced that immediate abolition was the only proper solution to slavery's wickedness. Channing's views carried great weight, especially among New England whites. Antislavery politicians such as John Quincy Adams and Charles Sumner would recall how Channing crystallized their views against slavery.

Proslavery advocates included many prominent Christian voices too, both Catholic and Protestant. Although Pope Gregory XVI condemned the slave trade in 1839, white southern Catholics still defended the institution as compatible with biblical and natural law. Bishop John England of South Carolina declared in 1840 that, all things considered, enslavement was not a bad arrangement for obedient slaves. Being a slave ensures that you have "food, raiment, and dwelling, together with a variety of little comforts." Slaves did not have to worry about being neglected when sick or being left utterly destitute. "In return, all that is required is fidelity and moderate labor," he said. England acknowledged that slavery had its "evils," but in his view "the above are no despicable benefits." As we have seen, Protestant leaders such as the Baptist Thornton Stringfellow adhered to a literalistic reading of Scripture on the slave question and contended that there were no Bible verses transparently hostile to slavery. Christ himself seemingly said nothing on the subject, so could slavery really be considered such an abomination?

Most whites stood somewhere between the abolitionists and the staunch proslavery advocates. Some disliked slavery but did not think that mass emancipation was safe. In 1817, the American Colonization Society (ACS) was formed to advocate for sending free blacks and emancipated slaves "back" to Africa. Yet after the legal importation of slaves ceased in 1808, most American slaves had never lived in Africa. Henry Clay of Kentucky, one of Congress's great dealmakers on slavery, supported colonizing blacks in Africa. He told the ACS that because blacks could never "amalgamate" with whites, it would be better to "drain them off." Sending American blacks to Africa would have the additional advantage of introducing "civilization and Christianity" to West Africa, Clay argued. Some African Americans, such as the Baptist pastor David George, had already gone to West Africa by the end of the eighteenth century. In 1822, the ACS began sending blacks to Liberia, the West African nation that gained its independence in 1847. African American interest in colonization remained limited. Colonization was mostly a dream of whites who wished to find a way out of the stark choice between slavery and abolition.

The breakup of national denominations over slave owning was not just a religious calamity. It struck at the coherence of the nation. In an era when the federal government was miniscule, denominations were the most vital national institutions for everyday Americans. Presbyterians had already divided in 1837 into traditionalist "Old School" and prorevival "New School" wings, but slavery was only a secondary precipitant of that schism. New School Presbyterians tended to be stronger in the North and more inclined toward antislavery activism. Both wings of the Presbyterian division would split again in 1857 (New School) and 1861 (Old School), this time into northern and southern factions.

In 1844, the Methodists became the first denomination to break apart over slavery itself. The Methodists had gained ecclesiastical independence from their English brethren in the 1780s, creating America's Methodist Episcopal Church. Black-led breakaway Methodist denominations included the African Methodist Episcopal Church (1816) and the African Methodist Episcopal Zion Church (1821), the latter founded by black Methodists in New York City. White Methodists began to bicker in the 1830s over whether people who owned slaves could remain in good standing with the church. In particular, Methodists debated whether bishops could own slaves or not. Methodist founder John Wesley had condemned slavery in the 1770s, but by the early 1800s most white southern Methodists no longer found his arguments persuasive.

A small faction of northern Methodists first broke away from the main body in 1843. These "Wesleyan Methodists" were frustrated with the denomination's reluctance to take a stand against slavery. The national Methodist schism in 1844 resulted from northern opposition to Georgia bishop James Andrew, who owned slaves by way of marriage. A strong majority of the Methodist General Conference voted to ask Andrew to resign rather than to continue to serve as a slaveholding bishop. This vote resulted in a walkout by southern delegates, who then formed the Methodist Episcopal Church, South.

In the midst of the furor over Bishop Andrew, one Virginia Methodist leader, Thomas Crowder, issued a remarkable prediction about the ramifications of national Protestant divisions. He worried that if the Methodist church broke apart, "a civil division of this great confederation [the United States] may follow that, and then hearts will be torn apart, master and slave arrayed against each other, brother in the Church against brother, and the north against the south—and when thus arrayed . . . civil war and far-reaching desolation must be the final results." Other southerners argued that a religious schism would actually help preserve national political union. White southerners insisted that they must protect themselves from the "pseudo-religious frenzy called abolitionism."

General conference of the Methodist Episcopal Church, South, May 1, 1858, Nashville, Tennessee

Agitation for and against slavery similarly divided the Triennial Convention, the chief Baptist organization. Some Baptist leaders tried to prevent the convention and its missionary boards from taking a position on slavery. Abolitionist northern Baptists, however, wished to exclude slaveholders from being missionaries. Baptists from Georgia and Alabama tested the convention's policies in the mid-1840s. They discovered that, functionally, known slaveholders were barred from official appointments as Baptist missionaries. In 1845, hundreds of (mostly) southern delegates announced the formation of the Southern Baptist Convention (SBC), as an alternative to the Triennial Convention. Delegates argued that slavery was not the root cause of the formation of the SBC. They said that they desired to focus on the gospel message alone, and did not wish to combat the political agitations of the "ultra northern brethren."

White Southern Baptists, wanting to demonstrate the sincerity of their commitment to the gospel, redoubled their efforts to evangelize African Americans. This resulted in the addition of hundreds of thousands of blacks in Baptist churches in the fifteen years prior to the Civil War. Many of those African Americans would leave white-led churches in favor of black-pastored Baptist congregations in the war's aftermath. Still, the SBC would become the nation's largest Protestant denomination by the mid-twentieth century. The legacy of slavery would continue to cloud the denomination's history, however. In 1995—one hundred fifty years after its founding—the SBC formally apologized for the role of slavery in the creation of the denomination.

Catholics were hesitant to get embroiled in the political controversy over slavery. European-background Catholic leaders tended to assume that slavery was permissible in theory, though they knew that it was morally problematic in practice. As with Protestants, Native American and African American slavery had been a feature of Catholic colonies from the Great Lakes to Mexico in the 1700s. On the eve of Confederate secession, the Paris-trained Bishop Augustin Verot, a key Catholic leader in Florida and Georgia, preached a sermon titled "Slavery and Abolitionism" that would circulate throughout the South. Bishop Verot denounced abolitionists as "modern fanatics." Slavery, he insisted, had received the "sanction of God, of the Church, and of Society at all times, and in all governments." Northern Catholic leaders, on the other hand, were cautious about endorsing the Union cause. They coalesced around the conviction that, at a minimum, southern rebellion against the national government was rash and sinful. Catholic clergy and nuns played an important role in the war as chaplains and as nurses on both sides of the war. Some 20 percent of all Civil War nurses were nuns.

Among the abolitionists' most powerful weapons in the years leading up to the Civil War were appeals to Christian sentiment. Literary trends associated with Romanticism suggested that the emotions, not cold rationality, were the best guide to moral truth. One of the most important Christian sentimental novels in American history was *Uncle Tom's Cabin* (1852) by Harriet Beecher Stowe. Stowe was part of the great Beecher clan of New England Congregationalists. The family had taken a leading role in moral reform movements including temperance and opposition to Indian removal. Stowe and other

Harriet Beecher Stowe

Library of Congress, Prints & Photographs Division, LC-DIG-ppmsca-49807

abolitionists were outraged when the Compromise of 1850 included a tough fugitive slave law. It helped ensure that slave masters could retrieve runaway slaves who had escaped to the North. One of the central themes of Stowe's novel was the horrid injustice of slave families being ripped apart when masters sold individual slaves away. The book was a bestseller, with more than 300,000 copies sold within a year of its release. Even more popular were the great number of stage adaptations of the novel, including a successful one on Broadway.

Other issues divided antebellum Americans besides slavery, of course, and some of those issues were explicitly religious. Anti-Catholic animosity grew in the 1840s in the wake of mass immigration from Ireland and other countries. In 1844, Philadelphia exploded in anti-Catholic violence, with Protestant mobs battling Irish Catholics in the streets. Irish people's homes were burned, and rioters destroyed two Catholic churches. Thirteen people died in the Philadelphia clashes. Hostility toward Catholics also undergirded the formation of the American or "Know-Nothing" political party in the 1850s. "Know-Nothing" alluded to the semisecret character of the organization. In the early 1850s, the national Whig Party, the rival of the Democrats, was disintegrating under pressure caused by sectional divisions over slavery. The Know-Nothings seemed briefly poised to take the Whigs' place as a major force in national politics, winning offices from Massachusetts to California. The Know-Nothings had pockets of strength in the white South, but many of its members were white Protestants worried both about the expansion of slavery and about the burgeoning number of Catholic immigrants. Ultimately, the Know-Nothings did not endure because of the same sectional pressures that undermined the Whigs. The northern-based Republican Party emerged by 1856 as the new rival to the Democrats. The Republicans opposed the expansion of slavery into the West, which meant that they had virtually no white southern support.

The Catholic Church sought to consolidate its flock in the Southwest even as its numbers and the anti-Catholic backlash burgeoned in the East. Bishop Jean-Baptiste Lamy, born and educated in France, had arrived in Santa Fe, New Mexico, in 1851. Lamy and other leaders such as the Spanish-born Bishop Thaddeus Amat y Brusi of Los Angeles sought to suppress local Hispanic forms of Catholicism in the 1850s. Of particular concern were the practices of *Los Hermanos de Nuestro Padre Jesús Nazareno*, widely known in the Southwest as the *Penitentes*. The *Penitentes* engaged in intense self-disciplinary practices that critics regarded as extreme and vicious. Yet groups like the *Penitentes* had supplied Catholics' pastoral needs across the Southwest for decades in the absence of European-born clerics.

Leaders such as Lamy believed that the work of the *Penitentes* and similar groups were "contrary to modern ecclesiastical order and harmful to the image of Catholicism in the eyes of newcomers from the East." Some European-born clerics feared that indigenized Hispanic church practices would only fuel anti-Catholic sentiment. Despite efforts to regulate the *Penitentes*, Protestant missionaries made much of the unfamiliar Hispanic rituals and folk beliefs they encountered in the Southwest. One missionary wrote, "The paganism in this land of Christian liberty would astonish Eastern people. . . . Could you see the blood streaming from the wounds of these 'Penitentes,' and many other acts of barbarism, your hearts would be touched—your prayers would be more earnest that the souls for whom Christ died may be saved from their sins." Protestants did not consider these Catholics to be real Christians.

Protestants generally found the West a less hospitable place than their eastern strongholds. Protestants could not assume the quasi-established status that they enjoyed in so many areas east of the Mississippi. Protestant leaders in the East, such as Lyman Beecher, had made Sabbath enforcement a major reform issue starting in the early 1800s. In new states and territories like California, however, Sabbath laws were contested. Catholic tradition had never enforced strict Sabbath observance in California, going back to the days when the state was part of Mexico. Unchurched gold miners and other California workers reportedly looked forward to Sundays as times of gaming and carousing. In the mid-1850s, Protestant ministers began pressuring the California legislature to pass Sabbath observance laws. A Jewish clothes merchant in Sacramento temporarily got a law overturned that prohibited commerce on Sundays, but the legislature reinstituted the Sabbath law in 1861. The spread of Protestantism on the western frontier made impressive gains, but Protestant Christianity would never exercise as uniform a hold in the western United States as it once had in the East.

Some Californians kept battling against the Sabbath law for the next two decades, led by a small but vocal group of Seventh-day Adventists in California, who, like Jews, observed a Saturday Sabbath. The Seventh-day Adventists had a strong commitment to religious liberty and did not appreciate the state trying to make a Sunday Sabbath the norm. The Sabbath law controversy came to a head in 1882 when California authorities made over 1,600 arrests of Sabbath violators, including Jews, Seventh-day Adventists, and Chinese merchants. The mass arrests led to a backlash against the Sabbath law, and in 1883 California repealed it. In the long run, the effort to create a Protestant establishment in California failed, and the state never adopted another Sunday law.

Across the nation, the economy remained a major political issue in the 1850s. In 1857, shady financial practices led to a collapse in the banking and real estate sectors, creating one of the worst economic crises in American history. This helped to precipitate a new wave of Christian awakenings, especially in northern cities. The revival of 1857–58 is often called the Businessmen's Revival or the Prayer Meeting Revival. Legions of businessmen went to prayer meetings, seeking solace amid the maelstrom. Although this revival had a distinctly urban cast, the Prayer Meeting Revival was part of the enduring quest for mass conversions associated with the long Second Great Awakening. The revival's effects were not restricted to cities. For instance, Presbyterians in Moore County, North Carolina, experienced the height of a revival in 1857 before the financial meltdown even commenced. Revivals in the late 1850s also impacted parts of Britain and Canada, indicating that the transatlantic paths of revival remained a fixture of Anglo-American religion.

The economy and anti-immigrant animus were major concerns, but in 1850s America slavery became the defining political controversy. The most provocative figure in the years leading up to the Civil War was the antislavery zealot John Brown. Brown, a New Englander, adhered to traditional Calvinist theology and abolitionist principles. He was also mentally unstable and had a cruel streak. In the mid-1850s, Brown and members of his family made their way to Kansas, then the epicenter of national controversy over slavery. In the Kansas-Nebraska Act (1854), Congress had given the Kansas territory the right to decide for itself whether to legalize slavery. Militant voters sought to establish residency in Kansas in order to participate in elections, and New England abolitionists sent many to try to turn the territory against slavery. Brown and his sons also got involved in the small-scale civil war that was engulfing "Bleeding Kansas." In 1856 Brown's righteous rage against slavery turned murderous, as he and his followers abducted five proslavery settlers at Pottawatomie Creek, Kansas, and executed them with broadswords.

Brown fled prosecution and ended up back in the East by the late 1850s. There he began plotting to free slaves en masse. Brown retained the support of key radical abolitionists, including Unitarian ministers Theodore Parker and Thomas Wentworth Higginson. Higginson would go on to serve as colonel of the First South Carolina Volunteers, an all-black Union regiment with white officers. Higginson commented that Brown was one of the only radical abolitionists he knew "who was not more or less radical in religious matters also. His theology was Puritan, like his practice." Parker and Higginson were part of the "Secret Six," a group of Brown's backers who helped fund his scheme to seize the federal armory at Harpers Ferry, Virginia.

Although his plan was ill-conceived, Brown improbably captured the armory in October 1859. He apparently hoped that word would spread to slaves in the surrounding region, but there were relatively few slaves living in western Virginia. Instead, his attack attracted the attention of federal authorities. Marines under the command of future Confederate general Robert E. Lee put down Brown's insurrection with little trouble. Prior to his execution, Brown gave a speech justifying his actions and casting himself as a Christian martyr. The Bible taught him "all things whatsoever I would that men should do to me, I should do even so to them," he said. "It teaches me further, to 'Remember them that are in bonds, as bound with them.' I endeavored to act up to that instruction. I say I am yet too young to understand that GOD is any respecter of persons." White southerners were horrified by Brown's actions, and resented the fact that abolitionists hailed Brown as a "Christian hero." Aside from the election of Abraham Lincoln, Brown's insurrection did more than anything else to push white southerners toward secession.

Like John Brown, Abraham Lincoln had grown up in a Calvinist family. Lincoln was reared in a frontier family of Calvinistic Baptists. Lincoln jettisoned his family's Calvinism, however, under the influence of skeptical writings such as Tom Paine's controversial *Age of Reason.* Lincoln's upbringing gave him indelible exposure to the Bible, much of which he knew by heart. Thus Lincoln drew easily on biblical rhetoric in his greatest speeches. Like many Americans, the spiritual beliefs of Abraham and Mary Todd Lincoln, his wife, were eclectic. The early deaths of two children fostered the couple's fascination with spiritualism and the use of mediums to communicate with the dead. On a number of occasions, mediums came to the Lincoln White House to hold séances. The president himself attended a few of the sessions.

Partisans and soldiers on both sides interpreted the Civil War with reference to the will of God. Such references peppered the papers of legions of Americans from well-known politicians, such as Lincoln, to humble soldiers, fathers, wives, and mothers. Secessionists portrayed the creation of the Confederacy as a Christian obligation. Even those white southerners who initially resisted secession came to see the Confederacy as the unfolding of God's providential plan. Alexander Stephens of Georgia, vice-president of the Confederacy, declared that the independent South's "cornerstone rests upon the great truth, that the negro is not equal to the white man. . . . It is the first government ever instituted upon the principles in strict conformity to nature, and the ordination of Providence, in furnishing the materials of human society. . . . It is, indeed, in conformity with the ordinance of the Creator."

Northern partisans painted the war in starkly different terms. Militant abolitionists saw the war as a holy crusade to end slavery. Massachusetts abolitionist Julia Ward Howe articulated this sentiment in her "Battle Hymn of the Republic," which became a popular Union army marching tune. Drawing on images from Isaiah and the book of Revelation, Howe focused on Christ as both redeemer and avenger and on the transformative power of holy death. Howe's anthem, first published in the *Atlantic Monthly* in early 1862, declared:

> Mine eyes have seen the glory of the coming of the Lord;
> He is trampling out the vintage where the grapes of wrath
> are stored;
> He hath loosed the fateful lightning of His terrible swift
> sword:
> His truth is marching on. . . .
> In the beauty of the lilies Christ was born across the sea,
> With a glory in His bosom that transfigures you and me.
> As He died to make men holy, let us die to make men free,
> While God is marching on.

African Americans in both North and South saw the war as the occasion of God's providential deliverance of the slaves. The Civil War was destined to result in emancipation and a biblical year of jubilee, they believed. Especially once Lincoln enacted the Emancipation Proclamation in 1863, African American activists insisted that blacks get behind the Union war effort. Commending the memory of slave rebels such as Denmark Vesey, Nat Turner, and the black followers of John Brown, Frederick Douglass summoned northern blacks to take up arms. "In a contest with oppression, the Almighty has no attribute which can take sides with oppressors," Douglass warned his audience.

A desperate Alabama slaveholder in the late stages of the war asked a young slave named W. B. Allen to pray that God would "hold the Yankees back." The emboldened Allen told his master that he would by no means pray for that. "I told my white folks [that] . . . I not only wanted to be free, but that I wanted to see all the Negroes freed! I told them that God was using the Yankees to scourge the slave-holders just as He had, centuries before, used heathens and outcasts to chastise His chosen people—the children of Israel."

As the long war drew to an end in 1865, Americans reflected upon God's purposes in the war. In his Second Inaugural Address, Lincoln cited Matthew 18:7 to suggest that God had brought a judgment on both North and South for the sin of slavery. "'Woe unto the world because of offenses; for it must needs be that offenses come, but woe to that man by whom the offense cometh.' If we shall suppose that American slavery is one of those offenses which, in the providence of God, must needs come," Lincoln said, "but which, having continued through His appointed time, He now wills to remove, and that He gives to both North and South this terrible war as the woe due to those by whom the offense came, shall we discern therein any departure from those divine attributes which the believers in a living God always ascribe to Him?" Soon thereafter, Lincoln's tragic death by assassination—he was shot on Good Friday in 1865—turned him into a Christian martyr for many in the Union. One Connecticut Baptist made the comparison explicit. "Jesus Christ died for the world," he said. But "Abraham Lincoln died for his country."

Lincoln emphasized the need for national reconciliation in the Second Inaugural, noting that "both sides read the same Bible and pray to the same God." Others were less equivocal about the meaning of Union victory. When Union general William T. Sherman concluded the 1864 "March to the Sea" by entering Savannah, Georgia, African Americans gathered at the city's Second African Church. One of the pastors stood before the packed audience and prayed, thanking God "that the black people were free, and forever free." The congregation, overcome with elation, sang the hymn

> Blow ye the trumpet, blow!
> The gladly solemn sound
> Let all the nations know.
> The year of jubilee has come.

Some white northerners crowed that the Union victory meant that God had been on their side. Others heralded Union victory as the signal of a new providential era and, perhaps, the beginning of Christ's millennial glory on earth. Horace Bushnell, a devotee of Romantic philosophy and one of the most influential theologians of the nineteenth century, spoke at Yale College in 1865 and extolled what the Union soldiers had done for the nation. "The dead of our war have done for us a work so precious, which is all their own—they have bled for us; and by this simple sacrifice of blood they have opened for us a great new chapter of life." By "this blood our [national] unity is cemented and forever sanctified," Bushnell insisted.

Devout white southerners struggled to understand why God had not let the Confederacy win. Most attributed the loss to a host of sins for which God must be chastising them, or simply to the inscrutable workings of God's providence. The young South Carolinian Grace Brown Elmore confessed darker musings in her diary. "Our Confederacy, our pride, our glory is departed, we as a people are no more. I know not how to bear it. . . . Hard thoughts against my God will arise." In her next entry, she asked "Has God forsaken us? . . . What have we done, in what have we failed, to be thus given to a people [the Union] wicked and cruel as devils in hell?"

The church divisions of the Civil War lasted well into the future. Southern and northern Methodists reconciled in 1939. Presbyterians did so in 1983. Northern and southern Baptists never did reconcile. With the conservative consolidation of the Southern Baptist Convention that began in the 1980s, reunion between the SBC and the mainline American Baptist Churches (once known as the Northern Baptist Convention) would be most improbable today.

Denominational rupture was not the only churchly legacy of the Civil War, however. For African Americans, the end of the Civil War signaled a great flowering of independent congregations and denominations. Many southern whites and blacks alike preferred that freed people have their own churches instead of the common prewar arrangement of black members attending white-pastored churches. The turn toward independent black congregations would also lead to a great influx of African Americans as church members. The number of African American denominational adherents rose by a million people from 1890 to 1906 alone, to a total of 3.6 million.

Northern whites sent missionaries, educators, and church planters into the postwar South to assist and evangelize the freed people. The Congregational Church formed the American Missionary Association in order to coordinate relief efforts, and by 1868 the AMA had more than five hundred teachers and missionaries working among the freed people. The AMA also helped to start freedmen's schools that eventually turned into historically black colleges such as Fisk University in Nashville (1866) and Hampton Institute in Virginia (1868). Black churches and denominations, such as the African Methodist Episcopal Church, also poured resources into the South. In 1865, AME bishop Daniel Alexander Payne returned to Charleston after a thirty-year absence. Payne had run a school for free black children in the city, but white hostility had forced him to leave. At the end of the war, Payne helped to build a new edifice for Charleston's AME church since the old church had been razed following Denmark Vesey's conspiracy in 1822. By 1866, Charleston had eleven independent black churches representing the Methodist, Baptist, Congregational, Presbyterian, and Episcopal traditions.

Baptists claimed the largest number of African American adherents, even though massive numbers of blacks left the SBC after the war. Before the war, for example, South Carolina Baptists counted twenty-nine thousand blacks among their members. By 1874 that number had dropped to under two thousand. Baptist polity allowed for flexibility in starting congregations and ordaining pastors, and black Baptists used freedom as an opportunity to found countless new churches. The formation of the National Baptist Convention in 1895 gave cohesion to the African American Baptist churches. Although that denomination would split just twelve years later, the Baptist tradition would remain the most common Christian affiliation among African Americans. Holiness and proto-Pentecostal churches also won many African American adherents, signaled by the founding of the Church of God in Christ (COGIC) in Memphis in 1897. COGIC would go on to become one of the nation's largest denominations of any kind.

NYPL, Public Domain

Daniel A. Payne

The Civil War was arguably the pivot point in American history, and it had profound implications for the American religious landscape. If the war led to a national new birth, that experience required unfathomable levels of suffering, with at least 620,000 Americans dead. The slavery issue did long-lasting damage to traditional white-led denominations. For African Americans, the travails of the war led to emancipation and the independence of much of the black church. Thus the violence of the Civil War transformed American society and religion.

WORKS CITED
AND FURTHER READING

A Home Missionary. "Paganism." *The Home Missionary* 62, no. 11 (March 1890): 500.

Channing, William Ellery. *The Complete Works of W. E. Channing*. London: Routledge, 1890.

Cherry, Conrad. *God's New Israel: Religious Interpretations of American Destiny*. Rev. and updated ed. Chapel Hill: University of North Carolina Press, 1998.

Elliott, Charles. *History of the Great Secession from the Methodist Episcopal Church*. Cincinnati: Swormstedt & Poe, 1855.

England, John. *Letters of the Late Bishop England*. Baltimore: John Murphy, 1844.

Frankiel, Sandra Sizer. *California's Spiritual Frontiers: Religious Alternatives in Anglo-Protestantism, 1850–1910*. Berkeley: University of California Press, 1988.

Goen, C. C. *Broken Churches, Broken Nation: Denominational Schisms and the Coming of the American Civil War*. Macon, GA: Mercer University Press, 1985.

Harvey, Paul. *Bounds of Their Habitation: Race and Religion in American History*. Lanham, MD: Rowman & Littlefield, 2017.

Kidd, Thomas S., and Barry Hankins. *Baptists in America: A History*. New York: Oxford University Press, 2015.

Koester, Nancy. *Harriet Beecher Stowe: A Spiritual Life*. Grand Rapids: Eerdmans, 2014.

Kornbluth, Gary J. *Slavery and Sectional Strife in the Early American Republic, 1776–1821*. Lanham, MD: Rowman & Littlefield, 2010.

Parker, David B. "'The Church Did Not Die': Religion in Florida during the Civil War." In *A Forgotten Front: Florida During the Civil War Era*, 115–34. Edited by Seth A. Weitz and Jonathan C. Sheppard. Tuscaloosa: University of Alabama Press, 2018.

Rable, George C. *God's Almost Chosen Peoples: A Religious History of the American Civil War*. Chapel Hill: University of North Carolina Press, 2010.

Raboteau, Albert J. *African-American Religion.* New York: Oxford University Press, 1999.

Reynolds, David S. *John Brown, Abolitionist: The Man Who Killed Slavery, Sparked the Civil War, and Seeded Civil Rights.* New York: Alfred A. Knopf, 2005.

Rugemer, Edward B. "Slave Rebels and Abolitionists: The Black Atlantic and the Coming of the Civil War." *Journal of the Civil War Era* 2, no. 2 (June 2012): 179–202.

Stauffer, John, and Henry Louis Gates Jr., eds. *The Portable Frederick Douglass.* New York: Penguin Books, 2016.

Stout, Harry S. *Upon the Altar of the Nation: A Moral History of the American Civil War.* New York: Viking, 2006.

Weiner, Marli F., ed. *Heritage of Woe: The Civil War Diary of Grace Brown Elmore, 1861–1868.* Athens: University of Georgia Press, 1997.

Chapter 8

IMMIGRATION
AND RELIGIOUS
DIVERSITY

From the Civil War to the Great Depression, immigration was arguably the most transformative factor in American history. Immigration brought millions of people with ethnicities and faith traditions that were unfamiliar to white Protestant Americans. The movement of these masses into America, as well as people moving within America, demanded a response from churches. The remarkable life of the Italian immigrant Sister Blandina Segale, for example, illustrated how immigration presented challenges and opportunities for people of faith. Sister Blandina's family emigrated from Genoa to Cincinnati, Ohio, around the time of the Civil War. When she was sixteen, she joined the Sisters of Charity in Cincinnati. The Sisters of Charity were a branch of a Catholic community originally founded in Maryland by Elizabeth Ann Seton. The entrepreneurial Sister Blandina was stationed at several missions throughout the West during the 1870s and '80s. She started a school for Native American girls and a hospital for railroad workers in Santa Fe, New Mexico. Along the way, Sister Blandina became friends with the legendary outlaw Billy the Kid. In the mid-1890s,

Sister Blandina returned to Cincinnati where she kept ministering to Italian immigrants. With her biological sister Justina, Sister Blandina opened the first Catholic settlement house, the Santa Maria Institute, in Cincinnati in 1897. The institute, alongside similar settlement houses across the nation, focused on immigrants' needs, giving them a "place to which they could turn in their perplexity." The Segales hoped to keep the new immigrants within the Catholic fold and provided them vocational and domestic training as well as material assistance.

Catholic immigrants from Ireland and later from Central and Eastern Europe are relatively well-known in American social history. American immigration prior to the Great Depression was also a story of Chinese, Japanese, and Mexican immigrants in the West, and African American immigrants moving from the rural South to northern and western cities. All these movements changed, challenged, and diversified religion in America. However, the religious vitality resulting from immigration also introduced new tensions and threats of violence on the cultural landscape.

As we have seen, the pre–Civil War years were marked by a surge of Irish and German immigration, which injected a great new Catholic presence into the American religious scene. The Irish were overwhelmingly Catholic, while the German immigrants were divided between Catholics and Lutherans. The Irish would come to dominate the Catholic hierarchy in America by the late 1800s, causing consternation among other Catholic ethnic groups. A German priest in Milwaukee wrote to the Vatican (the Roman seat of Catholic authority) in 1886, asking that "German parishes shall be entirely independent of Irish parishes" and that "rectors of Irish parishes shall not be able to exercise any parochial jurisdiction over Germans." Because the "manners and social customs of the two nationalities differ exceedingly," the priest argued, the Irish and Germans needed different kinds of Catholic parishes. The Irish "love simplicity . . . and do not care much for pomp and splendor," and the Germans loved the "pomp of ceremonies, belfries and bells, organs and sacred music, processions, feast days, sodalities [religious associations], and the most solemn celebration of First Communion and weddings." Many observers like this priest were quick to assign cultural and religious traits to whole ethnic groups.

This sort of assumption about the different styles of ethnic Catholics made the "national parish," or a congregation focused on one ethnic group, a standard feature of American Catholic life. As various Catholic cohorts immigrated into American cities, the church hierarchy thought it sensible to create parishes comprised mostly of Irish, Germans, Mexicans, and so forth. Sometimes those parishes offered services in a national language other than English, such as German or Spanish. The national parish was a product of large-scale immigration and was harder to sustain in places with few recent immigrants. African Americans sometimes also had black-majority Catholic parishes. As suggested in the Milwaukee priest's letter, the leaders of the national parishes did not always match the ethnicity of the majority of the parishioners.

In the 1880s, Catholic immigration to America became dominated by people from southern and eastern Europe. Italian priests and nuns were critical in forging a Catholic infrastructure in the West starting in the 1870s, due to efforts of people like Sister Blandina Segale. In the 1880s, the stream of Italian immigration to the United States became a flood, with about a million Italians coming to America in the last two decades of the nineteenth century. Three million more Italians immigrated in the first two decades of the twentieth century. As with the Irish, the vast majority of Italians were at least nominal Catholics. In the initial waves of Italian immigration, men frequently came by themselves. They hoped to make money and bring family members over to America later or to return to Italy (which they did by the millions in the early twentieth century).

One observer in the early twentieth century explained that Italian men "were not so church scrupulous as the women although they were

Catholic. . . . Basically they dislike the clergy, and if they dislike the Italian clergy they despise the American clergy." Nevertheless, most immigrants saw a deep connection between their Italian identity and Catholicism. This connection was illustrated by Italian community celebrations such as New York City's annual *festa* in honor of the Virgin Mary. As described by the *festa*'s best-known historian, Robert Orsi, the great "parade, with thousands of marchers, several bands, trailing incense and the haunting sounds of southern Italian religious chanting, made its way up and down every block in the 'Italian quarter' of Harlem."

Library of Congress, Prints & Photographs Division, LC-DIG-fsa-8d24204

Christmas midnight mass at an Italian Catholic church in New York City, 1942

Poles also came by the millions before the Great Depression. Until 1918, Poland was divided between Prussia, Austria, and Russia. Ethnic Poles came to the United States from all those nations. Polish immigrants, like the Irish and Italians, were mostly Catholics. Poles also wanted their own ethnic parishes, but different Polish regional cohorts fought over control of churches. Polish national parishes typically emerged from the initiative of local laypeople, who expected to have a voice in decisions about how to run the church. Some Poles grew so frustrated with the church hierarchy that they formed schismatic Catholic congregations in cities including Buffalo, Chicago, and Scranton (Penn.). In one of the most remarkable Catholic divisions in American history, schismatic Polish Catholics even founded the Polish National Catholic Church (PNCC) in Scranton in 1896. Although it has remained small, the PNCC is the only ethnic-based Catholic denomination in the United States to have survived a split from Rome. Much of the PNCC's theology is similar to that of the Roman Catholic Church, although since the early 1920s it has allowed priests to get married.

Some Polish immigrants were Jews, part of a swelling tide of Jewish immigration to America from Eastern Europe beginning in the 1870s and '80s. Tens of thousands of Jews were expelled from cities such as Moscow, Saint Petersburg, and Kiev in the 1870s and '80s. In 1881–82, hundreds of towns in the Russian empire witnessed anti-Semitic pogroms, or ethnic riots, that targeted Jews. Even worse violence against Jews transpired in Moldova and Romania in 1903. The recurring pogroms spurred many Jews to flee their homelands. Many ended up in the United States. Between 1880 and 1900, some 500,000 Eastern European Jews came to America, and another 1.5 million came to the United States between 1900 and the outbreak of World War I in 1914. Many of the new Jewish immigrants were Orthodox Jews, practicing traditional rituals and maintaining conservative enclaves of Jewish culture, and many arrived in New York City, with smaller numbers passing through ports such as Galveston, Texas. Emma Lazarus, a native-born Jewish poet, penned the lines that would be emblazoned on the Statue of Liberty in New York harbor.

> Give me your tired, your poor,
> Your huddled masses, yearning to be free,
> The wretched refuse of your teeming shore,
> Send these, the homeless, tempest-tost to me,
> I lift my lamp beside the golden door.

The anti-Semitic horrors of the Holocaust would engulf Europe in the 1930s and '40s. By that point America was less receptive to Jewish immigrants. The great era of Jewish immigration from 1881 to 1914, however, gave the United States the largest Jewish population of any country in the world. Depending on how one counts, the modern state of Israel (founded 1948) may now have a larger population of Jews than the United States. Yet after the genocide against Europe's Jews during the Holocaust, Israel and the United States would become home to a strong majority of the world's population of Jews.

Being Jewish was an ethnic identity, and (as with Irish, Italian, and Polish Catholics) sometimes ethnic identification did not entail devout religiosity. Most practicing Jews were part of Reform temples or of Orthodox or Conservative synagogues. Reform Judaism, more popular among American-born Jews, saw cultural adaptation as a natural part of religion. Orthodox Jews were overrepresented among the new immigrants from the Russian empire. They dismissed the notion of updating Jewish law and custom; instead, they wanted to find a place to practice their faith in freedom. In between the Reformed and the Orthodox were the Conservative Jews. They believed in conserving the heart of Jewish law and tradition, while also seeking to fit into modern society.

Jewish boy in prayer shawl, 1911

Library of Congress, Prints & Photographs Division, LC-DIG-ppmsca-06590

One of Conservative Judaism's most influential leaders was the Moldovan-born rabbi and scholar Solomon Schechter, who in 1902 became president of New York's Jewish Theological Seminary. Schechter explained that "there is nothing in American citizenship which is incompatible with our observing the dietary laws, and sanctifying the Sabbath . . . or our perpetuating any other law essential to the preservation of Judaism. . . . In this great, glorious and free country we Jews need not sacrifice a single iota of our Torah [the law of God], and in the enjoyment of absolute equality with our fellow citizens we can live out those ideals for which our ancestors so often had to die." The ethnic and theological diversity among American Jews forced them to compete with one another for adherents in the early 1900s. Shechter's followers, for example, fanned

out from New England to the Southwest, trying to convince synagogues
to hire rabbis from Jewish Theological Seminary.

Orthodox Christians from Russia, and from other parts of Europe,
were another strand of the vivid ethno-religious fabric of immigration.
The Orthodox split from the Roman Catholic Church had transpired
in the eleventh century's East-West Schism. Over time Orthodox
churches assumed strong national identities in countries such as Russia
and Greece. Historically, the Russian Orthodox Church's strongest
North American presence was in the Pacific Northwest and Alaska.
Small numbers of Orthodox Christians in San Francisco in the 1860s
united to form a combined Greek-Russian-Slavic Orthodox congregation. Portland, Oregon, and Seattle, Washington, likewise saw the
founding of multiethnic Orthodox churches in the 1890s. (The charter
members of Portland's Orthodox church were reportedly six Arabs,
four Serbs, and two Russians.) As soon as Orthodox numbers grew
large enough, ethnic groups tended to break away to establish their
own national congregations in American towns.

Immigrants in the eastern United States from the Russian empire
included many Orthodox Christians too. This growth led the Orthodox
archbishop of San Francisco, which had been the center of Orthodox
life in the United States, to move his diocesan see (or jurisdiction) to
New York in 1905. Still, the largest group of Orthodox Christians in
the United States were Greeks, with about 300,000 people of Greek
heritage living in America by 1920, most from an Orthodox background.
Orthodox leaders in the United States have sometimes sought to create
unified Orthodox church structures, but until the post–World War II
era, these efforts met with limited success. Greeks, Russians, and other
Orthodox groups found it difficult enough to contain disagreements
and splits among their own communions. Most ethnic groups with
significant numbers of Orthodox adherents were given (or they unilat-
erally established) their own dioceses in America prior to World War II,
including Orthodox churches of Serbia (1921), Romania (1930), and
Albania (1932).

In the Pacific West, Chinese and Japanese immigration also introduced new religious traditions in the mid- to late nineteenth century. Large numbers of Asian immigrants went to Hawaii and California starting in the 1840s. They sought jobs in the sugar industry in the Hawaiian Islands and in California's railroad industry and Gold Rush, which began in 1849. In early 1849, only fifty-five Chinese people reportedly lived in California. By 1854, the number of Chinese people in California had shot up to forty thousand. Resentment against Chinese and Japanese workers resulted in riots and hostile legislation, culminating in Congress's Chinese Exclusion Act (1882), which barred Chinese people from immigrating. The United States effectively cut off all Chinese immigration until World War II. Nevertheless, Chinese culture and religion had become a fixture of the Pacific West by 1882. European and American Christian missionaries had labored in China for many years, but most of the Chinese immigrants to America adhered to Confucianism, Buddhism, Taoism, or local Chinese religions. In 1853, Chinese settlers in San Francisco built the first Buddhist temple in America. A Buddhist temple also appeared in Oroville, California, a town swept up in the gold fever of the 1850s. The California temples were distinctively Chinese, pairing images of Buddha with Chinese gods such as Kuan Ti, the god of prosperity.

Japanese immigrants also brought Shinto and Buddhist practices with them. Seeking to mimic the success of the Young Men's Christian Association, Japanese Buddhists formed the Young Men's Buddhist Association (YMBA) in San Francisco in 1899. Seeking a broader profile, the YMBA began calling itself the Buddhist Mission of North America (BMNA) in 1914. As of 1930, the BMNA had thirty temples affiliated with it. These temples often began calling themselves *churches*, hoping that the term would seem less threatening to Anglo-American religious sensibilities.

Thousands of Sikhs also came to California and other areas of the

Pacific West during this period. Most originated from northern India, where the monotheistic Sikh religion had emerged in the early 1500s. Stockton, California, became the focus of Sikh settlement in America. Stockton saw the creation of America's first Sikh association (1912) and the first *gurdwara*, or Sikh place of worship, in 1915. The Sikh community remained small, however, and Stockton's *gurdwara* remained the only one in the United States until 1948. As with many Asian immigrants, the Immigration Act of 1965 would signal the beginning of a major new wave of Sikh immigration to America. Sikhs came to establish major urban enclaves in places such as Richmond Hill (Queens), New York, which today has the largest Sikh population in the New York metropolitan area.

Starting in the mid-1800s, the influx of Asian immigrants created concern among the native-born Christian population in America. One California congressman warned that the Chinese would never assimilate to dominant white Christian society because of their culture and religion. "We are a Christian civilization," the congressman said. "A pagan civilization is necessarily inconsistent with it." Some Protestant groups sought to evangelize Chinese and Japanese settlers, but white critics said it was no use trying to teach the "filthy and abominable heathens Christianity." Aside from generalized missionary work, Presbyterians and Methodists set up special female missionary homes in San Francisco by the mid-1870s to provide sanctuary for Chinese prostitutes. Relatively few Chinese people received Christian baptism prior to the Chinese Exclusion Act in 1882. Yet thousands of Chinese immigrants participated in missionary-sponsored English classes or went to the YMCA. San Francisco's YMCA was founded in 1853.

Chinese people who converted to Christianity were often zealous to spread their new faith among their countrymen. One Baptist missionary named Fung Chak in Portland, Oregon, in the early 1880s told the American Baptist Home Mission Society that more investment in Chinese-American missions was needed. "We can only with aching hearts see these thousands of precious souls sinking into hell, with never a hand to save or a voice to warn. . . . The Chinese must not be wholly left without the Gospel." However, conversion was often more complex than a wholesale transfer of allegiance from Chinese religious practices to a Christian church. Chinese Congregationalist missionary and minister Jee Gam reported that one Chinese convert in Oakland had "given up every thing to serve Christ except one thing, and that was the worship of ancestors." Christian adherents from many ethnic backgrounds retained heterodox practices that clergy found worrisome.

Christians with European ancestry also kept trying to reach Native Americans in the Midwest and Far West. One of the key players in Catholic evangelization of Native Americans in the late 1800s was Katherine Drexel, the heiress of a wealthy banking family who founded the Sisters of the Blessed Sacrament for Indians and Colored People (SBS) in 1891. Drexel may have donated as much as $20 million of her personal fortune, the equivalent of hundreds of millions today, to the SBS. Answering her own sense of religious calling, Drexel entered a convent in 1889 and took a vow of personal poverty, even as she continued to oversee a multimillion-dollar charitable enterprise. Drexel would eventually build dozens of Catholic schools for Indians in the West. Protestant politicians demanded that the government reduce funding to Catholic Indian schools. They wanted the money redirected to public schools, which, for practical purposes, inculcated a generic Protestantism with lessons from the King James Bible. The reduced funding to Catholic schools tested even Drexel's vast financial resources in the early twentieth century. Drexel was canonized as a saint by the Catholic Church in 2000, becoming only the second native-born American to receive that distinction (the first was Elizabeth Ann Seton).

White Protestants also kept working to educate and convert Native Americans. This effort generally produced small numbers of enduring conversions, but it did result in occasional revivals. One of the most spectacular and controversial Indian awakenings transpired at the Round Valley Indian Reservation, California's largest, in 1874. Under President Ulysses Grant's "peace policy" toward Native Americans, the

Department of the Interior in 1871 had given the Methodist Church administrative control of California's missions, including Round Valley. One of the missionaries there, Mary Colburn, reported that some eight hundred Indians had become Christians over the course of a few weeks. All of the tribal "chiefs"—representing varied groups including the local Yuki tribe—had professed faith in Christ, clearing the way for rank-and-file Indian conversions. "Nightly songs of praise and prayer ascend from the lips of these newborn souls," Colburn told the American Missionary Association, a northern missionary group originally connected to the abolitionist movement. Colburn had worked in previous assignments among freed people in the South, and among Chinese settlers in California. Those experiences were "rich and varied," she wrote, "but never have I witnessed such an outpouring of the Holy Spirit and such an ingathering of souls as now." Colburn's class and ethnic consciousness came out when she exulted that "these trophies are plucked from the lowest class of humanity—the *California Digger Indians.*" ("Digger" Indians reputedly dug for roots and insects as food.)

Methodist administrator and pastor J. L. Burchard instituted harsh discipline on the mission Indians at Round Valley beginning in 1872, sometimes subjecting disobedient natives to whippings. He sought to have the Round Valley residents live in Anglo-American style houses. Burchard eliminated the Indians' ritual sweathouses and demanded that they bury their dead in a cemetery instead of cremating them. Within two years, almost half of the 1,700 Indians there had left or died. Virtually all of the remaining Round Valley natives participated in the 1874 revival. Burchard was happy to report that "all dancing, swearing, drinking, gambling, Sabbath-breaking, and all the pagan practices and habits, have been abandoned; citizens' dress universally adopted." Six Indian men began working as Methodist preachers. The revival dwindled in coming years, though many of the reservation's Indians remained at least nominally Protestant.

The missionaries at Round Valley surely did not realize how contested the reservation's spiritual allegiances would become in the 1870s.

Round Valley Methodist Church, Round Valley Reservation, California
*The Burke Library Archives (Columbia University Libraries)
at Union Theological Seminary, New York*

That era saw the advent of the Indian "Ghost Dance" controversy. The Ghost Dance rites, starting in Nevada in the late 1860s, attracted Indians across the Mountain West and Great Plains, including some at Round Valley prior to the 1874 Methodist revival. Devotees believed that the dance itself would reconnect them with the spirits of deceased ancestors. Ghost Dance spirituality drew upon older Native American prophetic themes, rejecting the corruptions of the dominant white Americans. Some strains of Ghost Dance religion were apocalyptic, anticipating the end of the world (or at least the end of white Americans' power). Others were moralistic, promising that abstinence from alcohol and other debilitating influences would lead to a flourishing of native societies.

By 1890 the Ghost Dance movement had arrived among the Lakota Indians of South Dakota, where the Lakota leader Sitting Bull was killed in a clash over fears about the ritual. At the end of 1890, the US army attacked Lakotas affiliated with the Ghost Dance at Wounded Knee Creek in South Dakota, using cannon fire to bombard their camp. When the smoke cleared, 146 Lakotas, including dozens of women and children, were dead. It was another tragic instance of the conjunction of religious revitalization and oppressive violence in American history.

Hispanic immigrants, who were overwhelmingly Catholic, came to the United States in small numbers prior to the 1910s. In spite of their deep historic roots in Florida and the Southwest, circumstances did not yet favor large-scale Hispanic immigration. Nevertheless, Catholics did open a Spanish-speaking national parish in San Francisco in the mid-1870s. This parish served Mexican residents of the city, as well as diplomatic agents representing countries from Bolivia to Spain. Cuban settlers also sponsored the founding of a chapel to Nuestra Senora de la Caridad del Cobre, the national patroness of Cuba, in Key West, Florida, in 1879.

The first decade of the twentieth century saw notable growth in Mexican immigration. This was partly due to a need for railroad and agricultural workers to replace the banned Chinese. Then between 1910 and the Great Depression, millions of Mexican immigrants crossed into the United States, many escaping the turmoil of the Mexican Revolution in the 1910s. This surge in Mexican immigration was followed by the establishment of many new Hispanic churches, such as Houston's Our Lady of Guadalupe Church in the El Segundo barrio (neighborhood). Catholics built two more Houston churches catering to Mexicans by the mid-1930s. Although the number of Hispanic Protestants was small, Protestants opened missions stations and churches in barrios as well. Houston had at least five Protestant congregations ministering to Mexicans by the early 1920s.

Of special significance for Protestant outreach to Hispanics were churches representing the new Holiness and Pentecostal movements. These groups emphasized the "higher life" of holiness available to fully committed Christians. Holiness and Pentecostal churches raised up key Hispanic evangelists. They generally enjoyed more success in reaching fellow Hispanics than did Anglo missionaries. One of the most prominent early Protestant Hispanic evangelists was Francisco Olazábal, a native of Mexico. Olazábal's mother had converted to Protestantism in

1898. She became a lay Methodist preacher, and Francisco followed her into the ministry. He received Methodist seminary training in Mexico and became a pastor in El Paso, Texas, in 1911. Olazábal then began working as an itinerant evangelist based in California.

In San Francisco, Olazábal was persuaded to join the new Pentecostal movement. As we shall see, Pentecostal piety received a major boost from the 1906 Azusa Street revival in Los Angeles. Pentecostals spoke in tongues, and taught that Holy Spirit baptism was a postconversion experience and was key to personal holiness. They also prayed confidently for healing and testified to many healing miracles. Olazábal eventually left the Methodist Church and joined the Assemblies of God, a Pentecostal denomination. As a Pentecostal preacher, he held successful evangelistic and healing campaigns in Los Angeles and El Paso. After clashing with white Assemblies of God leaders, Olazábal founded the Interdenominational Mexican Council of Christian Churches (Pentecostal) in 1923. He went on to develop a national profile as an evangelist and healer, which culminated in a massive 1931 revival he led in Spanish Harlem in New York.

Before Olazábal switched to Pentecostalism, he studied at Moody Bible Institute in Chicago. The great evangelist Dwight Moody founded this school in 1889. If Olazábal represented the emerging Pentecostal and charismatic strain of American revivalism, Moody represented a more traditional evangelical strain. Moody's popularity in Britain and America approximated that of George Whitefield before him. Moody was a businessman in Boston and Chicago before committing himself fully to ministry at the beginning of the Civil War. Moody worked among Civil War soldiers and ministered to poor people in Chicago following the war.

Moody enjoyed his greatest success as an itinerant preacher. Moody and his associate, the singer Ira Sankey, engaged in a phenomenal evangelistic tour of Britain from 1873 to 1875. This model of pairing an evangelist with a singer would be followed by future American evangelists, most notably Billy Graham and George Beverly Shea. Moody and Sankey returned in triumph from Britain to the United States, barnstorming through northern cities to great acclaim. Moody preached simple, sober sermons on the need to give one's heart to Christ. He attracted the attention of powerful businessmen and politicians, with President Ulysses Grant even attending one of his meetings in Philadelphia. Moody was skeptical about the Christian social reform movements of his day, including those associated with the "social gospel," or the idea that the gospel must be lived out in loving service. Moody explained that he saw the world as "a vessel going to pieces on the rocks. God puts a life-boat in my hands, and says: 'Rescue every man you can.'" God wanted him to save souls, not reform society. Nevertheless, Moody did establish several Bible-based academies, including a girls and a boys school in Massachusetts and Moody Bible Institute.

Moody and Sankey's meetings, often held in cavernous meeting halls and opera houses, were typically somber. One reporter at a meeting wrote that "even the rough fellows who crowd the gallery passages make no sound." By contrast, Pentecostal meetings were not so quiet. The "rough fellows" at Moody's meetings signaled that he did resonate with the working class, even if his core support came from middle- and upper-class business interests. Pentecostals disproportionately attracted common whites, Hispanics, and African Americans, although Pentecostal interracial fellowship became less frequent after the initial fervor of Azusa Street wore off. The emergence of American Pentecostalism correlated with the beginning of mass Hispanic immigration, as well as African Americans' "Great Migration" in the early twentieth century. After Reconstruction ended in 1877, a steady stream of African Americans made their way out of the rural South to the cities of the Northeast, Midwest, and West. The pace of African American movement vastly accelerated during World War I. Immigrating Mexicans and African Americans proved especially receptive to Holiness and Pentecostal religion.

In the early 1900s, new centers of African American religious life began appearing outside of the South. During the nineteenth century, the First African Baptist Church in Richmond, Virginia, had been the nation's largest black church. By World War II, Olivet Baptist Church in Chicago had supplanted it. Holiness beliefs were taking root among African American Christians during this period, as signaled by the founding of the Church of God in Christ denomination in 1897. Then at the outset of the twentieth century, speaking in tongues took hold among some Holiness Christians, beginning at Bethel Bible College in Topeka, Kansas, in 1901. At a "watch night" service marking the dawn of the twentieth century, a Bethel student named Agnes Ozman began speaking in a language that sounded to observers like Chinese, though she did not know that language. Observers also noted that something like a "halo seemed to surround [Ozman's] head and face." Ozman was unable to speak English at all for three days. Pentecostals said that tongues, or glossolalia, were gifts of the Holy Spirit, who enabled believers to speak in unknown languages, or the language of the Spirit. This experience mimicked that of the earliest Christians in the book of Acts.

The founder of Bethel Bible College, Charles Fox Parham, itinerated and taught other Holiness Christians about the gift of tongues, which he saw as evidence of the baptism of the Holy Spirit. Parham influenced many followers across the Midwest and Southwest, including an African American waiter in Houston named William J. Seymour. The Pentecostal message began to spread to the Pacific Coast as Seymour moved to Los Angeles in 1906. Seymour began holding Pentecostal meetings there, including some in a warehouse on Los Angeles's Azusa Street. The Azusa Street revival began to attract national and international attention as people journeyed there to experience what seemed to be a dramatic manifestation of the Spirit's power.

One of those who came to Los Angeles was Charles H. Mason, a child of former slaves and one of the founders of the Church of God in Christ. During the revival, Mason prayed to be baptized in the Holy

Members of a Washington, DC, Church of God in Christ congregation

Spirit. Mason said that a brilliant light surrounded him, and "a flame touched my tongue which ran down in me. My language changed and no word could I speak in my own tongue." Mason returned to Mississippi teaching about tongues but found that many of his Holiness colleagues did not accept the restored practice. Mason eventually consolidated control of the Church of God in Christ, which became a distinctly Pentecostal, African American–led denomination. White Pentecostals largely became affiliated with the new Assemblies of God association of churches, which formed in Arkansas in 1914.

Many Christians responded to the new religions and new peoples in America with the time-honored responses of evangelism and education. Sometimes they advocated relief and social ministry, especially for the impoverished people of the crowded cities. One of the most distinctive responses to the new religious pluralism was the World's Parliament of Religions in Chicago in 1893, which many regard as the first American attempt at interfaith dialogue. Organizers came from the modernist or liberal wing of Protestantism. Some believed that all religions contained some divine truth, and others were confident that Christianity represented the one true and fully universal religion. Nevertheless, the parliament gave a stage to representatives of Buddhism, Islam, and Hinduism, among other world religions.

John Henry Barrows, a Presbyterian minister who introduced the parliament, was among those with assurance of Christianity's exclusive truth among the new faiths in America. Nevertheless, Barrows explained that "the influence of religion tends to advance the general welfare." He hoped that the parliament would show forth the "religious harmonies and unities of humanity" and "the moral and spiritual agencies which are at the root of human progress." By contrast, many traditionalist Christians, who were underrepresented at the Parliament, saw religion as something that fundamentally divided humanity, especially into the ranks of the saved and the damned.

World's Parliament of Religions, 1893

The late nineteenth and early twentieth century was a time of phenomenal growth in immigration (both into and within the United States) and religious diversity in America. Many Christians continued to use missions and evangelism to reach these new ethnic populations: the Catholics from eastern and southern Europe and from Latin America, non-Christians from East Asia, Native Americans, and freed people from the South, among others. Pentecostalism brought phenomenal new spiritual energy for many whites, blacks, and Hispanics. Pentecostals would play an increasingly prominent role in the story of American (and global) religion. However, the challenges of immigration and religious diversity threatened many Americans' aspirations for a unified Christian nation. The fear of new waves of Catholic and non-Christian immigration, paired with concern about secularizing intellectual trends, would generate a vociferous backlash among many traditionalist Protestants.

WORKS CITED
AND FURTHER READING

Baptist Home Missions in North America: 1832–1882. New York: Baptist
   Home Mission Rooms, 1883.

Barrows, John Henry, ed. *The World's Parliament of Religions.* Chicago:
   Parliament, 1893.

Barry, Colman J. *The Catholic Church and German Americans.* Milwaukee:
   Bruce, 1953.

Cohen, Michael R. *The Birth of Conservative Judaism: Solomon Schechter's
   Disciples and the Creation of an American Religious Movement.* New
   York: Columbia University Press, 2012.

Espinosa, Gastón. *Latino Pentecostals in America: Faith and Politics in
   Action.* Cambridge, MA: Harvard University Press, 2014.

Evensen, Bruce J. *God's Man for the Gilded Age: D. L. Moody and the Rise of
   Modern Mass Evangelism.* New York: Oxford University Press, 2003.

Fitzgerald, Thomas. "Eastern Christianity in the United States." In *The
   Blackwell Companion to Eastern Christianity*, 269–79. Edited by Ken
   Parry. Malden, MA: Wiley-Blackwell, 2010.

Hartley, Benjamin L. *Evangelicals at a Crossroads: Revivalism & Social
   Reform in Boston, 1860–1910.* Hanover, NH: University Press of New
   England, 2011.

LaGumina, S. J. *The Immigrants Speak.* New York: Center for Migration
   Studies, 1979.

Le Beau, Bryan F. *A History of Religion in America: From the End of the Civil
   War to the Twenty-First Century.* New York: Routledge, 2018.

Mann, Gurinder Singh, Paul Numrich, and Raymond Williams. *Buddhists,
   Hindus, and Sikhs in America: A Short History.* New York: Oxford
   University Press, 2008.

McGuinness, Margaret M. *Called to Serve: A History of Nuns in America.*
   New York: New York University Press, 2013.

Orsi, Robert A. *The Madonna of 115th Street: Faith and Community in
   Italian Harlem, 1880–1950.* 3rd ed. New Haven, CT: Yale University
   Press, 2010.

Paddison, Joshua. *American Heathens: Religion, Race, and Reconstruction in California*. Berkeley: University of California Press, 2012.

Ruth, Lester. *Longing for Jesus: Worship at a Black Holiness Church in Mississippi, 1895–1913*. Grand Rapids: Eerdmans, 2013.

Schechter, Solomon. *Seminary Addresses and Other Papers*. Cincinnati: Ark, 1915.

Synan, Vinson. *The Holiness-Pentecostal Tradition: Charismatic Movements in the Twentieth Century*. 2nd ed. Grand Rapids: Eerdmans, 1997.

Wacker, Grant. *Heaven Below: Early Pentecostals and American Culture*. Cambridge, MA: Harvard University Press, 2001.

Warren, Louis S. *God's Red Son: The Ghost Dance Religion and the Making of Modern America*. New York: Basic Books, 2017.

Chapter 9

EVOLUTION, BIBLICAL CRITICISM, AND FUNDAMENTALISM

Doubts about traditional Christian faith or the Bible were hardly new to post–Civil War America. But the trauma of the war itself, paired with evolutionary theory and higher criticism of the Bible, seemed to put unprecedented pressure on America's heavily Christian culture. Christians in the post–Civil War era offered a wide range of responses to Charles Darwin's *On the Origin of Species* (1859) and the theory of evolution. The book posed the basic scientific question of whether species had continuously evolved over long periods of time into their current forms. Most professional scientists had accepted that component of evolution by the mid-twentieth century. However, pastors and theologians, as well as some believing scientists, asked whether Darwin's theory excluded God from the evolutionary process. Was evolution naturalistic by definition? Could it be reconciled with traditional belief? Some argued that Christians could fold evolution into their understandings of the Bible and creation, just as Christians had once adjusted to heliocentrism, or the concept that the earth revolved around the sun.

Others were not sure about the validity of integrating evolution and Christian faith. The Catholic Church did not condemn the theory outright, but it registered doubts about whether evolution could mesh with traditional doctrine. In 1909, the Pontifical Biblical Commission at the Vatican insisted that no faithful Catholic could question "the creation of all things by God at the beginning of time; the special creation of man; the formation of the first woman from the first man; [or] the unity of the human race." In the 1890s, church authorities urged Notre Dame physics professor John Zahm not to publish his book *Evolution and Dogma*, which contended that Catholics could reconcile evolution with church teachings. Pope Leo XIII warned American church leaders about the individualistic heresy of "Americanism," including Zahm's brand of evolution, in an 1899 encyclical letter. By 1950, Pope Pius XII advised that the church should take a neutral position on evolution as a scientific matter. Catholics could accept evolution as long as they did not explicitly deny basic Christian beliefs such as God's special creation of Adam and Eve.

Protestant reactions to evolution ran along a broad spectrum because there was no central church authority to guide Protestant approaches to science. Even at Unitarian-dominated Harvard, two of the most prominent professors took different views of evolution. Scientist Louis Agassiz grew up as the child of a Protestant minister, but as an adult he did not have any church affiliation. Nevertheless, Agassiz rejected Darwinism because of its materialism, which he said could not stand before the "intellectual grandeur of the universe." Agassiz's devout colleague, Presbyterian botanist Asa Gray, was more open to evolution. Gray tended to separate his personal piety from his scientific views. Gray modeled a secular approach to science that would become the norm among university-based scholars in the twentieth century. Gray was also influenced by correspondence with Darwin himself, which made him disposed to accept the British scientist's theories.

At Princeton College and Princeton Theological Seminary, there was also sharp disagreement regarding how to react to evolution. Some, like the Presbyterian pastor and Princeton president James McCosh, believed that there was "nothing atheistic" in the theory if properly understood. He was confident that evolution, "like every other part of God's work, would illustrate his existence and his wisdom" once it was better comprehended. Princeton Seminary's Charles Hodge did not share McCosh's certitude. Hodge, one of the most influential theologians of his day, did not necessarily oppose evolution if one assumed that God was superintending the development of species. Yet he feared that "Darwinism," as a code of belief, excluded divine agency. "The great question which divides theists from atheists—Christians from unbelievers—is this," Hodge declared. "Is development an intellectual process guided by God, or is it a blind process of unintelligible, unconscious force, which knows no end and adopts no means? In other words, is God the author of all we see, the creator of all the beauty and grandeur of this world, or is unintelligible force, gravity, electricity, and such like?" Evangelical opponents of evolution would, by the mid-twentieth century, develop countertheories related to problems in demonstrating Darwin's evolution of lower forms of life into higher ones. Still, Hodge elaborated the core Christian objection to Darwinism: it posited a natural order in which God seemed absent.

Deists and other skeptics had long questioned God's role in the natural world. The American Revolution and the disestablishment of the state churches opened more cultural space for public attacks on the Bible. The most spectacular fusillade came from Tom Paine's *The Age of Reason* (1794). Paine called the Bible "a book of lies, wickedness, and blasphemy; for what can be greater blasphemy than to ascribe the wickedness of man to the orders of the Almighty?" Paine also contended that many of the books of the Bible were not actually written by the traditional authors. For instance, he challenged the notion that Moses wrote the Pentateuch, the first five books of the Old Testament. As we have seen, deistic ideas influenced founders such as Paine, Ben Franklin, and Thomas Jefferson.

Higher criticism of the Bible gathered momentum in early nineteenth-century Germany. The works of German scholars such as Friedrich Schleiermacher and his student David Strauss influenced theologians across Europe and America. Many regard Schleiermacher as the father of liberal Christian theology. He emphasized the importance of individual experience and feeling in discerning religious truth. In his pathbreaking *General Hermeneutics* (1809–10), Schleiermacher argued that the goal of studying any text—including biblical texts—was "understanding in the highest sense." The scholar might be able to "understand the writer better than he understands himself." For Schleiermacher, interpreting texts was no rigid, timeless exercise but a psychologically sensitive matter in which the reader sought to understand an author's context and motivation. Schleiermacher made the interpretation of any Bible verse a complicated and artistic endeavor. Certainty in biblical interpretation was, to Schleiermacher, normally elusive.

Strauss's *Das Leben Jesu* (1835) sensationally confronted the same question Jefferson had privately considered in his edition of the Gospels. Were the Gospel accounts reliable? Had Jesus's followers merely imagined his miracles and divinity after his death? Strauss initiated a long public debate about the "historical Jesus." Many scholars since have argued that the New Testament is not always a dependable source of information about Jesus of Nazareth. One of the more controversial recent efforts to assess the Gospels was the Jesus Seminar in the 1980s and '90s, in which dozens of left-leaning biblical scholars voted on the historicity of various sayings and actions of Jesus. Books like Strauss's opened the door for nineteenth-century American theologians to engage in broader discussions about the Bible's authority. German higher criticism also generated a backlash, in which traditionalist theologians defended the Bible's "infallibility" or "inerrancy." Charles Hodge, for example, asserted in his *Systematic Theology* that the whole Bible was "the Word of God, written under the inspiration of the Holy Spirit, and therefore infallible." To Hodge, the Bible was "free from all error, whether of doctrines, fact, or precept."

For decades, the influence of German higher criticism was largely limited to liberal American colleges and seminaries. Promising American pastors and seminarians continued to study theology in Germany, and those with traditionalist leanings could find congenial German professors with whom to work. Ironically, modernist theology won few adherents among German-background Lutherans in America. As of the 1920s, American Lutherans remained overwhelmingly traditionalist. In the 1870s, however, American seminaries began to debate whether they would permit instruction in evolutionary theory and higher criticism.

Although modernist beliefs made little impact on rank-and-file Southern Baptists, Professor Crawford Toy of Southern Baptist Theological Seminary became the first instructor in America fired for his advocacy of higher criticism. Toy undertook graduate work in Semitic languages at the University of Berlin after the Civil War. Influenced by Schleiermacher's work, Toy believed that good hermeneutics, or interpretation of the Bible, would account for both the spiritual and the human elements in Scripture. Toy grappled with Darwinism and with geological claims that the earth was far older than Christians traditionally believed. He became convinced that while the spiritual meaning of the Bible was completely true, the historical and scientific details were often marred by incorrect, time-bound information. Doubts regarding the Bible's scientific accuracy led Toy also to question the authorship and dating of some Old Testament books. He asserted that Isaiah was composed by three authors. He also denied that the Hebrew Bible's seemingly messianic prophecies were fulfilled in Christ. Toy resigned under pressure from Southern Baptist Seminary in 1879 and took a position teaching Semitic languages at Harvard.

In 1877, Toy wrote to Charles A. Briggs, a Presbyterian who had recently taken an Old Testament teaching position at Union Theological Seminary in New York. Toy and Briggs had studied together in Berlin. Toy told Briggs that he was "glad to find that we are in accord as to the spirit of Old Testament study, and rejoice that you have spoken so earnestly and vigorously on behalf of the spirit of broad, free, spiritual minded investigation. . . . It will require patient and wise effort to dislodge the tradi-tional narrowness that has obtained so firm a foothold in some quarters." Briggs would become the target of a high-profile heresy trial for teaching views that were similar to Toy's. Briggs, like Toy, made a distinction between the spiritual and human qualities of the Bible. Yes, he found errors in the Bible. Those errors were, Briggs contended, "beyond the range of faith and practice, and therefore they do not impair the infallibility of Holy Scripture as a rule of faith and practice." Many Presbyterians were not convinced by his distinction. The Presbyterian General Assembly suspended Briggs from the ministry in 1893. That decision prompted Union Theological Seminary to sever its ties with the Presbyterian Church.

Some attacks on Scripture also emerged from the women's rights movement. Although the movement held its first convention in 1848 at Seneca Falls, New York, legal and cultural reform for women came about slowly. The Fourteenth Amendment (1868), which guaranteed "equal protection of the laws" to US citizens, seemed to make voting rights an exclusively male privilege when it prohibited the denial of the vote to "male inhabitants." Seneca Falls delegates had criticized churchmen for "claiming Apostolic authority for [women's] exclusion from the ministry," but the vast majority of American churches continued to prohibit women's ordination as pastors or priests. Some skeptics argued that the Bible itself was to blame for much oppression of women. Ernestine Rose, a Jewish abo-litionist and women's rights advocate, proclaimed at an 1853 convention of biblical skeptics that the Bible was a "millstone" around women's necks, which has "subjected her to the entire control and arbitrary will of man."

Presbyterian Robert L. Dabney, a Virginia seminary professor, spoke for many church officials when he asserted that the New Testament assigned the "home as the proper sphere of the Christian woman. . . . She is not to be a ruler of men, but a loving subject to her husband." Thus Dabney argued that faithful Christians should regard the women's rights movement as "infidel."

A few denominations were open to women pastors. Quakers had long accepted women speaking in their meetings. Antoinette Brown

Blackwell received ordination in the Congregationalist Church in 1853, the first woman to be admitted to a pastor's role in one of America's mainstream Protestant denominations. Aside from these examples, most women who functioned as preachers usually did so under unusual circumstances, not as official ministers. The Kentucky Presbyterian Louisa Woosley had experienced conversion in 1874, and she immediately felt a call to evangelize and preach. Indeed, in 1889 her presbytery in the Cumberland Presbyterian denomination recognized her as a teaching elder. The Kentucky Synod objected, prompting Woosley to publish an 1891 text *Shall Woman Preach?*, in which she countered typical arguments that critics such as Dabney used against women preachers.

Elizabeth Cady Stanton, a pillar of the women's rights movement, also lamented how men had used the Bible to oppress women. In *The Woman's Bible* (1895, 1898), Stanton conceded that the letter of Scripture, which was flawed, did not boost women's rights. "The Bible teaches that woman brought sin and death into the world, [and] that she precipitated the fall of the race. . . . Marriage for her was to be a condition of bondage, maternity a period of suffering and anguish, and in silence and subjection, she was to play the role of a dependent on man's bounty. . . . Here is the Bible position of woman briefly summed up." Only a critical approach to the Scripture could discern its underlying benevolent principles. Only these principles would emancipate women, Stanton believed.

Of all the churches under the evangelical umbrella, the new Pentecostal movement gave the most latitude to women preachers. Sometimes Pentecostal women preachers were formally ordained, but others served as evangelists and healers in husband-wife tandems. Two of the key Spanish-speaking evangelists emerging from the Azusa Street revival in Los Angeles were Abundio and Rosa López. They wrote that, since the revival, they could "testify to the power of the Holy Spirit in forgiveness, sanctification, and the baptism with the Holy Ghost and fire." After Azusa Street, the Lópezes engaged in a widespread evangelistic ministry in the barrios of southern California.

One of the best-known evangelists of the 1920s was the Pentecostal preacher Aimee Semple McPherson. She was also based in Los Angeles, and her cavernous Angelus Temple could seat five thousand people. In 1923 she founded the International Church of the Foursquare Gospel, focused on McPherson's "foursquare" truths: Christ as Savior, Healer, Baptizer, and Coming King. McPherson was already a major media star when she mysteriously disappeared in 1926, only to resurface in Mexico a month later, claiming that she had been kidnapped. Although no one could prove what had happened to her, critics charged that the divorcée McPherson had run away for a liaison with a former employee. In any case, McPherson's controversial work demonstrated the potential openness in the Pentecostal movement for female preaching.

Aimee Semple McPherson speaking at Angelus Temple, circa 1923

❧

As illustrated by John Zahm and the fight over evolution, the Catholic Church endured its own "modernist" controversy beginning in the late nineteenth century. Catholic modernists tended to focus their criticisms on the church rather than the Bible. They adopted a progressive view of the church's role in history. The most articulate representative of Catholic modernism in America was Archbishop John Ireland of St. Paul, Minnesota. Ireland (who was born in Ireland in 1838, with his family coming to America in 1848) emphasized that the divinely inspired teachings of the church should not be altered but that the church had to adapt to new understandings of truth. "The Church never changes," he wrote, "and yet she changes. . . . We should never fail to distinguish in the life and action of the Church the absolute and the relative, . . . what she received of her Founder and what she assumed of her own accord." Ireland advocated an irenic approach on matters such as support for Protestant-dominated public schools and relations with Protestant churches. Ireland and other modernists attended the 1893 World's Parliament of Religions, eliciting criticism from exclusivist Catholics.

The 1899 papal letter against "Americanism" put Ireland and other American modernists on defense. The church took an even more decisive stance against modernism in a 1907 encyclical by Pope Pius X. Branding modernist thought as "agnosticism," Pius X condemned its influence and demanded that priests and seminary professors take an oath against modernism. The pope asserted that while modernists affirmed inspiration for the Scriptures in principle, "it is all mere juggling of words. For if we take the Bible, according to the tenets of agnosticism, to be a human work, made by men for men, but allowing the theologian to proclaim that it is divine by immanence, what room is there left in it for inspiration?" The 1907 encyclical against modernism signaled that, for at least the next half-century, the Catholic Church hierarchy would remain committed to the authority of Rome and conservative theology.

Among Protestants, debates over evolution and higher criticism precipitated the fundamentalist-modernist controversy, which agitated many white-led denominations. The controversy culminated symbolically in the 1925 Scopes Trial in Tennessee, which challenged the state's law banning the teaching of evolution in schools. In 1910, the (largely northern) Presbyterian Church (USA) had outlined five "essential" doctrines that they would enforce among churches and pastoral candidates. These doctrines were the inerrancy of Scripture, Christ's virgin birth, Christ's substitutionary atonement (the idea that Christ took the punishment that believers deserved to secure their forgiveness), Christ's bodily resurrection, and the veracity of the biblical miracles. Although the list differed slightly in various iterations, these doctrines became known as the "five points of fundamentalism."

Prior to the Scopes Trial, *fundamentalist* referred to those Protestants who defended the Bible against higher critical thought. Although the term was not coined until 1920, the twelve-volume series *The Fundamentals* popularized the concept. *The Fundamentals* were underwritten by California oil magnate Lyman Stewart, who also founded the Bible Institute of Los Angeles (later Biola University) in 1908. These developments, along with the flowering of the modern Pentecostal movement in Los Angeles, signaled that southern California was becoming a hotbed of fundamentalism and evangelical Christianity. And Stewart exemplified the striking financial connections between the oil industry and American evangelicalism (which continued with figures such as J. Howard Pew of Sunoco and H. L. Hunt of Hunt Oil Company).

Modernist thought tended to flourish most among college-educated whites, and fundamentalism's most prominent defenders were likewise white, college-trained men. Even so, modernist thought gained some traction among certain African Americans, such as the writer W. E. B. Du Bois. Du Bois grew up in a New England Congregationalist church, an unusual setting for an African American child in the 1800s. Though he retained respect for the Christian church, Du Bois's religious beliefs ranged somewhere between liberal Christianity and agnosticism. Du Bois went to Fisk University, Harvard, and the University of Berlin. Du Bois recalled that "by the time I went to Harvard, I was not orthodox at all." Yet he also attended church at Harvard and insisted that he was no radical modernist. He simply appreciated the moral code of Christianity more than its claims about miracles. "I was rather on the side of the Germans who at that time were beginning to reinterpret and retranslate the Bible," he explained.

Rank-and-file African American Protestants were more in line theologically with fundamentalists. Racial antipathy and mistrust, however, caused white fundamentalists to keep black Protestants at arm's length. Many black Protestants saw modernism as newfangled thought invented by elite whites. J. H. Frank, editor of the *National Baptist Union-Review*, scoffed at modernists as "White Infidels." Frank was dismissive of African Americans who dabbled in modernism, saying that liberal blacks were just demonstrating their "chronic tendency to imitate the ungodly white people." Antimodernists like Frank cast the black church as a guardian of theological orthodoxy against the temptations of white-invented liberal thought.

The "social gospel" was an activist movement that overlapped somewhat with modernist theology. Social gospel advocates argued that churches needed to respond to public problems by ministering to the "least of these" in America and around the world. The most obvious problems in the late 1800s were those posed by mass urbanization and immigration. Traditional Christian groups like the Salvation Army integrated evangelism in the cities with education, vocational training, and provision of food and shelter to those with desperate needs.

Some of the momentum behind the social gospel had carried over from pre–Civil War reform movements. The temperance or antialcohol crusade had made significant strides before the Civil War, and it was reinvigorated in 1874 with the founding of the Women's Christian Temperance Union (WCTU). Much of the WCTU's success was due to its energetic leader, Frances Willard. By the 1890s, the WCTU had become the country's largest association of women, with 150,000 members. The WCTU and groups like the Anti-Saloon League engaged in a campaign to prohibit the manufacture and sale of alcohol. They ultimately secured the Eighteenth Amendment to the Constitution, ratified in 1919. Prohibition lasted for thirteen years. Although it did reduce America's per capita consumption of alcohol, prohibition was widely viewed as a failure because of the black market for alcohol and the criminal syndicates, led by bosses such as Al Capone, it spawned.

The social gospel was a subset of the larger Progressive movement for reform. Progressives focused on alleviating the abuses of industry and big business, making government more democratic, and addressing the plight of America's poor. Social gospel advocates contended that America must apply Christian principles to everyday problems. This philosophy, in its simplest form, was popularized by Congregationalist minister Charles Sheldon's 1896 bestseller *In His Steps*. This book showed how church members changed the life of a town by just asking, "What Would Jesus Do?" and living out Christ's precepts. The slogan WWJD enjoyed a brief renaissance in 1990s Christian youth culture, though by then the concept was more tied to maintaining personal holiness than seeking social transformation.

More substantive social gospel treatises came from journalists, pastors, and theologians. One was British journalist William Stead's *If Christ Came to Chicago!* (1894). Stead stayed in Chicago for several months during the World's Columbian Exposition and its associated World's Parliament of Religions. In the book, Stead exposed terrible poverty, corruption, and crime in the city. He insisted that Jesus would never have countenanced Chicago's suffering, and neither should Christians. Stead indicted churches for failing to "interpret the full orbed revelation of the will of God toward us in all its bearings upon the social, political and national life of man." Stead joined a phalanx of "muckraking" writers who detailed the horrors of America's cities and factories. Some of the muckrakers were more overtly religious than others, but they all conveyed a moral obligation to respond to injustice.

Perhaps the most influential theologian of the social gospel movement was Walter Rauschenbusch, a German Baptist and a professor at Rochester Theological Seminary. Rauschenbusch had pastored a church near New York City's "Hell's Kitchen" neighborhood, and the experience made an indelible impression on him about the city's needs. In his celebrated book *Christianity and the Social Crisis* (1907),

Rauschenbusch argued that too many Christians saw Jesus's ethics as otherworldly or private. Instead, he believed that Christian morality should confront the abuses of the present age. "The spiritual force of Christianity should be turned against the materialism and mammonism of our industrial and social order," he contended. "Religious men have been cowed by the prevailing materialism and arrogant selfishness of our business world. They should have the courage of religious faith and assert that 'man liveth not by bread alone,' [Matthew 4:4] but by doing the will of God." Rauschenbusch's writings would later influence key American theologians and Christian activists, including Reinhold Niebuhr and Martin Luther King Jr.

Even though many African American Christians viewed modernism skeptically, black church leaders often embraced the social gospel. They were dismayed by black poverty and racial violence. Black leaders believed that Christian principles should engage such matters in a land that was supposedly filled with so many Christians. One African Methodist Episcopal editor insisted that the Bible revealed that the "so-called 'social gospel' is not new, but a most vital part of the old time religion." The social gospel, as taught by Christ and the prophets, was "the solution of the Negro Problem, the problem of poverty and all the social ills."

Other African American church leaders may not have had direct connections with social gospel icons such as Rauschenbusch, but their ministry fit the social gospel rubric nevertheless. While the most visible white social gospelers often neglected issues such as racial violence, segregation, or women's rights, African American church leaders did not. Perhaps the most compelling example of this type of African American leader was the National Baptist Convention's Nannie Helen Burroughs. Burroughs was not an ordained pastor or theologian, but she served in national leadership positions for six decades, focusing on the Women's Convention of the NBC. Burroughs was concerned about the plight of black women in America, and in 1909 she founded the National Training School for Women and Girls in Washington, DC. The institution offered vocational education for African American women, who typically had few opportunities for formal schooling. Burroughs delivered a landmark speech, "How the Sisters are Hindered from Helping," at an NBC meeting in 1900 and lamented how Christian women had been excluded from the full range of Christian service. "For a number of years," Burroughs said, "there has been a righteous discontent, a burning zeal to go forward in [Christ's] name among the Baptist women of our churches and it will be the dynamic force in the religious campaign at the opening of the 20th century." Burroughs advocated a conservative ethic of hard work and personal holiness for racial uplift. Her training school inculcated the "three Bs"—the Bible, the bath, and the broom—and the importance of piety and cleanliness. Her quest for African American women to gain dignity and independence illustrated her version of the social gospel.

Some theological conservatives worried about the social gospel. To them, the movement's charitable work seemed to substitute for the "good news" of salvation through Christ. Lost people living in improved societies still faced the wrath of God when they died, fundamentalists warned. Not all social gospel advocates embraced modernist theology, but enough did so to give the social gospel a reputation for liberalism. Rauschenbusch, for example, was a Universalist who denied that anyone would suffer hell's eternal torments. The Ohio

Nannie Helen Burroughs

Library of Congress, Prints & Photographs Division, LC-USZ62-79903

Congregationalist minister Washington Gladden likewise wrote dozens of books on the social gospel, and questioned Christians' traditional views of the Bible. He insisted that "intelligent pastors" no longer believed in the Bible's infallibility. Most fundamentalists would concede that the church should minister to the poor. One of the authors of *The Fundamentals* reminded readers that working among the poor did not require the "adoption of a so-called 'social gospel' which discards the fundamental doctrines of Christianity and substitutes a religion of good works."

The most formidable defender of conservative theology in the era was Princeton Seminary's J. Gresham Machen. Machen studied at elite universities including Johns Hopkins, Princeton, and schools in Germany before returning to teach at Princeton Seminary in 1906. In his best-known work, *Christianity and Liberalism* (1923), Machen argued that traditional Christianity and the new modernism did not just differ over points of theology. They were two different religions. "The great redemptive religion which has always been known as Christianity is battling against a totally diverse type of religious belief," Machen wrote, "which is only the more destructive of the Christian faith because it makes use of traditional Christian terminology. This modern non-redemptive religion is called 'modernism' or 'liberalism.'"

The Presbyterian Church attempted to downplay sharp divisions between modernist and fundamentalist theology. However, by the mid-1920s it appeared that Machen's standing at the Presbyterian Princeton Seminary was in jeopardy, as liberals rejected what they saw as his intolerance. When the seminary formally committed itself to a broad range of theological perspectives in 1929, Machen left Princeton and founded Westminster Theological Seminary in Philadelphia. Westminster has continued to serve as a bastion of conservative Reformed theology, along with institutions such as Covenant Theological Seminary in St. Louis (1956) and Reformed Theological Seminary (1966, multiple campuses).

By the early 1930s Machen came under increasing scrutiny from Presbyterian officials because of his involvement with Westminster Seminary. He also founded an alternative missions board for conservative Presbyterians. Finally in 1935 the Presbyterian General Assembly suspended Machen from the ministry. He established a new denomination in 1936 that would come to be called the Orthodox Presbyterian

Church (OPC). Shortly before the founding of the denomination, Machen wrote that, for conservative Presbyterians, "our rule or plumb line is the Bible. A thing is 'orthodox' if it is in accordance with the Bible." Machen preferred the term *orthodox* to *fundamentalist*, and the name stuck for the new Presbyterian fellowship. The OPC has remained a small denomination, with about 30,000 members as of the 2010s. Yet it has retained an outsized influence on conservative Protestantism, partly due to intellectual leadership from figures such as Machen.

Until the 1920s, evolution had been a concern of some fundamentalists, but it had not been a core issue in the movement. Machen, for instance, did not mention evolution in *Christianity and Liberalism*. Then the Presbyterian William Jennings Bryan, the three-time Democratic nominee for president, put evolution at the center of his flamboyant fundamentalist advocacy. Bryan and his supporters wanted laws passed banning the teaching of evolution in public schools. When Tennessee passed a law against teaching evolution, it set the stage for the 1925 Scopes "Monkey Trial." Virtually everyone involved had a vested interest in turning the trial into a media circus, including city leaders in Dayton, Tennessee, who wanted to see the small town get national attention. They encouraged John Scopes, the teacher in question, to break the law against teaching evolution to set up the show trial.

Scopes admitted that he had broken the law, so the real contest in Dayton was between Bryan, who volunteered to help the prosecution, and Scopes's defense lawyer, Clarence Darrow. Bryan was in desperately bad health by the time the trial started, and he foolishly agreed to take the stand in defense of the Bible. Darrow humiliated the ill-prepared Bryan, stumping him with questions about the Bible's reliability. The exhausted Bryan died just days after the trial concluded, symbolically suggesting the death of fundamentalism. As the dust settled in Dayton, modernists could point to many victories, and for the time being, modernism did seem ascendant in many of the large northern-dominated denominations. Traditionalism prevailed, however, in the Southern Baptist Convention, in Lutheran, Holiness, and Pentecostal denominations, and among the top leaders of the Roman Catholic Church. Of course, conservative theological opposition to modernism was hardly over. Within a half century of the Scopes Trial, it would be the modernist-led mainline denominations that seemed to be struggling for relevance and survival.

WORKS CITED AND FURTHER READING

Appleby, R. Scott. *Church and Age Unite! The Modernist Impulse in American Catholicism.* Notre Dame, IN: University of Notre Dame Press, 1992.

Blum, Edward J. *W. E. B. Du Bois, American Prophet.* Philadelphia: University of Pennsylvania Press, 2007.

Briggs, Charles Augustus. *The Defence of Professor Briggs.* New York: Scribner's, 1893.

Croce, Paul J. "Probabilistic Darwinism: Louis Agassiz vs. Asa Gray on Science, Religion, and Certainty." *Journal of Religious History* 22, no. 1 (February 1998): 35–58.

Dochuk, Darren. "Fighting for the Fundamentals: Lyman Stewart and the Protestant Politics of Oil." In *Faithful Republic: Religion and Politics in Modern America,* ed. Andrew Preston, Bruce J. Schulman, and Julian E. Zelizer, 41–55. Philadelphia: University of Pennsylvania Press, 2015.

Espinosa, Gastón. *Latino Pentecostals in America: Faith and Politics in Action.* Cambridge, MA: Harvard University Press, 2014.

Feurzeig, Lisa. *Shubert's Lieder and the Philosophy of Early German Romanticism.* New York: Routledge, 2014.

Grasso, Christopher. *Skepticism and American Faith: From the Revolution to the Civil War.* New York: Oxford University Press, 2018.

Gundlach, Bradley J. *Process and Providence: The Evolution Question at Princeton, 1845–1929.* Grand Rapids: Eerdmans, 2013.

Higginbotham, Evelyn Brooks. *Righteous Discontent: The Women's Movement in the Black Baptist Church, 1880–1920.* Cambridge, MA: Harvard University Press, 1993.

Hodge, Charles. *Systematic Theology.* New York: Scribner, Armstrong, and Company, 1873.

Ireland, John. *The Church and Modern Society: Lectures and Addresses.* Chicago: McBride, 1896.

Kern, Kathi. *Mrs. Stanton's Bible.* Ithaca, NY: Cornell University Press, 2001.

Larson, Edward J. *Summer for the Gods: The Scopes Trial and America's Continuing Debate Over Science and Religion.* New York: Basic Books, 1997.

Longfield, Bradley J. *The Presbyterian Controversy: Fundamentalists, Modernists, and Moderates.* New York: Oxford University Press, 1991.

Maas, A. J. "Hexaemeron." *The Catholic Encyclopedia.* 15 vols. New York: Appleton, 1910, 7: 313.

Machen, J. Gresham. *Christianity & Liberalism.* New ed. Grand Rapids: Eerdmans, 2009.

———. "What Is Orthodoxy?," in *Presbyterian Guardian,* November 4, 1935, 38.

Marsden, George M. *Fundamentalism and American Culture.* New ed. New York: Oxford University Press, 2006.

Mathews, Mary Beth Swetnam. *Doctrine and Race: African American Evangelicals and Fundamentalism Between the Wars.* Tuscaloosa: University of Alabama Press, 2017.

McCosh, James. *The Religious Aspect of Evolution.* New York: Scribner's, 1890.

Paine, Thomas. *The Theological Works of Thomas Paine.* Boston: Mendum, 1858.

Pope Pius X. "The Doctrines of the Modernists." In *The American Catholic Quarterly Review* 32 (January–October 1907): 705–30.

Rauschenbusch, Walter. *Christianity and the Social Crisis.* New York: Macmillan, 1913.

Stead, William Thomas. *If Christ Came to Chicago.* Chicago: Laird & Lee, 1894.

Vaughan, C. R., ed. *Discussions of Robert L. Dabney.* Vol. 2. Richmond, VA: Presbyterian Committee of Publication, 1891.

Wills, Gregory A. *Southern Baptist Theological Seminary, 1859–2009.* New York: Oxford University Press, 2009.

Chapter 10

THE RELIGIOUS
CHALLENGES OF
THE WORLD WARS

The mass expansion of American business and industry following the
Civil War led to a new era of American involvement in global affairs.
America had prided itself in not being a colonizer, despite its conquest of
northern Mexico in the 1840s. By the late 1800s, however, many believed
that America was destined to guide the worldwide spread of Christian
civilization. Some Americans, including William Jennings Bryan, still saw
colonization—especially by military force—as antithetical to the spirit
of Christianity. The great flashpoint of this debate came in 1899 when
the United States annexed the Philippines. President William McKinley,
a devout Methodist, reportedly told a group of his fellow Methodists
that God had shown him that America needed to "educate the Filipinos,
and uplift and civilize and Christianize them." McKinley was hardly
alone in this conviction about the divine purposes behind annexation.
Senator Alfred Beveridge asserted that God had destined America to
"administer government among savage and senile peoples" and to keep
barbarism at bay. God had "marked the American people as His chosen
nation to finally lead in the regeneration of the world." Many missionary

agencies, as well as social gospel advocates, believed that American power could open doors for the proclamation of true Christianity. One religious periodical called Jesus "the most imperial of the imperialists."

. In the first half of the twentieth century, America would face unprecedented global military crises, culminating in World Wars I and II. It would also confront its most crippling financial crisis during the Great Depression. Mass immigration and higher critical thought about the Bible had undercut the nation's Protestant dominance. Many elite politicians and others interpreted the unfolding of American history through the lens of God's providence. Leaders kept employing religious rhetoric to explain America's involvement in its extraordinarily demanding wars. The influence of traditional Protestantism, especially in elite circles, may have been on the wane, but the power of American civil spirituality in times of war showed no signs of flagging.

Christians in the World War I era tended to optimistically assess a nation possessed of such power as America. Some, including President Woodrow Wilson, saw democracy as uniquely compatible with Christianity and sanctified a national crusade for making the world "safe for democracy."

Yet other religious groups recoiled at such blending of faith and American national power, and the era of the world wars saw a new flowering of sectarian withdrawal and pacifist resistance. Anabaptist groups such as the Mennonites and Amish encouraged their young men to file as conscientious objectors so they would not have to take up arms. Seventh-day Adventists did likewise, although they did not object to members serving in noncombatant roles. More radical groups, especially the non-Trinitarian Jehovah's Witnesses (founded 1870s), refused to defer to the American government in virtually any way. This led to widespread arrests of the Witnesses' military-age members. Protestant fundamentalists, modernists, Quakers, and Jews all produced important pacifist advocates during the 1910s.

Early black and white Pentecostals were also disproportionately pacifist. African American pastors in the burgeoning Church of God in Christ, including its leader Bishop Charles Mason, attracted attention for critical comments about American entry into World War I. Many soldiers from such religious backgrounds must have endured struggles like those of Alvin York, a Tennessean and member of the Churches of Christ. He originally filed for conscientious objector status, but an officer convinced him that it was acceptable for a Christian to fight for a just cause. York would go on to win the Congressional Medal of Honor for heroic actions in the war.

On the whole, majorities of Protestants and Catholics supported World War I. They approached the war with levels of devotion ranging from a reluctant sense of duty to fanatical patriotism and anti-German loathing. Liberal Congregationalist minister Lyman Abbott declared that Christian love required that Americans hate what Germany represented. "I hate [Germany's power] for what it is. I hate it because it is a robber, a murderer, a destroyer of homes, a pillager of churches, a violator of women. I do well to hate it." Fundamentalists likewise indulged serious discussions about whether Kaiser Wilhelm, Germany's leader, was the Bible's prophesied Antichrist. Popular American revivalist Billy Sunday spoke for many American Christians when he described the war as a struggle of "Bill [Kaiser Wilhelm] against Woodrow, Germany against America, [and] Hell against Heaven."

America's victory in World War I seemed to confirm the wisdom of Wilson's decision to intervene and suggested that God really was on the Allies' side. For many fundamentalists influenced by dispensational theology, developments such as the 1917 Balfour Declaration, in which Britain expressed support for a Jewish homeland in Palestine, indicated that the war might even have prophetic significance for a restored nation of Israel. A. B. Simpson, founder of the evangelical Christian and Missionary Alliance denomination (1887), reportedly wept as he read the Balfour Declaration to his church.

For those committed to Wilson's idealistic views, the victory over

Germany was sweet. But the aftermath soured when America rejected membership in Wilson's proposed League of Nations, a precursor to the United Nations. Many modernists earnestly desired membership in the league. The mainline Federal Council of Churches told Wilson that they regarded the league as the "political expression of the Kingdom of God on earth." Others saw it as an invitation to get dragged into more foreign wars. After World War I, isolation as a national policy became fashionable again.

There has always been tension between the politics of faith, on the one hand, and the everyday work of congregations, on the other. Partisan politics has rarely been the lifeblood of individual congregations. Even as churches grappled with proper responses to war and (in the 1930s) economic catastrophe, the period saw continued interest in evangelism among many religious groups. The era saw great growth in many American churches, including in Pentecostal denominations such as the Assemblies of God and Aimee Semple McPherson's International Church of the Foursquare Gospel. As we have seen, Pentecostals made serious inroads among Mexican-Americans, who were mostly from a Catholic background. The African American–led COGIC also made gains among blacks moving north and west as part of the "Great Migration." Demand for black workers increased outside the South and swelled the nonsouthern urban black population. As southern blacks streamed into cities from New York to Los Angeles, black churches such as COGIC offered spiritual solace and material assistance to these new migrants. Riding the wave of the Great Migration, COGIC experienced a huge expansion of adherents between the world wars. For example, Chicago had no COGIC churches in 1915. By 1928, it had twenty-four, the same number of congregations as the venerable African Methodist Episcopal denomination in the city.

One of the most visible COGIC leaders was Sister Rosetta Tharpe, who became one of the early celebrities of gospel music. Tharpe was a brilliant vocalist and guitar impresario (the Rock and Roll Hall of Fame posthumously inducted her in 2017) who used her musical talents to proselytize for COGIC. Chicago became a seedbed of black gospel music. Both Tharpe and the great singer Mahalia Jackson, a Baptist, got their start performing in the city's churches. This was a common story, even for musical celebrities who eventually left gospel for secular music. During the Depression and World War II, Elvis Presley was reared in the musical traditions of his Assemblies of God church in Tupelo, Mississippi. "The Queen of Soul" Aretha Franklin likewise started her career singing in the Detroit Baptist church of her father, C. L. Franklin. C. L. Franklin, for his part, was a major radio preacher and sold many copies of his sermons on disc records. Gospel, blues, and country music all got their starts in black and white Protestant churches.

During the era of the world wars, Pentecostals and other American evangelicals also kept sending missionaries around the globe. The Azusa Street revival was a major impetus to Pentecostal missions. Within a year of the revival's beginning, native-language Pentecostal periodicals had been established in Brazil, China, Germany, Japan, and Palestine. By 1909, Pentecostals had already opened missionary stations in fifty countries outside the United States. Some non-Pentecostal missionaries got swept up in the fervor too. Methodist missionary Willis Hoover had been in Chile since 1889. There Hoover and his wife came under the influence of the writings of Minnie Abrams, an American-born Methodist missionary to India who taught Holy Spirit baptism as a postconversion event. Hoover presided over a major revival in Valparaiso, Chile, in 1909. His Methodist congregation spoke in tongues, engaged in "holy laughter," and experienced ecstatic visions. The revival attracted the attention of Christian and Missionary Alliance leader A. B. Simpson, who visited Hoover's church in 1910. Concerned Methodist officials pressured Hoover to leave the denomination because of what they saw as his Pentecostal excesses, so in 1910 Hoover became the head of the new Iglesia Metodista Pentecostal, a denomination that drew virtually all of its support from Chileans.

The Chilean revival heralded the global burgeoning of Pentecostal and evangelical faith that would mark the century after World War I.

Much of the increase was indirectly tied to American missionary work, but the most dynamic Christian growth generally happened when leadership passed from outside missionaries to locals. In 1800, virtually all Protestants lived in Europe or the United States. By 1900, the number of Protestants outside of America and Europe had grown to 10 percent.

Pentecostal service in Harlan County, Kentucky, 1946

By the early 2000s, two-thirds of Protestants were living outside of Europe and the United States. Pentecostals benefited from much of this increase, particularly in places such as Latin America and sub-Saharan Africa. Although Christianity had always been a universal faith, early Pentecostals had an especially strong sense of global endeavor, partly because many of them were unmoored from American patriotism. Women such as the Methodist Minnie Abrams found ministry outlets in the missionary movement. It was one of relatively few official capacities in which they could serve in Christian denominations. Women's missionary activism also produced denominational luminaries such as the Southern Baptists' Lottie Moon, who went to China in 1872 and worked there for four decades. The SBC named a Christmas missions offering for Moon, and today it brings in hundreds of millions of dollars a year for the SBC's International Mission Board.

Another new engine of missionary mobilization was the Student Volunteer Movement (SVM), founded in 1886. Its most influential leader was John R. Mott, a Methodist dynamo and future winner of the Nobel Peace Prize. Mott helped popularize the watchword of the SVM, "The Evangelization of the World in This Generation." Mott and other missions advocates argued that increased technological prowess and missionary organization had made possible the final dissemination of the gospel to all tribes, tongues, and nations, as the book of Revelation put it. Missionaries commonly believed that reaching all the nations would lead to Christ's return to earth. The Presbyterian Robert Speer told SVM leaders that "what we are doing will hasten the coming of that radiant morning when the eastern skies shall be full of the glory of [Christ's] coming."

The SVM convinced thousands of American college students to commit to missionary work. The most common destination of SVM missionaries, as with many evangelical organizations, was China. SVM missionaries (whom the SVM placed through the missionary departments of traditional denominations) were conversionist in their aims, but they also sought to introduce Western civilization to non-Western cultures. Thus many missionaries were educators. By 1922, Protestants from America were sponsoring 219 kindergartens, about 700 elementary schools, and 300 high schools in China alone. They also set up orphanages, leper colonies, colleges, and seminaries. In 1923, the American Bible Society sent 20,000 Bibles to China, as well as millions of tracts that included sections of the Bible. Arthur Smith, an American missionary who served in Shandong Province, explained that China needed "a new life in every individual soul, in the family, and in society. The manifold needs of China we find, then, to be a single imperative need. It will be met permanently, completely, only by Christian civilization." Missionaries generated some violent backlashes in China, especially during the 1900 Boxer Rebellion. A mass expulsion of outside missionaries finally followed the communist takeover of China in 1949.

Missions became a flashpoint of controversy in the late stages of the fundamentalist-modernist conflict as well. Modernists tended to downplay the need for non-Christians to convert. They were more prone than fundamentalists to see spiritual value in non-Christian religions. For example, in *Christ of the Indian Road* (1925), Methodist missionary E. Stanley Jones wrote that "the religious genius of India is the richest in the world," although he admitted that in some forms that genius was "degrading and cruel." As the Indian genius for religion "pours itself through Christian molds it will enrich the collective expression of Christianity," Jones asserted. "But in order to do that the Indian must remain Indian. . . . The expression of his Christianity will be essentially Eastern and not Western." This departed from the philosophy of those who saw eastern nations fundamentally in need of Christian civilization. Nevertheless, Jones still pled with Hindus and other non-Christian Indians—including his acquaintance Mohandas Gandhi—to convert to Christianity. The great Indian rights activist remained friends with Jones, but he saw conversionist missionaries as imperialists who forced outside religious traditions on indigenous peoples.

American critics of missions joined a growing chorus in the 1930s. One of the most prominent detractors was Pearl Buck, author of the Pulitzer Prize–winning *The Good Earth* and the daughter of missionaries to China. Buck wrote in *Harper's* magazine against conversionist missionary work. An older generation of missionaries "believed simply and plainly that all who did not hear the gospel, as they called it, were damned," Buck lamented. "It goes without question that for most of us this kind of creed has been discarded."

The most controversial anticonversionist critique was *Re-Thinking Missions* (1932), a publication of the Laymen's Foreign Missions Inquiry. This commission was headed by Harvard's William Hocking and funded by the modernist Baptist John D. Rockefeller. *Re-Thinking Missions* called for an end to overt evangelism in favor of benevolent Christian service. Its advice resonated with missionary agencies such as the American Board of Commissioners for Foreign Missions, which had dominated American missionary work in the 1800s, and which by the 1890s had become influenced by modernism. Traditional Protestants denounced the Laymen's Inquiry. For example, Clarence Macartney, pastor of First Presbyterian Church of Pittsburgh, declared that *Re-Thinking Missions* represented a "complete repudiation of historic and evangelical Christianity." As modernist missionary work morphed into service, medical care, education, and other tasks without overt evangelistic aims, theological liberals funneled their energy into nongovernmental organizations such as the Red Cross, which had Christian roots but no longer proselytized.

However, the era of conversionist missions was hardly over. In addition to efforts by denominations such as the Southern Baptist Convention and the Assemblies of God, evangelicals founded specialized ministries such as Wycliffe Bible Translators (1942) and World Vision (1950) to translate the Bible and to minister to children in poverty.

The best-known evangelical missionary of the post–World War II era was probably Jim Elliot, who served with the Plymouth Brethren's Christian Missions in Many Lands. Elliot's work among Ecuador's Waorani Indians highlighted the continuing global ambitions of American missionaries. His death in 1956 alongside four missionary colleagues in an attack by Waoranis made Elliot famous to many Americans. Secular outlets such as *Life* and *Reader's Digest* covered the incident. Elliott once wrote in his journal that "he is no fool who gives what he cannot keep to gain that which he cannot lose." This became one of the most cited inspirational quotes for American Christians involved in missions. After World War II, evangelicals and Pentecostals came to dominate American Protestant missionary ranks. By 1980, about thirty-two thousand of the thirty-five thousand American missionaries were from conservative denominations and agencies.

In spite of their challenges and divisions, Protestants retained a dominant influence in many sectors of American culture. However, higher criticism, modernism, and rising Catholic and Jewish immigration since the late 1800s seemed to threaten America's de facto Protestant establishment. The growing ranks of non-Protestants drove many Americans to support the Ku Klux Klan and similar groups committed to white Protestant domination. The Klan of the 1910s and '20s remained hostile toward African Americans, but it was just as concerned with preserving Protestant power. Devoted Christians were well-represented in the Klan, alongside many Protestants who rarely attended church. The Klan flourished across the nation, not just in the South but in states from New Jersey to Oregon. In the early 1920s, the Klan sought to promote "100 percent American" candidates into office. In Oregon, Klan supporters undermined Catholic schools, which had become a fixture in American education by the early twentieth century. Catholics saw their parochial schools as essential to keeping their children within the church. Wary Catholics tended to regard public schools effectively as Protestant institutions. With the Klan's backing, the Oregon legislature passed a law that required all children from ages eight to sixteen to attend public school. The law was a direct assault on parents' ability to send their children to religious schools, especially Catholic ones. The law would have also devastated Lutheran and Seventh-day Adventist schools. Oregon officials defended the law by claiming that the Constitution required "an absolute and unequivocal separation of church and state." Before it went into effect, the Supreme Court struck down the Oregon public school law in the unanimous *Pierce v. Society of Sisters* decision (1925), a landmark ruling for religious liberty and against anti-Catholic bigotry.

The height of anti-Catholic turmoil during the interwar era came in 1928 when Alfred E. Smith, a well-known New York Democrat, became the first Catholic to run for president as a major party nominee. Smith denounced the flood of anti-Catholic sentiment he faced from the Klan and other antagonists. It was a grievous mockery of Christianity, he said, to use "the blazing cross [a hallmark of the Klan], the cross upon which Christ died, as a symbol to install into the hearts of men hatred of their brethren." To Klansmen, Catholics were not their "brethren." Herbert Hoover trounced Smith in the 1928 election, and Smith could not even carry his home state. Anti-Catholicism was not the whole story of the election, of course. Smith did carry the Protestant-dominated Deep South states, the traditional Democratic base of the era. But Smith's Catholicism was a major factor in his loss.

The number of Jews in America was growing quickly in the pre–World War I era too, and widespread anti-Semitism led Jews to shore up their communities in America. Under the leadership of Rabbi Isaac Mayer Wise, Jews founded the Hebrew Union College in Cincinnati in 1875, the oldest enduring Jewish seminary in America and a center for Reform Judaism. New York City's Yeshiva University was founded in 1886, serving as a bastion of Orthodox Jewish learning, while Solomon Schechter's Jewish Theological Seminary in New York (also founded 1886) became a key Conservative Jewish institution.

Jews in America were divided over Zionism, or the promotion of a Jewish state in their traditional homeland of Palestine. Reform Jews in America generally opposed the concept, with some saying that Zion "is not our hope of the future. America is our Zion." As World War I approached, Zionism took on new life among American Jews, especially with the famous lawyer and soon the first Jewish Supreme Court justice Louis Brandeis adopting Zionist principles. Brandeis was personally agnostic, but secular Jews like him often saw a Zionist state as a refuge for persecuted Jews and a great hope for Progressive social and political aims. Devout Jews likewise saw a reestablished state of Israel as a fulfillment of divine promises in the Hebrew Bible, or "the land of Israel for the people of Israel according to the Torah of Israel," as one Zionist organization put it. In spite of the Balfour Declaration of 1917, a Jewish state in Palestine would not generate sufficient international support until the Holocaust's horrors came to light at the end of World War II.

In spite of the growing respectability of figures such as Brandeis, American Jews still had to endure anti-Semitic attacks and lurid conspiracy theories about them. The communist revolution in Russia stoked fears about an international Bolshevik/Jewish plot to rule the world. The most infamous of the anti-Semitic conspiracy tales was *The Protocols of the Elders of Zion*, a forgery originally published in Russia in 1905. In America, the *Protocols* got a wide hearing due to their coverage, starting in 1920, in automobile magnate Henry Ford's *Dearborn Independent* newspaper. A multivolume set of books titled *The International Jew* followed and was printed in hundreds of thousands of copies. Ford, an Episcopalian, later apologized for publicizing "gross forgeries" about Jewish conspiracy. Such theories continued to appeal to a segment of American society. President Richard Nixon, for example, was taped making a number of anti-Semitic comments during his presidency. In one conversation with the evangelist Billy Graham in 1972, Graham affirmed Nixon's sentiments and insisted that the Jewish "stranglehold" on the nation had to be broken. Graham apologized for these comments when the tapes went public. Such outbursts of anti-Semitism were often connected, at least indirectly, to the perceived decline of Protestant domination in America.

The Great Depression of the 1930s was economically disastrous for the nation, and it tested churches and other religious agencies' capacity for ministering to the poor. Abyssinian Baptist Church, Harlem's largest congregation, had always served the poor and elderly in its neighbor-hood, as many American congregations sought to do. The Depression brought a surge of needs that the African American church struggled to address. Pastor Adam Clayton Powell Sr. insisted that their witness for Christ was at stake, so he determined to give a third of his income to poverty relief. His congregation upped their giving too, even though many of them were also affected by the Depression. In 1930–31, Abyssinian Baptist assisted more than forty thousand people in need of clothing, food, and home-heating fuel. Powell's son, Adam Clayton Powell Jr., would become pastor at Abyssinian Baptist in 1937 and would go on to become a major civil rights leader and New York's first African American congressman.

Few congregations could match Abyssinian's scale of response to the Great Depression. Too often the churches' efforts were not enough. Millions of Americans, devout and irreligious alike, could identify with the plight of people such as an Iowa Lutheran Sunday school teacher who wrote to Eleanor Roosevelt in 1936, asking if she could spare some used clothes. "I know we must not let our clothes keep us from church (neither do I), but sometimes I feel so badly when I see all the others dressed so nice. . . . I never thought the time would come when I would find it necessary to do this. . . . Oh please help me."

Benefit church supper in Bardstown, Kentucky, 1940

Agencies such as the YMCA, YWCA, Salvation Army, the Catholic Society of St. Vincent de Paul, and the Jewish Welfare Board also sought to address material deprivations during the Depression. Some groups, such as Dorothy Day's Catholic Worker movement, publicized by her newspaper, the *Catholic Worker*, offered relief to the poor alongside a thoroughgoing critique of the capitalist system that had seemingly produced America's suffering. Day believed that the *Catholic Worker*'s emphases on the common worker and interracial ministry made critics suspect that her movement was driven by dangerous radicals. She sensed that while most American Catholics were willing to give money to the poor, they did not question the system that oppressed so many workers. As Day wrote, "Our insistence on worker-ownership . . . , on the need to de-proletarize the worker, all points which had been emphasized by the popes in their social encyclicals, made many Catholics think we were Communists in disguise, wolves in sheep's clothing."

Reinhold Niebuhr, one of the most influential Protestant theologians of the era, was wary of Christian attempts to fundamentally change social and economic systems. As a professor at New York's Union Theological Seminary, he became the best-known advocate of "Christian realism," a reaction against the optimistic Progressive naïveté prior to World War I. Niebuhr and other advocates of theological "neoorthodoxy" followed the example of the Swiss theologian Karl Barth by insisting that sin had more debilitating consequences than most modernist theologians admitted. Applying Christian principles to social problems was noble, but Christians also had to accept the world as it was, broken by sin and beset with enormously complex problems.

Niebuhr worried about the Great Depression, but he also believed that most white-led churches in America were too fundamentally committed to their class and ethnic interests to be of much help. "It is a bit of unwarranted optimism to expect them to make any serious contribution to the reorganization of society," Niebuhr wrote. In books such as *The Irony of American History* (1952), Niebuhr explained how difficult it was for nations to assess the morality of their actions, or for leaders to anticipate the results of their policies. Niebuhr was a much-noted commentator on American foreign affairs during World War II and the Cold War. He advocated American intervention against the Nazis in 1940, before many Americans were ready for that fateful step. Yet he saw the

American use of atomic weapons against Japan as morally indefensible. Niebuhr, whose views received widespread media coverage, was one of the last theologians to approach "household name" status in America.

As seen in Niebuhr, World War II would garner its share of criticism from American religious figures, especially when America used nuclear bombs against Hiroshima and Nagasaki. Though the Pearl Harbor attack of 1941, and the totalitarian ambitions of Nazi Germany had made the war easy to justify for most, members of Anabaptist groups, the Quakers, and Seventh-day Adventists filed for conscientious objector status once again. Jehovah's Witnesses were the most frequently imprisoned for resisting the World War II draft, often because they would not serve in noncombatant roles either.

Japanese Americans came under suspicion as the war unfolded, resulting in the notorious Executive Order 9066. This led to the detention of some 111,000 Japanese Americans in internment camps. More than half of the Japanese detainees were Buddhists, although significant numbers were Christians too. Some Japanese Buddhists reportedly burned sutras (Buddhist scriptures) and family altars to avoid scrutiny from authorities. Buddhists could still hold religious services in the camps, but government officials initially required the services to be in English. Nyogen Senzaki, a Zen Buddhist leader from California who was taken to a camp at Heart Mountain, Wyoming, wrote poems documenting the internment experience. In 1943 he wrote

> Sons and daughters of the Sun are interned
> In a desert plateau, an outskirt of Heart Mountain,
> Which they rendered the Mountain of Compassion or
>   Loving-kindness.
> They made paper flowers to celebrate Vesak, the birthday
>   of Buddha.

American-born, English-speaking Japanese leaders took on more responsibility in the Buddhist community than they had before the war because American officials trusted them more than the Japanese-born who spoke little English.

Buddhist church, Japanese internment camp, 1943

As some debated the moral questions raised by internment camps and atomic bombs, most Americans rallied behind the war and appreciated the civil-religious rhetoric employed by political and military leaders. General Dwight Eisenhower, one of the most avid crafters of such rhetoric, told the Allied troops participating in the 1944 D-Day invasion, "You are about to embark upon the Great Crusade, toward which we have striven these many months." Evoking the "Model of Christian Charity" speech of colonial Massachusetts governor John Winthrop, Eisenhower told them, "The eyes of the world are upon you. The hopes and prayers of liberty-loving people everywhere march with you. . . . Let us all beseech the blessing of Almighty God upon this great and noble undertaking." The successful D-Day invasion and defeat of Germany and Japan gave Americans more reason to suppose that God had providentially ordained the Allies' victory.

In the wake of the war, as the horrors of it and the extermination wrought upon Europe's Jews became more known, many Americans were left perplexed and adrift. Similarly to how Reinhold Niebuhr had urged theological humility and realism, post-Holocaust writers such as the Romanian Jew Elie Wiesel, an Auschwitz survivor who moved to the United States after the war, wondered about God's silence. Where was God during the Nazis' murderous rampage? In his book *Night*, translated into English in 1960, Wiesel wrote of the spiritual devastation wrought by the Nazis' death camp: "Never shall I forget the little faces of the children, whose bodies I saw turned into wreaths of smoke beneath a silent blue sky. Never shall I forget those flames which consumed my faith forever. Never shall I forget that nocturnal silence which deprived me, for all eternity, of the desire to live. Never shall I forget those moments which murdered my God and my soul and turned my dreams to dust."

The Depression, the world wars, and the Holocaust resulted in a loss of spiritual innocence for many as it did for Wiesel. The conclusion of World War II also left America as an economic and military superpower locked in a global struggle with the forces of Soviet communism, and the Cold War would come to exert a powerful influence on the shape of American religion and Americans' sense of national purpose.

WORKS CITED
AND FURTHER READING

Abbott, Lyman. *Outlook* 19 (May 15, 1918): 99.

Adams, Henry. *The Education of Henry Adams.* Introduction by Edmund Morris. New York: Modern Library, 1996.

Anderson, Allan Heaton. *To the Ends of the Earth: Pentecostalism and the Transformation of World Christianity.* New York: Oxford University Press, 2013.

Bays, Daniel H. *A New History of Christianity in China*. Malden, MA: Wiley-Blackwell, 2012.

Buck, Pearl S. *Is There a Case for Foreign Missions?* New York: John Day, 1933.

Day, Dorothy. *The Long Loneliness*. New York: Harper & Brothers, 1952.

Gamble, Richard M. *The War for Righteousness: Progressive Christianity, the Great War, and the Rise of the Messianic Nation*. Wilmington, DE: ISI Books, 2003.

Gaustad, Edwin S., and Leigh E. Schmidt. *The Religious History of America*. Rev. ed. New York: HarperOne, 2004.

Greene, Alison Collis. *No Depression in Heaven: The Great Depression, the New Deal, and the Transformation of Religion in the Delta*. New York: Oxford University Press, 2016.

Hamburger, Philip. *Separation of Church and State*. Cambridge, MA: Harvard University Press, 2002.

Jackson, Jerma A. *Singing in My Soul: Black Gospel Music in a Secular Age*. Chapel Hill: University of North Carolina Press, 2004.

Jenkins, Philip. *The Great and Holy War: How World War I Became a Religious Crusade*. New York: HarperOne, 2014.

Jones, E. Stanley. *The Christ of the Indian Road*. Nashville: Abingdon, 1925.

Long, Kathryn T. *God in the Rainforest: A Tale of Martyrdom and Redemption in Amazonian Ecuador*. New York: Oxford University Press, 2019.

Longfield, Bradley J. *The Presbyterian Controversy: Fundamentalists, Modernists, and Moderates*. New York: Oxford University Press, 1991.

McElvaine, Robert S., ed. *Down and Out in the Great Depression: Letters from the Forgotten Man*. 25th anniv. ed. Chapel Hill: University of North Carolina Press, 2008.

Niebuhr, Reinhold. *Leaves from the Notebook of a Tamed Cynic*. Chicago: Willett, Clark, and Colby, 1929.

Preston, Andrew. *Sword of the Spirit, Shield of Faith: Religion in American War and Diplomacy*. New York: Alfred A. Knopf, 2012.

Sarna, Jonathan D. *American Judaism: A History*. New Haven, CT: Yale University Press, 2004.

Seager, Richard Hughes. *Buddhism in America*. Rev. ed. New York: Columbia University Press, 2012.

Smith, Alfred E. *Campaign Addresses*. Washington, DC: Democratic National Committee, 1929.

The Student Missionary Appeal. New York: Student Volunteer Movement for Foreign Missions, 1898.

Wacker, Grant. *Heaven Below: Early Pentecostals and American Culture*. Cambridge, MA: Harvard University Press, 2001.

Walther, Karine V. *Sacred Interests: The United States and the Islamic World, 1821–1921*. Chapel Hill: University of North Carolina Press, 2015.

Wiesel, Elie. *Night*. London: MacGibbon & Kee, 1960.

Chapter 11

CIVIL RELIGION AND THE COLD WAR

The best-known religious figure of the post–World War II period was the evangelist Billy Graham. Graham's gospel message was not substantially different from that of George Whitefield during the Great Awakening a couple centuries before. But Graham was deeply conditioned by his mid-twentieth-century context, not least the specter of the Cold War clash between Soviet communism and Western democracy. During the 1949 Los Angeles crusade that launched Graham to national fame, he preached in the shadow of President Truman's announcement that Russians had successfully tested a nuclear weapon. This announcement crystallized the Soviet-American conflict like never before. America had a godly heritage, Graham told the audience, while the communists had "decided against God, against Christ, against the Bible, and against all religion. . . . Communism is a religion that is inspired, directed, and motivated by the Devil himself." He warned the people of Los Angeles that they had many communist sympathizers among them. "In this moment I can see the judgment hand of God over Los Angeles," he proclaimed. "I can see judgment about to fall." Their only hope was in repentance and revival. Graham's anticommunism was hardly unique. Many mainline Christians and Catholics agreed with it. The Catholic archbishop of Dubuque, Iowa, for example, called the Soviets the "Christ-haters of Moscow."

Graham stood at the intersection of a number of trends that made his message resonate. In addition to his anticommunism, he mastered electronic media, especially television. Although Graham spoke live before more people than anyone in history, far more people saw his sermons on television or listened to him on the radio. He also reflected the beginning of a powerful neoevangelical movement in America, one that would forge an alliance with the Republican Party, based partly on shared anticommunism. Graham was hardly the first celebrity pastor in American history. That phenomenon dated back at least to George Whitefield. Graham was one of a cadre of ministers who adapted their message to the new communications technologies and political concerns of the Cold War.

Graham's attitude toward the human condition was grimly traditional, though he always closed messages with the hope of forgiveness in Christ. Some of the radio and TV pioneers in religion took a more cheerful approach. One of America's earliest radio and TV preaching stars was Elder Lightfoot Solomon Michaux. His Depression-era radio show attracted Saturday evening audiences of twenty-four million people by 1934. He adapted quickly to television, getting his own TV program at the end of World War II. This made Michaux the first African American star on television and the first minister in America to have his own program. Michaux emphasized holy living and a positive mindset. "The sun is shining. The birds are singing. They're not complaining 'bout the depression," he said. "Why should we?" Michaux and other radio and TV evangelists such as the Baptist E. W. Kenyon injected a powerful New Thought strain into the evangelical culture of the early twentieth century. New Thought adherents taught that people had powerful creative abilities they could harness through godly thought and speech.

Positive thinking improved one's material and medical circumstances. William James, an influential philosopher of religion at Harvard, called Kenyon and Michaux's faith the "religion of healthy-mindedness." New Thought formed the foundation for what would later become known as the "prosperity gospel."

Elder Lightfoot Solomon Michaux

Reformed Church pastor Norman Vincent Peale preached a version of New Thought that became associated with the "self-help" movement. Through the radio, newspaper columns, and his magazine, *Guideposts*, Peale emerged as a major figure in mainline Christian circles even before the publication of his *The Power of Positive Thinking* (1952), which became one of the bestselling books of the twentieth century. Although Peale did not advocate as transactional of a relationship between faith and prosperity as some New Thought ministers, he nevertheless instructed readers to "believe in yourself and release your inner powers." Peale's ideas would influence millions of Americans, including future president Donald Trump, whose family began attending Peale's Marble Collegiate Church in the 1960s. Peale "would bring real-life situations, modern day situations into the sermon," Trump recalled. Peale officiated at Trump's first wedding.

Protestants were not the only ones focused on positive thinking in the post–World War II era. The most prominent Catholic exponent of it was Monsignor Fulton J. Sheen. Sheen's popular radio and TV programs emphasized the contrast between a peaceful life of serving God and the "anxiety complex" that beset so many modern people. A person converted to Christianity, Sheen insisted, would project peace, health, and confidence. That "peace of soul . . . makes somebodies out of nobodies. . . . It improves his health by curing the ills that sprang from a disordered, unhappy, and restless mind; for trials and difficulties, it gives him the aid of Divine power; it brings him at all times a sense of harmony with the universe." Sheen and Billy Graham both pushed for more space for religion in public life during Dwight Eisenhower's administration. Partly due to Sheen's urging, Eisenhower declared July 4, 1953, a National Day of Prayer.

Fulton Sheen

Although Eisenhower was not especially devout, he wanted to reenergize American civil spirituality. Sheen and Graham helped him do that. Graham assured Eisenhower, whom he had urged to run for president in 1952, that as president the general could "do more to inspire the American people to a more spiritual way of life than any other man alive." For Graham, Eisenhower, and their supporters, the Judeo-Christian tradition represented a shield against the atheistic menace of communism. The term *Judeo-Christian* first became popular during the period. Although Graham's preaching was as explicitly Christian as any minister's, the civil religion favored by Eisenhower was generically theistic, not Christian. Anticommunist civil spirituality reached its height in the mid-1950s when Congress added the phrase "one nation under God" to the Pledge of Allegiance and made "In God We Trust" the national motto. Some secularist organizations registered concern, noting that the motto might represent a religious test for officeholders, something explicitly banned in Article VI of the Constitution. However, these civil religious initiatives won broad support from Protestant, Catholic, and Jewish leaders, so they passed without much controversy.

Americans in the 1950s wanted to demonstrate their anticommunist bona fides. This was the fearful era of Senator Joseph McCarthy's investigations of suspected communists in America. Among the many segments of society that came under scrutiny were clergy, including mainline ministers. J. B. Matthews, chief investigator of the House of Representatives' Committee on Un-American Activities, charged that Protestant ministers were the single largest cohort supporting the Communist Party. Without much evidence, he claimed that seven thousand Protestant pastors had been drawn "into the network of the Kremlin's conspiracy." Their communist sympathies grew out of the "'social gospel' which infected the Protestant theological seminaries more than a generation ago," Matthews argued. "Many graduates of the 'liberalized' Protestant seminaries abandoned religion altogether in favor of the 'social gospel.'" One of the most prominent clergymen accused of communism was Methodist bishop G. Bromley Oxnam. Before the House committee, Oxnam protested that he was innocent and that he condemned communism because it was atheistic. He denounced the Committee on Un-American Activities because of its circulation of unsubstantiated charges against him and many other clergy.

Congressional investigators of procommunist clergy overextended themselves in Oxnam's case and many others'. Even sober observers, such as Reinhold Niebuhr, worried that some liberal American pastors really did have communist leanings, even if they were not technically communists themselves. Niebuhr acknowledged that Oxnam did not have direct connections with communists, but he insisted, "There are in fact Communist sympathizers and fellow travelers in the church." He was mindful of theologians such as his Union Seminary colleague Harry F. Ward, a Methodist who undoubtedly qualified as a "fellow traveler" with communists. Ward was the first chairman of the American Civil Liberties Union but resigned from that organization in 1940 when it prohibited communists from joining.

Many Americans saw the Cold War as a zero-sum conflict between incommensurate options: the godless Soviets and the Judeo-Christian democratic West. In such a global conflict, hedging was intolerable. The former communist spy Whittaker Chambers, a convert to Quakerism, explained the gulf between the two systems in his popular memoir *Witness* (1952). To Chambers, communism was an ancient faith that competed against the true religion of God. "Its promise was whispered in the first days of the Creation under the Tree of the Knowledge of Good and Evil: 'Ye shall be as gods.' It is the great alternative faith of mankind. . . . The Communist vision is the vision of Man without God."

Anticommunism became one of the pillars of conservative political and religious thought in the 1950s. The Catholic William F. Buckley, founder of *National Review* magazine, argued in his popular *God and Man at Yale* (1951) that his undergraduate institution was a bastion of aggressive secularism and "collectivism." Like Chambers, Buckley asserted that "the duel between Christianity and atheism is the most important in the world." Instead of equipping the students against Soviet ideology, his Yale professors undermined confidence in "moral absolutes" and "intrinsic truths," Buckley wrote. Of course, universities and seminaries themselves did not lack anticommunist advocates. One of the most prominent was Notre Dame economics professor Louis Budenz, who had once abandoned the Catholic faith of his childhood and for a time became a leader in the American Communist Party.

In 1945, Budenz renounced communism, partly through the influence of Fulton Sheen, returned to the Catholic Church, and became a key witness in trials of Americans accused of communist ties.

The connections between communism, universities, and white mainline churches were overstated, but they did exist, at least in indirect ways. Communist cultivation of American churches was not just a story within white-led mainline congregations and seminaries. Even before the Cold War, communists made halting efforts to build bridges with the African American church, hoping that the oppression they faced might make blacks more open to a radical critique of capitalism. Communists often found black ministers wary of their atheism. Baptist pastor Milton Sears sought to root out communist influence in his Birmingham, Alabama, church in the early 1930s. He drew contempt from communist organizers in the city and from communist sympathizers within his congregation. The animosity came to a head in 1933 when a procommunist mob confronted Sears during a service, and Sears ran them out of the building as he brandished a shotgun. Leaders of the civil rights movement, including Martin Luther King Jr., would face incessant charges from white adversaries and federal investigators that they were communist sympathizers. Fannie Lou Hamer, a devout Christian and civil rights activist, noted, "If Christ were here today, he would be branded a radical, a militant, and would probably be branded as 'red.'" Fiercely anticommunist Christians rejected those who questioned the moral legitimacy of the American order, while Christian civil rights leaders and workers' rights advocates often criticized the racial and economic inequalities that they saw as endemic to the system. These disparate views account for these groups' differing levels of comfort with American civil spirituality and with the blending of Christian faith and the American nation.

One of the founders of the civil rights movement was Howard Thurman, a pastor and professor who advanced a socialist critique of capitalism for the way it perpetuated ethnic and class inequality. Although Thurman grew up in southern African American Baptist churches, as an adult he trended toward a nonsupernatural, activist approach to Christianity. He adopted Unitarian-style modernism, as he doubted the Bible's miracles and the idea that Jesus was the unique Son of God. In 1935 Thurman met the Indian nationalist leader Mohandas Gandhi, who urged him to introduce the African American community to the concept of nonviolent resistance. In his most influential book, *Jesus and the Disinherited* (1949), Thurman lamented the way that religion was used to sanction racial inequality: "Most of the accepted social behavior-patterns assume segregation to be normal—if normal, then correct; if correct, then moral; if moral, then religious." Religion undergirded these assumptions by painting a racially segregated picture of the divine order. "God, for all practical purposes, is imaged as an elderly, benign white man, seated on a white throne. . . . Angels are blonds and brunets. . . . Satan is viewed as being red with the glow of fire. But the imps, the messengers of the devil, are black. . . . The implications of such a view are simply fantastic in the intensity of their tragedy." Martin Luther King was deeply influenced by Thurman, whom King encountered during his doctoral work at Boston University where Thurman was dean of chapel. King reportedly carried a well-worn copy of *Jesus and the Disinherited* with him during the Montgomery bus boycott of 1955–56.

The "baby boom" following World War II, along with surging religious interest associated with the popular preachers of radio and television, helped spawn church growth in America for two decades after the war. America's population growth was strong, but church adherence was even stronger. By the end of the 1950s, 65 percent of Americans said they were members of a religious congregation. This was the highest rate in American history. Nine out of ten Americans said they believed in God and in the efficacy of prayer. The vast majority of Americans were affiliated with Protestantism, Catholicism, or Judaism. At least until

1965, the role of religions outside of the Judeo-Christian fold remained numerically small. The Catholic Church was the largest Christian group in the United States. The Southern Baptist Convention became America's largest Protestant denomination sometime in the mid-twentieth century, and the SBC's tradition of evangelism and strength in the burgeoning postwar South helped it keep growing in the second half of the twentieth century, with its total reported members increasing from about seven million to fifteen million between 1950 and 1990.

Immigration and suburbanization also spurred denominational change, growth, and diversification during the post–World War II era. Although Catholic ministry to Hispanic immigrants was an older story in America, the Catholic Church's attention to Latinos became more conspicuous with the creation of the Bishops' Committee for the Spanish Speaking in 1945. This committee enhanced the church's efforts at ministering to Hispanic immigrants, especially migrant workers. Mindful of attempts by evangelical and Pentecostal churches to attract Hispanics, the Catholics' Office for the Spanish Speaking helped to build clinics, educational centers, and settlement houses in Latino neighborhoods.

Mexicans were the primary immigrant group in the Southwest, but Puerto Ricans were an increasingly visible presence in New York City and other urban centers after World War II. By the 1950s, the Catholic Church in America was gravitating away from the "national parish" model in which congregations catered to individual ethnic groups, yet Puerto Ricans and other immigrants still saw value in that model and shaped Catholic congregations that were effectively national parishes. One impoverished Puerto Rican immigrant, Encarnación Padilla de Armas, came to New York City in 1945. Unusually, she was able to express concern to a New York priest about the church's neglect of Puerto Ricans. The priest asked her and other Puerto Ricans to prepare a report on the matter. Padilla de Armas's 1951 report emphasized how Protestants were constantly reaching out to Puerto Rican Catholics. Many of the Protestant competitor churches had Puerto Rican pastors.

Meanwhile, the Catholic hierarchy remained reluctant to ordain Hispanics as priests. Indeed, Hispanic Pentecostal pastors and congregations had established a major presence in New York by the time of Padilla de Armas's report. The largest Protestant church in the city in the 1950s was La Sinagoga, a congregation of the Pentecostal Church of God. In light of Protestant incursions, Padilla de Armas insisted that "Puerto Ricans must be received as regular parishioners" in Catholic parishes and that longtime members of Catholic congregations needed to accept Hispanic immigrants as "brothers in Christ."

The spread of suburbs away from urban cores was fueled by population growth, prosperity, and the widespread ownership of automobiles and building of interstates. Middle-class white families in particular began to move to the peripheries of American cities. Churches went along with the suburbs, sometimes as entirely new congregations, and sometimes as relocated inner-city churches. Orange County, California, south of Los Angeles, was one of the epicenters of suburban growth in the 1950s. The county saw a remarkable flowering of churches, especially Protestant ones. Although mainline denominations were about to enter a multidecade pattern of membership decline, they showed little sign of that trend in the 1950s in Orange County. Episcopalians went from six to thirteen congregations there during the decade; Presbyterian churches grew from eight to fourteen. Methodists and Congregationalists saw a spate of new churches too. Pastor Robert Schuller, who would become nationally known for his preaching on positive thinking, in 1955 founded the church that became Orange County's Crystal Cathedral.

Conservative churches enjoyed even greater growth. A disproportionate number of the new Lutheran churches in Orange County were affiliated with the conservative Missouri Synod denomination, as opposed to the mainline Evangelical Lutheran Church in America. Baptists went from six churches in 1950 to fifty-seven in Orange County by 1960. Most of them were affiliated with the Southern Baptist Convention or were independent/fundamentalist congregations.

The Assemblies of God went from two to thirteen Orange County churches between 1950 and 1960.

Some areas, especially the Northeast, saw notable growth in suburban Jewish congregations too. In the New York City metropolitan area alone, Jews founded fifty-seven new Reform congregations, sixty-eight Conservative, and thirty-five Orthodox synagogues between 1945 and 1959.

St. Mark's Episcopal Church, Glendale, California

Library of Congress, Public Domain

These new congregations were not necessarily filled with uniformly devout people. Affiliation was not the same as activity, and membership did not always equate to consistent attendance. It is difficult to determine the number of people for whom faith functioned as an ethnic, political, or familial identity as much as a set of doctrinal convictions. For many it could function as some or all of these at once. Many Americans presumably agreed with Dwight Eisenhower's sense that Judeo-Christian faith was a part of being American. The American political tradition required "deeply held religious faith," Eisenhower said. "And I don't care what it is!"

The Jewish sociologist Will Herberg offered some of the most trenchant observations about post–World War II Americans' seemingly double-minded approach to religion. For example, why did huge majorities of Americans affirm the Bible as the Word of God, but many of them knew little about the Bible itself? Why did the president recommend "deeply held" faith, but did not care what that faith was? Herberg attributed Americans' contradictory inclinations to the close ties between America's religion and society. In effect, being American meant being religious, but that faith often did not have deep roots in the Christian or Jewish traditions. Thus "America seems to be at once the most religious and the most secular of nations," Herberg wrote in his classic book *Protestant-Catholic-Jew* (1955). He did not think that most Americans were hypocritical about their religious commitments, but "the religion which actually prevails among Americans today has lost much of its authentic Christian (or Jewish) content. . . . Americans think, feel, and act in terms quite obviously secularist at the very time that they exhibit every sign of a widespread religious revival. It is this secularism of a religious people, this religiousness in a secularist framework, that constitutes the problem posed by the contemporary religious situation." This combination of vitality and vacuity helped to explain why many religious people routinely behaved in ways that seemed to contradict their faith commitments.

Throughout the upsurge in religious fervor in the 1950s, American civil religion thus sat, sometimes uneasily, alongside traditional forms of American religion. Whether civil religion is part of, or separate from, Judeo-Christian faith is a disputed issue. In his 1967 article which popularized the term *civil religion*, sociologist Robert Bellah noted that while "some have argued that Christianity is the national faith, and others that church and synagogue celebrate only the generalized religion of 'the American Way of Life,' few have realized that there actually exists alongside of and rather clearly differentiated from the churches an elaborate and well-institutionalized civil religion in America." Civil religion appeared most distinctly on patriotic holidays and during occasions such as presidential inaugural addresses, Bellah explained. American politicians across the denominational and party spectrum typically invoked a supreme God, though not one with distinctively Christian or Jewish attributes, who had a special concern for the United States.

Exhibit A of Bellah's civil religion was the inaugural address of John Kennedy in 1961 when Kennedy affirmed the "belief that the rights of man come not from the generosity of the state but from the hand of God." As the first Catholic president, Kennedy was pressured by Protestant critics to deny that his Roman Catholic beliefs would influence his presidency. Yet Protestant critics still expected Kennedy to invoke the language of civil religion. Kennedy's election also illustrated how fear of communism could smooth over America's historic hostility between Catholics and Protestants. The specter of atheistic communism blunted some of the anti-Catholic animosity that had helped to defeat Alfred Smith in the 1928 election.

Still, Kennedy did face significant Protestant resistance to his candidacy, not only because of some ministers' (like Billy Graham's) preference for the GOP's Richard Nixon, but also because some wondered whether a Catholic president would divide his loyalties between the United States and the Vatican. Kennedy's election did not mark the end of anti-Catholicism in America, but it certainly signaled a stronger presence for Catholics in national politics. The Boston Catholic politicians John McCormack and Tip O'Neill would both serve terms as Speakers of the House of Representatives in the 1960s, '70s, and '80s, with McCormack being the first Catholic to serve in that position. By 2018, two-thirds of the justices of the Supreme Court had been raised as Catholics, with most of them still active in the church.

President Kennedy's election also came during a transformative era for the Catholic Church. From 1962 to 1965, the Second Vatican Council, often simply called Vatican II, met in Rome and adopted far-reaching changes, including an affirmation of religious liberty and a softening of the church's tone toward Jews and non-Catholic Christians. Perhaps the greatest difference Vatican II made on a weekly basis was authorizing vernacular languages instead of only Latin for the liturgy of the mass. By the early 2000s, this would mean that priests said mass in more than forty different languages in Los Angeles alone. Although devout Catholics before the 1960s might have understood the Latin liturgy, Catholic services in local languages assumed a more populist, accessible feel. A number of traditionalist Catholics, however, were uncomfortable with the changes inaugurated by Vatican II, including the vernacular-language mass. In 2007, Pope Benedict XVI authorized priests to use the Latin mass in private services or even in public when a sufficient number of parishioners wanted it.

The results of Vatican II's reforms for Catholic life turned out to be mixed. The Catholic Church in America endured a significant decline following 1970, especially in numbers of people in religious vocations and attendance at mass. The total number of priests in America declined from almost 60,000 in 1970 to less than 40,000 in 2010. The number of religious sisters and nuns in the United States has plummeted more precipitously, from more than 160,000 in 1970, to less than 50,000 by 2015. The percentage of self-identified Catholics attending mass every week dropped by half from 1970 to 2010, from 48 percent to 24 percent. The declines in Catholic life were later exacerbated by repeated scandals related to priestly sexual abuse. Reports of sexual abuse in the church began in the 1960s, but they exploded into national notoriety starting in 2002, when exposés by the *Boston Globe* began to unearth the horrifying depths of the problem and the coverups. The American Catholic Church's deterioration likely would have been more severe were it not for steady infusions of Catholic immigrants to the United States, especially from Latin America, since the late 1960s.

Much of the anxiety among American Protestants during the Cold War resulted from fallout over the fundamentalist-modernist controversy, which crested in the 1920s. The Scopes Trial of 1925 had represented a symbolic transition point for Protestant fundamentalists in America. Fundamentalists had largely failed to exclude theological modernists from seminary faculties in the northern denominations, and the theological wars within the Southern Baptist Convention would not come until the late twentieth century. So while a number of conservatives had stayed within the mainline denominations like the Presbyterian Church (USA) and the United Methodist Church, many others, such as the former Princeton Seminary professor J. Gresham Machen, broke away from the modernist-influenced Protestant denominations and joined conservative ones like Machen's Orthodox Presbyterian Church.

In the 1930s and '40s, fundamentalists confronted the question of whether they should pursue theological purity in isolation. Some of them wished to engage with broader secular culture, even if it meant occasional cooperation with modernists and Catholics. Those who came to be called "neoevangelicals," or just evangelicals, took the path of engagement. Those who insisted upon separation from modernists continued to adopt the label "fundamentalists," but now they represented a narrower constituency than the fundamentalists of the 1910s and '20s. Of course, lines between evangelicals and fundamentalists could be blurry. Moderate fundamentalists and hardline evangelicals could assume nearly identical stances, and by the 1970s white fundamentalists and evangelicals grew closer again as culture war politics became salient.

In the 1940s and '50s, battles between fundamentalists and evangelicals could still be as fierce as those between theological conservatives and liberals. Billy Graham's ministry was the greatest source of controversy. Graham had grown up in a thoroughly fundamentalist environment, but as his fame ascended he proved willing to accept the assistance of mainliners and modernists. When he agreed to let the New York City council of Protestant churches, which included liberal congregations, sponsor his 1957 crusade, it was the final straw for some fundamentalist leaders. John R. Rice, the Baptist editor of *The Sword of the Lord*, a flagship newspaper for fundamentalists, broke with Graham over his partnership with modernists. Graham also received criticism from his theological left for harping too much on individual sin and salvation. Reinhold Niebuhr saw Graham's preaching as immature and embarrassing. Even though the president of Niebuhr's Union Seminary supported Graham's 1957 crusade, Niebuhr refused to meet with Graham. The theologian believed that Graham was peddling an intellectually bankrupt view of an infallible Bible.

Graham and the neoevangelicals sought to present themselves as theologically traditionalist, culturally up-to-date, and politically formidable. An early milestone in securing the neoevangelical identity was the founding of the National Association of Evangelicals (NAE) in 1942. The NAE would serve as an institutional alternative to the mainline denominations' Federal Council of Churches, founded in 1908 as a predecessor to the present-day National Council of Churches. The Federal Council dominated Protestant public advocacy up to 1942 and did not support evangelical voices in popular culture, even arguing that government regulators and media networks should limit the access of evangelical radio preachers. The NAE's founders hoped it could defend the political and cultural interests of "evangelicals," a term that began to be used more commonly as a noun. Harold John Ockenga, pastor of Boston's Park Street Church, was one of the key players in the formation of the NAE. He remained concerned about the threat posed by modernist theology, but he also believed that the best answer to modernism was presenting a hopeful, united evangelical front. The NAE allowed any evangelical entity or individual to join. It also fashioned itself as a resource to conservatives who remained within mainline denominations.

The NAE made the critical decision from the outset to allow Pentecostals to join, a decision that was unpopular with fundamentalists. They viewed Pentecostals warily, as did many evangelicals themselves, because of the issue of speaking in tongues. After the Azusa Street revival and the rise of modern Pentecostalism, many evangelicals had embraced the doctrine of "cessationism," or the idea that the New Testament's "sign gifts," especially tongues, had ceased with the passing of Christ's apostles. Those gifts were not to be expected today. However, Ockenga's key partner in the founding of the NAE, the New Englander J. Elwin Wright, was heavily influenced by Pentecostals. Wright and Ockenga wanted the NAE to bridge the evangelical-Pentecostal divide.

On the other hand, although the NAE did not erect formal barriers to multiethnic membership or perspectives, it did little to reach out to African Americans or other evangelical people of color. Although many black churches remained theologically conservative, and many new Hispanic Protestants were Pentecostal, churches led by nonwhite pastors tended to develop separately from white-led evangelical organizations. Large African American denominations such as the National Baptist Convention and the Church of God in Christ did not join the NAE, and the relative lack of interest by the NAE in civil rights reform led a number of African American evangelicals and Pentecostals to form the National Black Evangelical Association in 1963.

Other milestones in evangelicals' quest for cultural influence were the founding of Fuller Seminary (1947) in Pasadena, California, and of the magazine *Christianity Today* (1956). Carl Henry, a Northern Baptist theologian, was a key player in both developments. Henry had a PhD from Boston University and was associated with Ockenga, who convinced Henry to become a charter faculty member at Fuller. Ockenga would serve in absentia as Fuller's first president. With funding and publicity from the radio evangelist Charles Fuller, the seminary's founders hoped that it would become a hub for prominent evangelical scholarship, especially in biblical studies. It would come to achieve that goal but not without enduring terrible internal conflict over the Bible's inerrancy, or its complete factual reliability.

Inerrancy had been one of the chief flashpoints in the earlier fundamentalist-modernist controversy, with fundamentalists and their evangelical heirs normally upholding the doctrine of Scripture being error-free against modernist doubts. However, moderate evangelicals at Fuller Seminary, including Daniel Fuller, the son of Charles, came to doubt the literalistic version of inerrancy framed by early twentieth-century fundamentalists. Daniel Fuller had studied for his doctorate under the neoorthodox luminary Karl Barth at the University of Basel. Although he retained more traditionalist convictions than Barth, Fuller insisted that the Bible did contain falsehoods, but only ones that did not relate to the message of salvation. At a tense faculty meeting in 1962, Harold Ockenga asked the professors, "Well, what are we going to do then? Dan Fuller thinks the Bible is just full of errors." Daniel Fuller and moderate administrators began to facilitate a mass departure of inerrantists from the Fuller faculty. While the seminary continued to embrace an evangelical identity, it now stands on the liberal side of the evangelical continuum.

At the time of the 1962 showdown over inerrancy, though, Carl Henry had already left Fuller Seminary. He was more comfortable as a public intellectual among evangelicals than as a seminary professor, so he agreed to become the founding editor of *Christianity Today*. This magazine effectively served as a flagship periodical for post–World War II American evangelicals. In the founding issue's editorial, Henry wrote that the magazine would "apply the biblical revelation to the contemporary social crisis, by presenting the implications of the total Gospel message for every area of life. This, Fundamentalism has often failed to do. . . . The Gospel of Jesus Christ is a transforming and vital force. We have the conviction that consecrated and gifted evangelical scholarship can provide concrete proof and strategic answers." Harold Lindsell, one of the inerrantists who left Fuller Seminary, served as the magazine's editor during a decidedly conservative phase for the magazine from 1968 to 1978. Over time, *Christianity Today* gravitated toward more of a general interest evangelical genre than just theological writing, but it still affected a culturally refined style.

Leaders such as Henry, Ockenga, and Lindsell made a major mark on twentieth-century evangelicalism, but Billy Graham stood above them all as evangelicals' most commanding voice. In a sense, Graham simply adapted the historic evangelical message of Jonathan Edwards, John Wesley, and George Whitefield to a new cultural setting. During his 1949 Los Angeles revival, Graham paid homage to Edwards by preaching Edwards's famous sermon "Sinners in the Hands of an Angry God." In Boston, Graham self-consciously emulated Whitefield when he gave a concluding sermon on Boston Common. Yet Graham's preaching also reflected Cold War–themed concerns particular to the 1950s and the decades following.

Billy Graham

Graham got his start in the mid-1940s preaching for Youth for Christ (YFC), an evangelistic ministry that focused on reaching young people returning from service in World War II. A Memorial Day 1945 YFC rally at Chicago's Soldier Field attracted seventy thousand people. Graham was one of the ministers there, joined by a five-thousand-voice choir standing under a large neon sign proclaiming, "Jesus Saves." Through YFC assemblies like this one, Graham caught a vision for mass evangelism. George Whitefield had pioneered this kind of ministry in the fields of Britain and America, but Whitefield did not have Graham's technological accoutrements of microphones, stadiums, airplanes, radio, and television. Like Whitefield, the tireless Graham presented the Christian gospel in stark, affecting terms, warning sinners of the impending judgment of God and assuring them of the rescue available in Christ. Graham himself briefly grappled with questions about the reliability of the Bible. Graham finally came to the conclusion that he did not need answers to all questions, and that he would simply accept the

Bible as the inspired Word of God. This removed any nuanced hedging in his preaching, and Graham projected total confidence that the Bible was trustworthy and of divine origin.

Infused with this renewed assurance, Graham became a national evangelical icon following widespread coverage of his 1949 crusade in Los Angeles. Media magnates William Randolph Hearst and Henry Luce gave priority to Graham in periodicals such as Luce's *Time* and *Life* magazines. This guaranteed Graham large crowds wherever his crusades took him. It seemed that Graham's work might signal the outbreak of a revival reminiscent of those in the 1740s or early 1800s. As Graham took Boston by storm, Ockenga speculated that the burgeoning awakening could "be the revival of the last time. It may be that God is now taking out his elect . . . before the awful wrath of God will be loosed in the atomic warfare of this day."

In the end, it is dubious to compare the post–World War II era to what happened in earlier "Great Awakenings" in American history. There is no doubt that the latter period saw huge church growth that followed suburbanization and produced talented Pentecostal and evangelical preachers, led by Graham. Graham's early ministry also represented one of the last times that evangelical faith received news coverage as faith per se.

Untold thousands of people around the world became born-again Christians due to Graham's preaching and that of other evangelical and Pentecostal ministers during the era. But in retrospect one of the most salient developments associated with Graham's work and the neoevangelicals is their growing identification with politics and the Republican Party. Evangelicals had often been engaged in politics before the 1950s, of course, but Graham facilitated the transformation by which American evangelicals—especially white evangelicals—would become known primarily for their political behavior. To Graham, this transformation was understandable, given the existential threat he perceived in global communism. He later expressed regret about his turn to politics as a distraction from the pure spirituality of his preaching. The gospel always remained the core message of his crusades, but the specifics of that preaching received relatively little media coverage after 1949. Graham would receive much more secular coverage for appearances at patriotic occasions and for his friendship with politicians, usually (though not exclusively) Republican ones, beginning with his fateful courtship of Dwight Eisenhower to run for office in 1952. Graham's remarkable access to presidents from Eisenhower to George W. Bush helped other evangelicals envision permanent proximity to powerful politicians. It was an enticing prospect. A desire to acquire and sustain political influence became one of the distinguishing marks of white evangelicals.

WORKS CITED
AND FURTHER READING

Allitt, Patrick. *Catholic Intellectuals and Conservative Politics in America, 1950–1985.* Ithaca, NY: Cornell University Press, 1993.

Bellah, Robert. "Civil Religion in America." *Daedalus* 96, no. 1 (Winter 1967): 1–21.

Bowler, Kate. *Blessed: A History of the American Prosperity Gospel.* New York: Oxford University Press, 2013.

Carpenter, Joel. *Revive Us Again: The Reawakening of American Fundamentalism.* New York: Oxford University Press, 1997.

Dochuk, Darren. *From Bible Belt to Sunbelt: Plain-Folk Religion, Grassroots Politics, and the Rise of Evangelical Conservatism.* New York: Norton, 2011.

Espinosa, Gastón. *Latino Pentecostals in America: Faith and Politics in Action.* Cambridge, MA: Harvard University Press, 2014.

Harvey, Paul. *Freedom's Coming: Religious Culture and the Shaping of the South from the Civil War through the Civil Rights Era.* Chapel Hill: University of North Carolina Press, 2005.

Herberg, Will. *Protestant-Catholic-Jew: An Essay in American Religious Sociology.* Rev. ed. Chicago: University of Chicago Press, 1983.

Herzog, Jonathan P. *The Spiritual-Industrial Complex: America's Religious*

Battle against Communism in the Early Cold War. New York: Oxford University Press, 2011.

Kruse, Kevin M. *One Nation Under God: How Corporate America Invented Christian America.* New York: Basic Books, 2015.

Marsden, George M. *Reforming Fundamentalism: Fuller Seminary and the New Evangelicalism.* Grand Rapids: Eerdmans, 1987.

Matovina, Timothy. *Latino Catholicism: Transformation in America's Largest Church.* Princeton, NJ: Princeton University Press, 2012.

Matthews, J. B. "Reds and Our Churches." *American Mercury* 77 (July 1953): 13.

McGirr, Lisa. *Suburban Warriors: The Origins of the New American Right.* Rev. ed. Princeton, NJ: Princeton University Press, 2015.

Niebuhr, Reinhold. *Essays in Applied Christianity.* Edited by D. B. Robertson. New York: Meridian, 1959.

Peale, Norman Vincent. *The Power of Positive Thinking.* New York: Prentice-Hall, 1952.

Rosell, Garth. *The Surprising Work of God: Harold John Ockenga, Billy Graham, and the Rebirth of Evangelicalism.* Grand Rapids: Baker Academic, 2008.

Sheen, Fulton J. *Peace of Soul.* New York: McGraw Hill, 1949.

Stanley, Brian. *The Global Diffusion of Evangelicalism: The Age of Billy Graham and John Stott.* Downers Grove, IL: InterVarsity Press, 2013.

Thurman, Howard. *Jesus and the Disinherited.* New York: Abingdon-Cokesbury Press, 1949.

Wacker, Grant. *America's Pastor: Billy Graham and the Shaping of a Nation.* Cambridge, MA: Harvard University Press, 2014.

Chapter 12

CIVIL RIGHTS AND CHURCH-STATE CONTROVERSY

The nearly universal popularity of Dr. Martin Luther King Jr. today has obscured the prophetic confrontation and spiritual transcendence of civil rights leaders like King. That prophetic edge made the civil rights movement unpopular among many whites in the 1950s and '60s. Southern white Christian responses to King mostly ranged from nervous reluctance about his cause to outright hatred for him. And the civil rights movement's spiritual transcendence might seem peculiar to many Americans today if they recognized it.

Yet the spiritual vitality of civil rights helps to explain the violent reaction against it. King had no doubt about the spiritual nature of the movement. His own conversion experience into a civil rights stalwart came in early 1956. King had already begun to emerge as a major leader calling for an end to segregation in public facilities, knowing that his leadership entailed horrible risks and could lead to physical harm for his young family. As he endured endless insults and menacing warnings, he entered a crisis of faith. King came to realize that much of his faith was casual, inherited from the long family line of Baptist preachers in which he stood. After another late-night phone caller threatened to murder him and his family, King came to the point of desperation and despair. He recalled,

> I had to know God for myself. . . . I prayed out loud that night.
> I said, "Lord, I'm down here trying to do what's right. I think I'm right. I think the cause we represent is right. But Lord, I must confess that I'm weak now. I'm faltering. I'm losing my courage. And I can't let the people see me like this. . . ." And it seemed at that moment that I could hear an inner voice saying to me, "Martin Luther, stand up for righteousness. Stand up for justice. Stand up for truth. And lo I will be with you, even until the end of the world [Matthew 28:20]."

The experience transformed King into one of the most steadfast advocates for human rights the world has ever known.

The civil rights movement was not entirely new in the 1950s. Its vitality flowed from the same ethos that had fueled the abolitionist campaign. The thirteenth through fifteenth amendments during the Reconstruction era ended slavery and guaranteed all American citizens—including native-born blacks—"equal protection of the laws." Practically, though, the amendments left a lot of unfinished work to address inequality between whites and people of color. As both the North and South became more urbanized and public transportation on trains and streetcars became more pervasive, the "Jim Crow" system of racial segregation became more entrenched. When freedpeople called for basic rights and privileges, they generated a white supremacist backlash, led by terrorist groups such as the Ku Klux Klan. Thousands of African Americans fell victim to white lynch mobs between the 1880s and 1920s. Many lynchings were grotesque spectacles, with hangings and burnings transpiring in front of crowds of thousands of white men, women, and children.

The writer and activist Ida B. Wells became among the most

powerful voices in the pre–civil rights campaign against lynching. She tried to move the consciences of white and black pastors to speak out. Too often she was met with equivocation or silence about racial violence, especially from white Christians. Exasperated, Wells commented that many churches were "too busy saving the souls of white Christians from future burning in hell-fire to save the lives of black ones from present burning in flames kindled by white Christians." Some white pastors did occasionally condemn lynching, if only to lament the lawlessness it reflected. Black pastors were more consistent in their denunciations of vigilante violence, even though speaking publicly put them at risk as well. A National Baptist Convention newspaper raged that the South seemed to be in the "deadly and diabolical grip of blood-thirsty delirium of lynching." The piece presented the white perpetrators as driven by demonic fury to commit their "inhuman and bloody night orgies." The church periodical warned that the lynchings were part of "an ever-growing horrid condition for the Negro race group in portions of the South."

Episodes of black resistance against white supremacy appeared regularly throughout the Great Depression and World War II. King's grandfather and father had both led protests against voter and educational discrimination, and King's family was hardly the only one resisting Jim Crow. Outcries against injustice flowed from the black church, which functioned as the key social and political institution in African American life. Before King and Rosa Parks's well-known Montgomery bus boycott, the National Baptist Convention USA pastor T. J. Jemison had led a similar campaign against the public transportation system of Baton Rouge, Louisiana, in 1953. Churches and pastors helped African Americans in Baton Rouge to coordinate a ridesharing system so that they could avoid riding the city buses, leading Baton Rouge officials to make concessions to the protestors.

Yet the civil rights movement coalesced resistance into a strategic, organized, and ultimately effective tool to bring about change. While pastors such as King and Jemison were the spokespeople of the black community, black Christian women often represented the ground forces of campaigns for racial justice. One of these women was Parks, who refused to give up her seat on a Montgomery bus to white passengers. Parks was a respected member of an African Methodist Episcopal congregation in the city, serving there as a "stewardess," or an assistant at communion services. Her fame can obscure other women's roles, but she was not alone. For instance, Jo Ann Robinson, an English professor in Montgomery and a member at King's Dexter Avenue Baptist Church, was one of several Baptist and Methodist women who served on the Women's Political Council of Montgomery, founded just after World War II to help educate and mobilize the city's African American community. Until the bus boycott, the Women's Political Council was the most vocal black civic group in Montgomery. Robinson naturally supported the burgeoning campaign against the segregated bus system, and she and other church women distributed boycott literature throughout the city. When the female council's work came to the attention of the ministers, the pastors "decided that it was time for them, the leaders, to catch up with the masses," Robinson recalled. When King and other ministers formed the Southern Christian Leadership Conference (SCLC) in 1957, however, they appointed no women to the group's board.

Although the civil rights movement would attract legions of black Christians, not all African American churches supported the boycotts and sit-ins. King and many other activist pastors were part of the National Baptist Convention, USA, but their denomination's leader, J. H. Jackson, opposed King's methods of direct resistance. Jackson preferred passing civil rights legislation and then suing segregationists for violating the laws, an approach taken by the National Association for the Advancement of Colored People since the early twentieth century. King did not oppose such measures, but he and many younger black clergy believed that direct confrontations and nonviolent resistance would stir the consciences of Americans who might be persuaded to oppose Jim Crow. Jackson outmaneuvered King and his allies for control of the National Baptist Convention, and in 1961 the differences between rival ministers over civil rights became so bitter that King and his associates left the National Baptist Convention and formed the Progressive National Baptist Convention. In spite of this split, the National Baptist Convention USA remained one of the largest African American–led denominations, along with the Church of God in Christ. The National Baptist Convention was hardly cut off from civil rights activism, as Baton Rouge pastor and former bus boycott leader T. J. Jemison succeeded Jackson as president in 1982.

As the white Christian South watched black Christians demanding civil rights reform, the dominant white reaction was caution and reluctance. This is why King directed much of his "Letter from Birmingham Jail" in 1963 to the southern "white moderate," who to King posed more of an obstacle than the Ku Klux Klan. The white moderate, King wrote, "is more devoted to 'order' than to justice" and "constantly says 'I agree with you in the goal you seek, but I cannot agree with your methods of direct action.'"

When TV cameras caught Alabama authorities turning attack dogs and water cannons on black protestors, it undoubtedly helped turn national opinion in favor of civil rights. In an episode that came to be known as "Miracle Sunday," March 5, 1963, some white Birmingham firefighters refused to fire water cannons on a prayer march led by Baptist pastor Charles Billups. Billups himself had once been beaten and branded by members of the Ku Klux Klan. A tearful Billups led the protestors in chanting, "Turn on your water, turn loose your dogs, we will stand here till we die." Even though police commissioner Bull Connor ordered the firemen to disperse the crowd, the protestors passed through the phalanx of police and firemen without incident. King, who was not there that day, insisted that "Miracle Sunday" taught him for the first time the conscience-moving power of nonviolent resistance.

Apart from the white moderates, some white Christians in the South were adamant segregationists and sought to defend the Jim Crow racial order on biblical grounds. The Ku Klux Klan always positioned itself as a Christian organization, and it had untold numbers of Methodists, Baptists, and other southern churchgoers in its ranks. A number of white pastors excoriated attempts to desegregate schools and other facilities. In the aftermath of the 1954 *Brown v. Board of Education* ruling, which struck down state laws sanctioning separate black and white schools, pastors such as W. A. Criswell vowed not to cooperate with the desegregation mandate. "If you want this group, or that group . . . brother, it's a free country," Criswell said. "If I want my group, let me have it. . . . Don't force me to cross over in those intimate things where I don't want to go." Criswell presided over First Baptist Dallas, one of the largest churches in the country at the time, with eleven thousand members. First Baptist Dallas was also the church where Billy Graham kept his membership, though Graham was rarely there due to his travel schedule. Criswell's ideas were complemented by more exotic segregationist views such as those of Atlanta Methodist pastor Lawrence Neff, author of the 1958 pamphlet "Jesus: Master-Segregationist." According to Neff, Jesus's instructions to his disciples to focus ministry on Jews, not gentiles, proved that he was the "most consistent and inflexible segregationist the world has ever known."

Many white Christians would have squirmed at Neff's outlandish exegesis. Yet when white churches and denominations did act against segregation, they risked a backlash. The Christian Life Commission of the Southern Baptist Convention, for example, attempted to inform SBC churchgoers about the immorality of racial discrimination. They circulated packets of information to SBC pastors on questions related to ethnicity, with titles such as "The Unity of Humanity" and "The Racial Problem is My Problem." Some Baptists in the Deep South found these packets offensive and threatened to withhold contributions from the Christian Life Commission if they did not desist. One Mississippi pastor complained to the commission, saying that he resented them using "mission money to tell me something that I do not believe."

Black Christians, of course, were taking the greatest risks by participating in struggles for civil rights. A number of black activists were tortured by Klansmen or police. Some paid for their involvement with their lives. One of the most horrific moments came when Klansmen planted a bomb outside Birmingham's 16th Street Baptist Church. During the Sunday service on September 15, 1963, the bomb exploded and killed four girls inside the building. King memorialized the girls as "martyred heroines of a holy crusade for freedom and human dignity." The bombing came just two weeks after King's stirring speech at the March on Washington. In an oration filled with biblical allusions, King had proclaimed that the marchers would not be satisfied until "justice rolls down like waters and righteousness like a mighty stream [Amos 5:24]."

The entrenched racism and viciousness that the civil rights movement confronted led some activists to criticize King's philosophy of nonviolent resistance. Anne Moody was one of the Mississippi activists at the March on Washington, but she found it dissatisfying. When Klansmen bombed the 16th Street Baptist Church, she found herself questioning God about whether it was right to forgive the murderers. Finally she resolved that she would no longer submit to beatings in the name of nonviolence. "Nonviolence is out," she told God. Moody and others began to advocate a more aggressive, retaliatory approach.

The most controversial black-led group that rejected King's Christian nonviolence was the Nation of Islam (NOI). The NOI's leader was Elijah Muhammad, but its most compelling spokesperson was Malcolm X. The NOI, founded in the 1930s in Detroit, blended some traditional Muslim beliefs with Black Power doctrines promoted by Elijah Muhammad and his prophetic mentor, Wali Fard Muhammad. The NOI especially appealed to poor urban African Americans. It reached a number of followers while they were in prison, including Malcolm X. In time, it also attracted a number of celebrity athletes. The most prominent was the champion boxer Muhammad Ali, formerly Cassius Clay. Elijah Muhammad preached an ascetic moral code, believing that the black community was being decimated by alcohol, crime, and drugs. Members of the NOI preferred black separatism over integration, and Malcolm X scoffed at King's march as the "Farce on Washington." Elijah Muhammad and Malcolm X portrayed white people as devils. In his autobiography, Malcolm explained that whites used Christianity to brainwash blacks "to always turn the other cheek, and grin, and scrape, and bow, and be humble, and to sing, and to pray, and to take whatever was dished out by the devilish white man; and to look for his pie in the sky, and for his heaven in the hereafter, while right here on earth the slavemaster white man enjoyed *his* heaven." Malcolm X eventually became disillusioned with the NOI and Elijah Muhammad and adopted a more traditional form of Islam after making the Muslim pilgrimage to Mecca in 1964. Malcolm was assassinated in 1965. King too was felled by an assassin in 1968.

Martin Luther King Jr. and Malcolm X, 1964

Two of the most powerful public voices contending for black dignity and equality were thus silenced by 1968, but others carried the movement forward. James Cone, a professor at Union Theological Seminary, became one of the most influential proponents of distinctly black theology. Like Howard Thurman and Malcolm X, Cone objected to the white domination of theology and whitened images of God. In books such as *Black Theology and Black Power* (1969) and *A Black Theology of Liberation* (1970), Cone explained that authentic Christianity was best understood by those who knew the experience of oppression. Black theology, he wrote, was "possibly the only expression of Christian theology in America" because "there can be no theology of the gospel which does not arise from an oppressed community." Cone and other theologians of black liberation posited that God himself was black.

Hispanics' efforts at civil rights reform and labor activism in the 1960s and 1970s were often inspired by the example of African American advocates, but they were also deeply rooted in the culture of Latino Catholicism. The most visible Hispanic activist of the era, César Chávez of the United Farm Workers, was successful in part because he drew upon Catholic culture and principles in his efforts to secure fair working conditions for agricultural laborers. Some Hispanic radicals had become suspicious of the Catholic Church's traditionalism. But Chávez warned that multitudes of Hispanic workers "desperately need some help from that powerful institution, the church, and we are foolish not to help them get it." Chávez sought to enlist the church as an ally. "We ask the church to sacrifice with the people for social change, for justice, and for love of brother. We don't ask for words. We ask for deeds." Our Lady of Guadalupe was an ever-present symbol in the public demonstrations of Chávez's movement.

While the civil rights movement continued, many white Christians in America in the early 1960s were more concerned with questions about religion in schools than about desegregating them. Religion, usually in Protestant form, was omnipresent in most American schools well into the twentieth century. The King James Bible was routinely read to students, and frequently used textbooks such as the *McGuffey Readers* were filled with biblical content, especially in their early editions in the 1800s. Catholics developed their own parochial school system partly as a reaction to the Protestant culture of public schools. After World War II, the increasing diversity of the American student population and the growth of a vocal community of religious skeptics made the de facto Protestant educational establishment more problematic.

Since the case of *Reynolds v. United States* (1879), the Supreme Court had not commented much on the First Amendment's religion clauses. In the 1940s, that began to change. As with other sections of the Bill of Rights, the court "incorporated" the no-establishment and free exercise of religion clauses, meaning that they applied them to states, not just the federal government. Decisions after World War II began to set clearer boundaries between state governments and religious institutions. For example, in 1947's *Everson v. Board of Education*, the court narrowly ruled in favor of a New Jersey law that reimbursed parents for the cost of transporting children to private schools. The provision benefited Catholic school parents almost exclusively. The court reasoned that because no money was going directly to the religious schools, and because the law was broadly applicable in theory, it did not represent an establishment of religion. However, citing Thomas Jefferson's 1802 metaphor, the court's majority affirmed that the "First Amendment has erected a wall between church and state. That wall must be kept high and impregnable. We could not approve the slightest breach." They simply did not see the New Jersey law as a breach.

As public expressions of "Judeo-Christian" religiosity became more pervasive in the anticommunist atmosphere of the 1950s, the Supreme Court proved hesitant about approving state-sanctioned religious activities on public school campuses. In 1951, the New York Board of Regents recommended that the state's schools begin each day with the prayer "Almighty God, we acknowledge our dependence upon Thee, and we beg Thy blessings upon us, our parents, our teachers, and our Country." A group of skeptic and Jewish parents sued over the prayer, insisting that it represented a violation of the no-establishment clause. The Supreme Court agreed, striking down the prayer in *Engel v. Vitale* (1962). Hugo Black, the liberal Baptist justice from Alabama who had also written the majority opinion in *Everson*, insisted that it was not the "business of government to compose official prayers for any group of the American people." Reactions from Christian leaders to *Engel* ranged from horror to enthusiastic support. Many evangelical leaders expressed dismay, but some admitted that the prayer was not theologically specific enough anyway. Martin Luther King, drawing on his Baptist convictions, regarded *Engel* as a "sound and good decision reaffirming . . . separation of church and state."

Then in the 1963 case of *Abington School District v. Schempp*, the court overwhelmingly ruled against school-sponsored Bible readings. This development was of deeper concern to many, as Bible reading had been a fixture of American schools since the colonial era. A dozen states mandated daily Bible readings in schools as of 1963, and in most other states Bible readings were permitted though not required. A Philadelphia-area Unitarian family, the Schempps, filed suit against the school district when it disciplined their teenage son for refusing to stand for the daily Bible reading. A related case emerged in Maryland when the son of the atheist activist Madalyn Murray protested against Baltimore's Bible reading policy. Lawyers for the American Civil Liberties Union (ACLU) focused more on the Schempps' case because they perceived Madalyn Murray as combative and an unappealing representative because of her atheism. Murray had written that the Bible was "replete with the ravings of madmen." The court majority followed the ACLU's lead and marginalized Murray's role. In its ruling, the court said that Bible reading represented a mandatory religious exercise, something the government could not require without violating the establishment clause.

Jews and mainline Christians tended to welcome *Abington School District*, while Catholics, evangelicals, and fundamentalists reacted negatively. The Catholic archbishop of Boston regarded it as a "great tragedy that the greatest book ever published . . . cannot be read in the public school system." Even though defenders of the decision noted that it did not forbid the Bible from being studied as history or literature, nor did it stop individual students from bringing and reading the Bible for themselves, fundamentalist pastor Carl McIntire maintained that the decision brought into question whether "America may continue to honor and recognize God in the life of the nation." A "school prayer amendment" to the Constitution initially generated bipartisan support, but by the 1980s it had become a more distinctively Republican cause. Although a majority of Americans sympathized with such an amendment for a time, it never got the supermajority needed to pass in Congress.

While the court's decisions restrained some expression of Christian faith in schools, it left in place expressions of American civil religion, such as the phrase "under God" in the Pledge of Allegiance. Repeated attempts by secularist groups to excise such expressions from public life made less headway in the decades following *Abington School District*. As long as the expression in question was theologically generic and connected to patriotism as much as religion, the courts usually deemed it acceptable.

Courts frowned upon direct government aid to religious groups, however. In the landmark case of *Lemon v. Kurtzman* (1971), an 8–1 majority sought to establish rules for when government connections to religion could be constitutional. The "Lemon Test" contended that permissible statutes must have a "secular legislative purpose," must not be designed to aid or undermine religion, and must avoid "excessive government entanglement" with religion. In decisions such as *Marsh v. Chambers* (1983) and *Town of Greece v. Galloway* (2014), court majorities also permitted government-funded chaplains and prayers at public meetings. The Supreme Court was less inclined, however, to permit student-led prayer in schools or at public schools' athletic events.

Cases such as *Engel* and *Abington School District* suggested to many American Christians that powerful forces were excluding faith from central institutions of American life. Some traditionalists found it similarly disconcerting when the protest movements of the 1960s spawned new iterations of Christian theology focused around feminist or ethnic perspectives, such as the black liberation theology of James Cone. Among the most controversial feminist theologians was Mary Daly, who taught at the Jesuit-run Boston College and became known for works such as *The Church and the Second Sex* (1968) and *Beyond God the Father* (1973). Daly lamented the way that Christians traditionally associated "God" with masculinity and invested both God and man with power over woman. "If God is male, then the male is God," Daly concluded. Too often the image of God "functions to legitimate the existing social, economic, and political status quo, in which women and other victimized groups are subordinate."

Perhaps the most troubling theological development of the 1960s and '70s for traditional Christians was the so-called "death of God." A number of liberal theologians posited that historic Christianity was becoming so outdated in the modern world that it must undergo fundamental change to survive. Going back to the deist movement of the 1700s, skeptical critics had advanced versions of Christianity in which supernatural belief was marginalized. The death of God theologians posited a kind of Christianity in which virtually all recourse to the supernatural vanished. Syracuse University professor Gabriel Vahanian argued in his book *The Death of God* (1961) that "the essentially mythological world-view of Christianity has been succeeded by a thoroughgoing scientific view of reality, in terms of which either God is no longer necessary, or he is neither necessary nor unnecessary: he is irrelevant—he is dead." A more irenic and popular version of radical theology appeared in Harvey Cox's bestselling *The Secular City* (1965). Cox, a Northern Baptist who taught at Harvard Divinity School, contended that Christianity itself was a major culprit behind secularization. There was still a place in the world for an authentic church engaged in "God's permanent revolution in history," Cox wrote, but the church as an organization was fated to become irrelevant in the contemporary urban environment.

Time helped to popularize the academic writings of the death of God theologians when the magazine's Easter cover in 1966 asked, "Is God Dead?" This signaled a new cultural openness to radical theology as well as a more public role for atheism. One advocate of atheism exulted that "God is a myth, like Santa Claus. The God-myth is dying." The comparison of God to Santa Claus was not new, but this kind of popular apologetic for atheism became increasingly prominent in the decades following the 1960s. The trend was exemplified in the early 2000s by "new atheists" such as Richard Dawkins and Tufts University philosopher Daniel Dennett. For traditional Christians and Jews, the provocative views of atheists and death of God theologians were both alarming and energizing. Conservatives in the 1960s realized they could no longer take the existence of God and his importance in America for granted. Billy Graham told *Time* that he knew that God was real "because of my personal experience. I know that I know him."

Graham helped to forge an evangelical partnership with Richard Nixon and the Republican Party to fight against cultural trends represented by the death of God, court decisions on religion in schools, urban riots, anti-Vietnam marches, and other protests of the 1960s. The Republicans' "culture war" was not theologically specific: there was never much room in the GOP platform for Graham's exhortations about the need to be born again through Christ. Yet Graham, Nixon, and their allies touted the idea that a "silent majority" of Americans still believed in God, America, and biblical morality. In this spirit, Graham and the celebrity comedian Bob Hope hosted "Honor America Day" in July 1970. Graham gave a sermon titled "The Unfinished Dream," in a nod to the slain Martin Luther King, while at the same time denouncing extremists in America who "desecrated our flag, disrupted our educational system, laughed at our religious heritage, and threatened to burn down our cities." Graham insisted that the vision of America's Founders was rooted in the Bible and that all liberty-loving citizens should defend "God and the American dream."

The alliance between religious conservatives and the Republican

Party would become more conspicuous in the decades following the 1973 *Roe v. Wade* decision, which struck down state restrictions on abortion. The culture wars would attract much media attention, especially after the founding of Jerry Falwell's Moral Majority in 1979. But there were other more spiritual trends in the 1960s and '70s that would infuse life into the broader evangelical and charismatic movements, aiding those movements' enduring strength. One of those spiritual trends was a charismatic renewal. Dating back to the Azusa Street revival of 1906 in Los Angeles, Pentecostals had been a force within Protestantism, with their distinctive emphases on the baptism of the Holy Spirit and speaking in tongues. The charismatic renewal touched all major Christian denominations and was focused on individual Christians' experiences of God's presence and power. While being charismatic did not always entail speaking in tongues, the charismatic movement involved new depths of spiritual experience for many Catholics, mainliners, and evangelicals.

Some trace the charismatic renewal to the controversial Episcopal priest Dennis Bennett, who informed his Los Angeles parish in 1960 that he had received the baptism of the Spirit and had spoken in tongues. Bennett was ultimately removed from his pastorate, and his bishop tried to ban speaking in tongues from the diocese. Bennett found work in a small Seattle Episcopal church where he also introduced charismatic practices. His congregation's membership boomed. Episcopal charismatics influenced other mainline congregations, including Lutheran and Presbyterian churches, and Catholics also experienced charismatic revivals that broke out at the University of Notre Dame and other Catholic colleges.

One of the most distinctive trends associated with charismatic renewal was the Jesus movement, which sought to reach the burgeoning youth culture and "hippies" of the 1960s and '70s. The movement was decentered without a unified leadership, but it flourished especially in California. One of the Jesus movement's most colorful leaders was the Mississippi Baptist Arthur Blessitt, who in the late 1960s began ministering to the denizens of Los Angeles's Sunset Strip. He especially sought to turn teenagers away from drugs, exhorting them to find true satisfaction in Jesus. Blessitt and other Jesus preachers put the traditional evangelical message into hippie vernacular, telling proselytes that they needed to start "tripping on Jesus." Blessitt himself preached in flowery shirts and bell bottoms. When Blessitt relocated his ministry to New York's Times Square, he trekked across the country on foot, hauling a huge cross.

Two of the most enduring organizations birthed from the Jesus movement were Calvary Chapel churches, founded by Chuck Smith, and Vineyard churches, founded by John Wimber. Smith was a product of the International Church of the Foursquare Gospel, Aimee Semple McPherson's denomination. Frustrated by what he perceived as the denomination's inflexibility, Smith decided to found the independent Calvary Chapel in Costa Mesa, California, in 1965. Soon Smith's church began outreach to hippie youths in nearby Huntington Beach, and a hippie-inflected style of ministry became Calvary Chapel's calling card.

Calvary Chapel in Montesano, Washington

Meanwhile, John Wimber, a former rock musician and Calvary Chapel pastor in Yorba Linda, embraced the principle of "power evangelism," or the idea that the exercise of charismatic gifts was one of the church's most effective tools for attracting new adherents. His church would become the flagship congregation of the Vineyard movement, founded in 1982. Calvary Chapel and Vineyard churches both illustrate modern evangelicalism's combination of up-to-date ministry styles with conservative, biblicist teaching.

The Jesus movement's most pervasive contribution to American religion was musical, both within congregations and in popular recordings. Traditional gospel music had been a staple of radio and recordings for decades, but the Jesus movement showed that a rock style could take religious music into unexplored commercial territory. Probably the key pioneer in Christian rock was Larry Norman. A former member of a modestly successful San Francisco secular band, Norman first experienced the filling of the Holy Spirit in 1967 and soon became a sought-after performer in Jesus movement circles in California. In 1972, he released the album *Only Visiting This Planet* (1972), one of the most influential Christian music albums ever recorded. It became a 2014 addition to the Library of Congress's prestigious National Recording Registry. The Jesus movement's music heralded the commercial successes of other Christian artists in the following decades, from Amy Grant to Jars of Clay, and more recently, to Christian rappers such as Lecrae.

By the 1970s, traditional Christians had become uncertain about their place within mainstream American culture. At least since the Second Great Awakening, evangelical Protestants had tended to see themselves as stewards of American society. In causes such as antislavery and the prohibition of alcohol, they had imagined that they might enhance the Christian character of the nation. In the face of Cold War communism, evangelicals joined with mainliners, Catholics, and Jews in elevating American civil religion to a more heightened status than ever before in American history.

Yet the 1960s and '70s gave conservative people of faith reasons to believe that their quasi-established status was under attack. Some whites were unsettled by the tactics of civil rights reformers. Others worried that the forces of "secular humanism," as popular evangelical philosopher Francis Schaeffer called it, had forced prayer and the Bible out of schools and legalized abortion in *Roe v. Wade*. Traditionalists grasped for ways to retain their claim on American culture. Many of them, especially starting with the founding of the Moral Majority, would seek to do so through politics and the courts. Evangelicals still believed, however, that spiritual transformation remained the essential solution to Americans' troubles. As Larry Norman put it in a 1972 song, "Why don't you look into Jesus? He's got the answer."

WORKS CITED
AND FURTHER READING

Allitt, Patrick. *Religion in America Since 1945: A History.* New York: Columbia University Press, 2003.

Bay, Mia, ed. *Ida B. Wells: The Light of Truth, Writings of an Anti-Lynching Crusader.* New York: Penguin, 2014.

Carson, Clayborne, and Kris Shepard, eds. *A Call to Conscience: The Landmark Speeches of Dr. Martin Luther King, Jr.* New York: Grand Central, 2001.

Chappell, David L. *A Stone of Hope: Prophetic Religion and the Death of Jim Crow.* Chapel Hill: University of North Carolina Press, 2004.

Cone, James H. *A Black Theology of Liberation.* Philadelphia: Lippincott, 1970.

Cox, Harvey. *The Secular City: Secularization and Urbanization in Theological Perspective.* New York: Macmillan, 1965.

Daly, Mary. *Beyond God the Father: Toward a Philosophy of Women's Liberation.* Boston: Beacon Press, 1973.

Dupont, Carolyn Renée. *Mississippi Praying: Southern White Evangelicals and the Civil Rights Movement, 1945–1975.* New York: New York University Press, 2013.

Eskridge, Larry. *God's Forever Family: The Jesus People Movement in America.* New York: Oxford University Press, 2013.

Garrow, David J. *Bearing the Cross: Martin Luther King, Jr., and the Southern Christian Leadership Conference.* New York: William Morrow, 1986.

Hassett, Miranda K. "Charismatic Renewal." In *The Oxford Handbook of Anglican Studies,* 301–13. Edited by Mark D. Chapman et al. New York: Oxford University Press, 2015.

King, Martin Luther, Jr. *Why We Can't Wait.* Introduction by Dorothy Cotton. Boston: Beacon, 2010.

Kruse, Kevin M. *One Nation Under God: How Corporate America Invented Christian America.* New York: Basic Books, 2015.

Long, Emma. *The Church-State Debate: Religion, Education, and the Establishment Clause in Post-War America.* New York: Continuum, 2012.

Malcolm X with Alex Haley. *The Autobiography of Malcolm X.* New York: Grove, 1965.

Mathews, Mary Beth Swetnam. *Doctrine and Race: African American Evangelicals and Fundamentalism Between the Wars.* Tuscaloosa: University of Alabama Press, 2017.

McWhorter, Diane. *Carry Me Home: Birmingham, Alabama, The Climactic Battle of the Civil Rights Revolution.* New York: Simon & Schuster, 2001.

Moody, Anne. *Coming of Age in Mississippi.* New York: Random House, 1968.

Robinson, Jo Ann Gibson. *The Montgomery Bus Boycott and the Women Who Started It.* Knoxville: University of Tennessee Press, 1987.

Stavans, Ilan, ed. *Cesar Chavez, An Organizer's Tale: Speeches.* New York: Penguin Books, 2008.

Stephens, Randall J. *The Devil's Music: How Christians Inspired, Condemned, and Embraced Rock 'n' Roll.* Cambridge, MA: Harvard University Press, 2018.

Vahanian, Gabriel. *The Death of God: The Culture of Our Post-Christian Era.* New York: George Braziller, 1961.

Witte, John, Jr., and Joel A. Nichols. *Religion and the American Constitutional Experiment.* 4th ed. New York: Oxford University Press, 2016.

Chapter 13

THE CHRISTIAN
RIGHT AND THE
CHANGING FACE OF
AMERICAN RELIGION

In 1976, it remained unclear exactly what form conservative Christian political alliances would take. Billy Graham had helped to secure the white evangelical nexus with the Republican Party starting in the early 1950s. Yet many of Graham's fellow white southern evangelicals remained attached to the Democrats' traditional coalition, if they were politically active at all. Then in the aftermath of Richard Nixon's resignation over Watergate, Democrats in 1976 nominated Georgia governor Jimmy Carter, one of the first evangelicals since William Jennings Bryan to run for president. The Baptist Carter did not mind telling reporters about his born again experience. Charles Colson, a convicted former Nixon aide and new evangelical believer, also helped to popularize evangelical conversion in his popular and controversial 1976 memoir *Born Again*. *Newsweek* pronounced 1976 the "year of the evangelical," and suddenly it seemed that evangelicals were one of the nation's hottest news stories.

In a move that would dramatically change the perception of evangelicals, the Gallup polling organization in 1976 began asking respondents if they were born again. From then on, polling organizations usually wanted to identify evangelicals (typically meaning white evangelicals) in order to track their political behavior. By 1980, the term *evangelical* carried heavy political baggage, just as white evangelicals decisively embraced what would become a decades-long pattern of dependence upon the Republican Party.

Carter was an adult Sunday school teacher and an intellectual disciple of the theologian Reinhold Niebuhr. He represented the moderate wing of the Southern Baptist Convention, a denomination that Carter's presidency would help to split. The folksy Carter spoke freely about his own spiritual struggles, but he could come across as naïve to the media. In an interview with the soft-core pornographic magazine *Playboy*, a venue that raised eyebrows among critical pastors,

Jimmy Carter leaving church

Carter readily admitted that he had not always been pure. "I have looked on a lot of women with lust," he confessed. "I've committed adultery in my heart many times." This sort of talk would have made sense in Carter's Sunday school class, but in the national media it caused chortling and perplexity. Carter's frankness was refreshing after Nixon, however, and he went on to defeat Nixon's successor Gerald Ford in November 1976. Carter initially enjoyed considerable support from his fellow white southern evangelicals. Yet Carter supported abortion rights and the Equal Rights Amendment, which would have constitutionally mandated equal legal rights for women. These positions, along with

Carter's seeming ineffectiveness as president, began to erode southern evangelicals' support for him.

By 1980, abortion had emerged as perhaps the defining concern for conservative Protestant voters. In the early 1970s, Catholics were more unified in opposition to legalized abortion than were many white evangelicals, especially Baptists. Led by Catholic physicians such as Dr. John Willke, the number of pro-life organizations in America reportedly swelled from just six before *Roe v. Wade* to about a thousand by 1974. Willke founded pro-life organizations in Cincinnati and the state of Ohio before serving for a decade as the head of the National Right to Life Committee. African American Christians were also initially more likely than white Protestants to be pro-life. Dr. Mildred Jefferson, who grew up in the Methodist church in Texas, became the first African American female graduate of Harvard Medical School in 1951. Even before *Roe*, she strenuously opposed efforts to liberalize state laws against abortion. Jefferson explained that because of her Christian upbringing, she felt obligated to stand up for the most vulnerable members of society. She lamented that *Roe v. Wade* "gave my profession an almost unlimited license to kill."

Evangelicals' first responses to *Roe v. Wade* were mixed. Some scholars have incorrectly concluded that most evangelicals were initially silent about abortion. Actually, many white and black evangelicals did express immediate opposition to *Roe*. The National Association of Evangelicals denounced the decision "in the strongest possible terms." *Christianity Today* proclaimed that "the decision runs counter not merely to the moral teachings of Christianity through the ages but also to the moral sense of the American people." Southern Baptists, however, were divided over abortion. Even some conservative pastors such as First Baptist Dallas's W. A. Criswell initially expressed support for almost unlimited abortion rights. The SBC newspaper *Baptist Press* commended *Roe*, interpreting it through the hardy categories of anti-Catholicism. "The Roman Catholic hierarchy insists that the Supreme Court blundered by making an immoral, anti-religious and unjustified decision. It has vowed to continue the fight against relaxed abortion laws," *Baptist Press* reported. "However, most other religious bodies and leaders, who have expressed themselves, approve the decision. Social, welfare and civil rights workers hailed the decision with enthusiasm."

Not all Southern Baptists agreed with *Baptist Press*. Robert Holbrook, pastor of First Baptist Church of Hallettsville, Texas, admittedly a far smaller platform than Criswell's church, founded Baptists for Life in 1973 and devoted much of his time trying to stir the consciences of fellow Baptists about abortion. Evangelical mobilization in the pro-life cause began slowly, but it was aided by popular Christian philosophy writer Francis Schaeffer. In 1979, Schaeffer produced the pro-life film *Whatever Happened to the Human Race?* along with the future Surgeon General and Presbyterian layman C. Everett Koop. Schaeffer argued that secular humanism had undermined the concept that each human life was created in God's image. Schaeffer's writings, films, and speeches had a massive impact on a generation of evangelicals, including Jerry Falwell Sr., who soon founded the Moral Majority. Schaeffer also helped to convince the Southern Baptist Convention that abortion was morally abominable. SBC leaders, not coincidentally, launched the "conservative resurgence" the same year as Schaeffer's film.

Library of Congress, Prints & Photographs Division, LC-DIG-ppmsca-09752

March for Life, 1979

This resurgence would transform the SBC into a uniformly evangelical denomination, as well as a pro-life one. Increasingly, liberal and moderate Baptists like Jimmy Carter felt alienated within the SBC. Carter formally broke with the SBC in 2000, aligning with the Cooperative Baptist Fellowship, an alliance of Baptist churches which formed in 1991 in opposition to the conservative resurgence.

In 1980, the declining popularity of Carter opened the door for white evangelical and fundamentalist defection to the Republicans and Ronald Reagan. The founding of Falwell's Moral Majority was a key moment in this switch. Falwell was popular in fundamentalist circles, but he had few connections to the worlds of Billy Graham and the National Association of Evangelicals. Until the late 1970s, Falwell's chief foray into politics had been opposing racial integration during the civil rights movement, a stance he later repudiated. Like many conservative Protestants, Falwell's reaction to *Roe v. Wade* was delayed. He began speaking out on the issue by 1976, however, and Schaeffer and Koop's work helped convince Falwell to make the pro-life issue a top priority.

Falwell's radio show had previously focused on spiritual and biblical issues, but in 1976 he began to criticize Jimmy Carter. By 1979, Falwell partnered with Paul Weyrich, a Catholic and the founder of the Heritage Foundation, a conservative activist group. Weyrich insisted that there was a "moral majority" of Americans who did not support the cultural changes sweeping America. Falwell had previously used the term *moral majority* too, and the concept was reminiscent of Richard Nixon's "silent majority" mantra. Falwell's cooperation with evangelicals, Catholics, and a small number of Jews in the Moral Majority drew the ire of some fellow fundamentalists, who had prized separation from all those outside the fundamentalist fold, but this did not deter him. Bob Jones Jr., president of South Carolina's Bob Jones University, averred that the Moral Majority was a satanic device which would help "build the world church of Antichrist."

Scholars have debated which issues were the most important in the founding of the Moral Majority. A host of concerns animated Falwell, including abortion, the Equal Rights Amendment, pornography, school prayer, and others. Yet Weyrich suggested that the most pressing issue to southern fundamentalists and evangelicals was fear that the Internal Revenue Service might revoke the tax-exempt status of Christian schools and colleges, as it had already done to Bob Jones University in 1976. Claiming a biblical case against interracial marriage, the university had imposed a number of discriminatory policies against nonwhite students. Under the Carter administration, the IRS indicated that it would crack down on similar Christian schools that maintained segregationist policies. A number of Christian academies had opened in the 1960s and '70s, some with the goal of evading the integration of public schools. Falwell's Lynchburg Christian Academy, founded in 1967, did not have overtly discriminatory rules, but it did not initially admit any nonwhite students. The local newspaper described it as a "private school for white students." The IRS did not, in fact, aggressively pursue action against the so-called segregation academies, but the mere prospect of federal regulation of such schools was a seminal factor in the Moral Majority's inception.

Given Carter's unreliability on abortion, the ERA, and Christian schools' tax status, Falwell and other Christian conservatives rallied around the Republican Party and its new standard-bearer, former California governor Ronald Reagan. At first glance, Reagan was not the most obvious candidate to become a favorite of the new Christian right. He was divorced, and he had signed liberal laws in California regarding abortion rights and no-fault divorce. But Reagan was affiliated with the evangelical-hued Bel Air Presbyterian Church in Hollywood and became connected with Billy Graham. Over time evangelical and Pentecostal leaders in California had become some of Reagan's strongest supporters. From them he learned about the concerns of evangelicals and, more importantly, the way to talk to evangelicals. Reagan was even known to share his Christian faith with others in an evangelical style.

Unlike Billy Graham, most traditionalist Protestant pastors were not used to being courted by national politicians. Thus it was exhilarating when Reagan made appearances at events such as the Religious Round-table's National Affairs Briefing in Dallas in August 1980. Tens of thousands of evangelical and fundamentalist leaders were there, including Falwell and the Christian Broadcasting Network's Pat Robertson. Reagan told the assembly that he knew they could not endorse him, but "I want you to know that I endorse you." Northern white evangelicals and Billy Graham had long leaned toward the Republican Party anyway, but Reagan's fall 1980 campaign signaled the rise of a nationally unified white evangelical cohort that would back the GOP under virtually any circumstances.

Eventually, some Christian right leaders became impatient with Reagan, because his talk of sympathy for their causes was not always matched with action. His early nomination of C. Everett Koop as surgeon general was heartening to them, but other appointments, such as Sandra Day O'Connor for the Supreme Court, were not. O'Connor had a pro-choice record as a legislator in Arizona, and she became one of the "swing votes" on the court that helped keep the basic principles behind *Roe v. Wade* intact. Attempts to pass constitutional amendments restricting abortion or permitting school prayer languished as the administration focused on more pressing priorities related to the economy and the Cold War.

The debate over abortion was one part of a broader clash over the respective roles of women and men in society, church, and families. The Equal Rights Amendment formed battle lines over such issues in the 1970s. The ERA passed through Congress and went out to the states for ratification in 1972. Mainline denominations tended to support the ERA, seeing it as related to women's ordination as pastors, which they also generally supported. The United Methodist Church began ordaining women clergy in the 1950s, and in the mid-1970s they adopted a pro-ERA statement at their quadrennial General Conference.

"The Gospel makes clear that Jesus regarded women and men as being of equal worth. Nowhere is it recorded that Jesus treated women in a different manner than he did men. . . . All United Methodists [should] work through the appropriate structures and channels toward ratification of the amendment." Conversely, evangelicals, fundamentalists, Mormons, and Catholics tended to oppose the ERA.

Phyllis Schlafly

Traditional Christian women were at the forefront of opposition to the ERA. Most prominent was the Catholic activist Phyllis Schlafly, likely the person in America most responsible for the ERA's demise. Schlafly thought the ERA was based on a fundamentally flawed assumption about the equivalence of men and women. Males and females, fathers and mothers, and boys and girls were not the same, Schlafly insisted. She believed that there were important differences between the sexes that needed to be reflected in law. If men and women were exactly the same, she asked, would women become subject to the military draft and fight on the front lines of battles? Would courts no longer compel child or spousal support from negligent fathers? Would activist lawyers make men and women share public bathrooms? Schlafly convinced many Americans that the ERA was a Trojan horse that radical liberals wanted to sneak into the Constitution. "If the women's libbers want to reject marriage and motherhood, it's a free country and that is their choice," Schlafly said. "But let's not permit these women's libbers to get away with pretending to speak for the rest of us. Let's not permit this tiny minority to degrade the role that most women prefer." For Schlafly, Falwell, and other Christian conservatives, the transformations of the 1970s were being imposed by a secular elite. Traditionalists could stop them, but they needed to mobilize to do so.

Questions about women's roles also helped precipitate the most tumultuous denominational controversy of the late twentieth century, the conservative resurgence in the Southern Baptist Convention, the nation's largest Protestant denomination. Small numbers of women had received ordination as pastors in northern Baptist churches since the 1880s, but the SBC did not ordain any female pastors until the 1960s. By the 1980s, the SBC had ordained hundreds of women, though relatively few of them became senior pastors. Progressives within the SBC were following the example of mainline Protestant denominations in slowly accepting women's ordination, while conservative Protestants and the Roman Catholic Church prohibited women from formal pastoral roles. Traditionalist Christians interpreted a variety of Bible passages as limiting senior spiritual leadership in the church to men.

Concern over women's roles and over the Equal Rights Amendment bolstered SBC traditionalists' efforts in the conservative resurgence. They sought to take control of SBC agencies and seminaries and to make the SBC leadership uniformly conservative on women's roles and the inerrancy of Scripture. Mobilizing pastors and "messengers" to the SBC annual meeting, conservatives repeatedly elected their candidates as SBC president, who appointed reliably conservative faculty and officials at SBC schools and agencies. Prior to 1979, the SBC tended to equivocate about culture war questions—or even to adopt liberal resolutions on them. By 1980, the SBC began to assert consistently conservative positions. That year, they adopted a resolution calling for a pro-life amendment to the Constitution. They also opposed the Equal Rights Amendment, saying that they affirmed the "biblical role which stresses the equal worth but not always the sameness of function of women." Changes to the SBC's Baptist Faith and Message, a foundational statement of Southern Baptist beliefs, stipulated that a wife should "submit herself graciously to the servant leadership of her husband" (1998) and that "the office of pastor is limited to men as qualified by Scripture" (2000). By the time of these changes, the triumph of the SBC conservatives was complete.

The SBC's dominance in southern culture had made it an exceptional denomination even before the conservative resurgence. Before 1979, the SBC was neither a mainline denomination nor a fully evangelical one. SBC conservatives took control of the denomination not only in hopes that they could preserve biblical faithfulness but also to prevent the kind of precipitous decline in attendance that had devastated mainline churches since the 1960s. Major mainline denominations included the United Methodist Church, the Presbyterian Church (USA), the Evangelical Lutheran Church in America, and the Episcopal Church. These groups had enjoyed disproportionate resources and cultural power, and in the 1950s they still claimed a large portion of American Protestant church attendees. Mainline churches' membership hit its high point in 1966, when together they represented more than 28 million members. In the decades that followed, mainline churches saw a decline in membership and attendance, shrinking to about 20 million members by 2003.* The SBC would face its own decline ahead, though, as its membership peaked in 2003 at 16.3 million and dropped to about 15.2 million by 2016.

A number of other conservative and Pentecostal denominations, as well as independent "megachurches," would enjoy significant growth beginning in the 1970s. Leading Pentecostal denominations, including

---

* Estimates of denominational adherents can vary widely, but these numbers are taken from Charles Lippy, *Faith in America* (Westport, CT: Praeger, 2006), 1:4.

the Assemblies of God and the Church of God in Christ, grew by millions globally. In the United States, the expansion of the Assemblies of God was marked especially among Hispanics. Throughout the Americas, including in the United States, there was a sharp increase in the number of Hispanic Protestants, most of it benefiting Pentecostal congregations. Meanwhile, much of the white growth in the Assemblies of God was among immigrants from Eastern Europe. Some historically white and native-born denominations, such as the traditionalist Presbyterian Church in America, founded in 1974 as the result of schism within the mainline Presbyterian denomination, also advanced in numbers.

The SBC and the Presbyterian Church in America would also witness a renewal of Calvinist and Reformed theology. After the conservative resurgence, the role of Calvinist theology became one of the most divisive issues within the SBC, driving a wedge between some Southern Baptist traditionalists. Some SBC conservatives argued that Calvinist theology and its emphasis on predestination did not accord with "traditional" Baptist beliefs and evangelism. Baptists sympathetic to Calvinism pointed out that in the aftermath of the First Great Awakening of the 1700s, most Baptists in America were Calvinists. Under the leadership of Albert Mohler, Southern Baptist Theological Seminary in Louisville, Kentucky, eventually became one of the strongholds not only of the conservative resurgence but also of Reformed theology among Baptists. The northern Baptist pastor and writer John Piper, founder of the popular Desiring God ministry and website, would also advocate Calvinist belief in evangelical circles. Likewise, The Gospel Coalition, a multidenominational, multiethnic evangelical website, where I currently blog, became a center for Reformed evangelical perspectives.

Many denominations grew partly due to people switching from one church to another. Religious increases in modern America have been disproportionately due to immigration, however. This immigrant-led ascendancy transpired across a number of faiths, not just Christianity. Changes in American law in 1965 meant that immigration to the United

States followed a more fully global pattern than in previous decades. Immigrants from the Middle East and Asia established a more vital presence for Islam, Buddhism, and Hinduism, and other non-Christian religions. Estimates suggest that more than a million Muslims moved to the United States in the three decades following the 1965 immigration law, for example. By the beginning of the twenty-first century, two-thirds of American Muslims were first-generation immigrants. Many of these Muslims were fleeing war and persecution in their homelands, including places such as Lebanon, Iran, and Somalia. Other Muslim people came for economic opportunity in the United States. By the 2000s, the largest cohort of immigrant Muslims in the United States had come from Arab nations, and the second largest from South Asian nations such as Pakistan. More than 10 percent of American Muslims were from Iran alone, with many Iranians fleeing to the United States in the wake of the 1979 fundamentalist Iranian revolution of the Ayatollah Khomeini. Many non-Muslim Americans have worried about the threat of jihadist terrorism related to Muslims in America, especially after the terrorist attacks of September 11, 2001. But most Muslim immigrants, especially those who escaped from Iran after 1979, have been resistant to Islamic fundamentalism, and many came to the United States due to their own fear of jihadist violence and persecution in their home countries.

Judaism remained the largest non-Christian religion in the United States in the 1970s and '80s, as it has until the present day. Yet immigration, birth rates, and marriage patterns for Muslims and adherents of other non-Christian religions have caused them to grow faster than American Judaism. Orthodox Jews have also tended to have more children than their moderate and liberal counterparts, so practicing American Jews became more traditionalist as time passed.

After 1965, immigration and declining commitment to "cultural" Christianity made the American religious landscape more diverse, with growing numbers of Americans no longer fitting Will Herberg's classic 1950s triad of "Protestant-Catholic-Jew." But immigration to the United States was still dominated by Christians, bolstering the ranks of American Catholics and Protestants, groups which would have seen more significant declines if they were attended by native-born Americans alone. Such immigration became one of the most significant developments in twentieth-century American religious history, a development often overlooked. Mexicans and other Central American immigrants, overwhelmingly Christian at least by background, were the largest cohort of immigrants to America. Most Hispanics were affiliated with Catholicism, but Latinos who were not Catholics increasingly joined Pentecostal or other kinds of Protestant churches. Christians were also overrepresented among immigrants from East and southeast Asia (China, South Korea, Vietnam), sub-Saharan Africa, and the Middle East.

Chaldean Church and Center, Sterling Heights, Michigan

In addition to Muslims, many Eastern Orthodox and Maronite and Chaldean Catholic Christians immigrated to the United States. Arab Americans were divided roughly in half between people of Muslim and of Christian background. Starting in the late nineteenth century, the metropolitan Detroit area had developed distinctive pockets of Muslim and Christian Arab communities in suburbs such as Dearborn and Sterling Heights. Detroit would become the American center of the Iraqi-based Chaldean Catholic Church, with the diocese, or "eparchy," of St. Thomas the Apostle of Detroit numbering more than 100,000 adherents in 2014. Many Iraqi Christians fled their homeland during the Iran-Iraq War of the 1980s, or in the years following the 2003 US invasion of Iraq and the Islamic State of Iraq and Syria persecution during the 2010s.

The decades since the 1970s saw the advent of many "megachurches." Evangelical and Pentecostal Christians have often gravitated toward large congregations with an array of resources that most smaller congregations could not match. Scholars conventionally have counted a megachurch as one with more than two thousand attenders or members. Some of these congregations attracted substantial numbers of new converts or formerly unaffiliated Christians, but many of their attendees switched from other churches. Some of what would become the largest megachurches, such as Houston's Second Baptist Church, the Los Angeles–area Saddleback Church, and Dallas-area Fellowship Church, were at least nominally connected with the Southern Baptist Convention or another traditional Protestant denomination. Saddleback was founded in 1980 by Pastor Rick Warren, who later became known for his bestselling 2002 book *The Purpose Driven Life*. Other congregations, such as Fellowship Church, came to meet in multiple locations, sometimes across multiple states, and became such large organizations that they took on the character of a small denomination themselves. Fellowship, Saddleback, and the Chicago-area Willow Creek Community Church were all heavily influenced by the "seeker-sensitive" movement, which held that churches should be as accessible as possible to people who did not grow up in church. Contemporary music and media were omnipresent in seeker-sensitive churches, some of which also downplayed technical or grim details of Christian theology, such as sin and hell, in their main Sunday services. Mainline megachurches, however, were rare. Those that did come about tended to be evangelical-leaning congregations of denominations such as the United Methodist Church.

Many of the largest megachurches were independent, and were frequently affiliated with what critics call the "prosperity gospel." The teaching of such churches focused on how to have a godly, successful mindset, and they attributed struggles, poverty, and sickness to Satanic attacks or defeatist, ungodly thinking. By the 2010s, about half of the American congregations with 10,000 members or more were influenced by the prosperity gospel. Although prosperity gospel churches have often been considered "evangelical," many evangelicals and some Pentecostals, the traditions from which many prosperity gospel churches sprang, regard them as theologically aberrant, at best. By the early twenty-first century, the largest megachurch was Joel and Victoria Osteen's Lakewood Church in Houston, which met in an arena that was formerly home to the Houston Rockets professional basketball team. Attendance at Lakewood in the early 2010s approached forty thousand for weekend services.

Joel Osteen's Southern Baptist father, John, founded Lakewood in the 1950s, but John later embraced charismatic theology and broke ties with the SBC. John Osteen developed a popular television program, but Lakewood shot to new heights of fame when Joel Osteen succeeded his father in 1999. Osteen still articulated some traditional evangelical emphases on salvation and the importance of the Bible, but his signature messages focused on victory and embracing "your best life now," as he put it in his wildly popular book of the same name. Osteen proclaimed that Christians had victorious living as their birthright. "You have the DNA of Almighty God," he said. "You need to know that inside you flows the blood of a winner."

By the Reagan era, much of American Christianity displayed a peculiar combination of continued demographic growth (at least outside of the mainline denominations) and a nearly desperate sense of embattledness. Intensifying the cultural battles of the 1970s and '80s were continuing controversies over religion and education. Dating back at least to the Scopes Trial, children's education was often a forum for fierce cultural-religious combat. Following the school prayer and Bible rulings of the 1960s, parents and educators continued to fight over what to teach children about human origins and evolution. In some states, antievolution educational laws remained on the books. A unanimous Supreme Court struck down such laws as unconstitutional in the 1968 case *Epperson v. Arkansas*. The court judged that an Arkansas law forbidding the teaching of evolutionary theory raised problems related to free speech. The law also represented an establishment of religion, the court averred, in the form of religiously based teaching about human origins.

Christian opponents of evolution realized they could no longer rely on biblical interpretation alone to make the case for God's creation of humanity, as biblical authority no longer commanded the cultural respect it had in the 1950s and earlier decades. Many antievolution activists also wanted to demonstrate that, contrary to the conclusions of most geologists, the Earth was relatively young. Thus began what came to be called "creation science." A "young Earth" would confirm the literal six days of creation and the generations of mankind in the Hebrew Bible, and creation science advocates calculated that the world was less than ten thousand years old, as opposed to the mainstream consensus that Earth was billions of years old. Perhaps the most influential proponent of creation science was the engineering professor Henry Morris, whose *The Genesis Flood* (1961) interpreted the layers and fossils of Earth's geology as resulting from the catastrophe of Noah's flood rather than eons of slow-developing strata and sediment.

Other traditional Christians accepted "old Earth" theory, just as William Jennings Bryan had. However, they rejected evolution as unduly speculative and theologically corrosive to beliefs such as the special creation of men and women in God's image. Morris and other critics of evolution commonly possessed earned doctorates at research universities, though their degrees were often in engineering and other fields besides biology or geology. Together they forged an alternative scholarly apparatus for creation science that many Christian schools and homeschoolers used. Morris and other creation scientists founded the Institute for Creation Research in 1972, which became one of the leading disseminators of antievolutionary beliefs.

Since *Epperson* had struck down laws forbidding the teaching of evolution, some states began adopting new laws that required teachers to balance the teaching of evolution with creation science. The American Civil Liberties Union initiated lawsuits against such "balance" laws in Arkansas and Louisiana. In 1987's *Edwards v. Aguillard*, a Supreme Court majority found that balancing evolution and creation science also represented a violation of the First Amendment's establishment clause. The laws in question advanced a religious purpose, the court insisted, in the teaching of creationism. Justices William Rehnquist and Antonin Scalia dissented, however, with Scalia writing that he believed that the "Court's position is the repressive one. The people of Louisiana, including those who are Christian fundamentalists, are quite entitled, as a secular matter, to have whatever scientific evidence there may be against evolution presented in their schools, just as Mr. Scopes [of the Scopes Trial in 1925] was entitled to present whatever scientific evidence there was for it." By 1987, conservative judges such as Rehnquist and Scalia had begun to question whether the establishment clause was being used to place special disadvantages on religious belief, especially in schools. Opponents of creation science argued, however, that it was traditionalist theology posing as science, and it had no place in credible scientific instruction.

Distraught by the removal of prayer and Bible reading, and by the promulgation of evolutionary theory, conservative Christians developed their own system of schools and curricula starting in the 1960s and '70s. Catholics had long cultivated parochial schools in response to the Protestant-dominated public school system of the 1800s and early 1900s. Now many traditionalist Protestants suspected that public schools effectively represented a secularist and proevolution establishment. Thus they developed new evangelical and fundamentalist academies. Evangelicals had maintained a network of institutions of higher learning for decades, such as Wheaton College (1860) in Chicago and Gordon College (1889) in Massachusetts. Fundamentalists had also created schools such as Bob Jones University (1927). Distinctively Christian education became more common at the elementary and secondary levels. Catholic and Protestant parents often argued that they should receive tax relief or "vouchers" to help pay for private schooling, since school districts still required that they pay taxes to support public schools. Teachers' unions and secularist organizations such as the American Civil Liberties Union objected that doing so would undermine the public schools and entail government aid to religion.

Homeschooling became more common starting in the 1980s. Homeschooling attracted a wide variety of adherents, but it especially appealed to Christian parents who believed they should personally offer holistic religious education to their children. Christian homeschool pioneers Raymond and Dorothy Moore wrote in *Home Grown Kids* (1981) that "the family was given to us by the same God in whom our country trusts." Americans had "gone a long, long way toward putting it down and substituting parenting-by-state. . . . We would do well to look again to God and the home," they advised. Michael Farris founded the Home School Legal Defense Association in 1983, which served as a legal resource for prospective homeschool parents, who often found that school districts put up legal barriers to homeschooling. States would adopt a wide variety of approaches toward homeschooling families, varying from imposing heavy bureaucratic requirements on them to allowing them to operate with virtually no oversight. Farris later founded the evangelical Patrick Henry College in Virginia in 1998, which catered to students from Christian homeschooling backgrounds.

Traditionalist Christians in the 1970s and '80s vacillated in their stance toward dominant American society. The Moral Majority and the evangelical alliance with the Republican Party signaled a renewed establishmentarian impulse in which Christians sought to influence the political order and to bring their values back into the public sphere. Their record in the culture war battles was mixed. *Roe v. Wade* and decisions about teaching creation science suggested to conservative Christians that they were being pushed to the margins of American society. On those margins, some Christians built alternative schools and forged subcultural educational realms such as creation science and homeschooling. Overall, the educational and cultural changes of the post-1965 era left many Christian traditionalists wondering whether they should seek to reclaim the nation or retreat from a secular American Babylon.

WORKS CITED
AND FURTHER READING

Allitt, Patrick. *Religion in America Since 1945: A History*. New York: Columbia University Press, 2003.

The Book of Resolutions of the United Methodist Church. Nashville: Abingdon, 1996.

Bowler, Kate. *Blessed: A History of the American Prosperity Gospel*. New York: Oxford University Press, 2013.

Critchlow, Donald T., and Nancy MacLean, eds. *Debating the American Conservative Movement, 1945 to the Present*. Lanham, MD: Rowman & Littlefield, 2009.

Dowland, Seth. *Family Values and the Rise of the Christian Right.* Philadelphia: University of Pennsylvania Press, 2015.

Gaither, Milton. *Homeschool: An American History.* 2nd ed. New York: Palgrave Macmillan, 2017.

Garrett, W. Barry. "High Court Holds Abortion to be 'A Right of Privacy.'" *Baptist Press*, January 31, 1973, 1.

Hankins, Barry. *Uneasy in Babylon: Southern Baptist Conservatives and American Culture.* Tuscaloosa: University of Alabama Press, 2002.

Harding, Susan Friend. *The Book of Jerry Falwell: Fundamentalist Language and Politics.* Princeton, NJ: Princeton University Press, 2000.

Harvey, Paul, and Philip Goff, eds. *The Columbia Documentary History of Religion in America Since 1945.* New York: Columbia University Press, 1945.

Hevesi, Dennis. "Mildred Jefferson, 84, Anti-Abortion Activist, Is Dead." *New York Times*, October 18, 2010, B19.

Leonard, Bill J. *Baptists in America.* New York: Columbia University Press, 2005.

Miller, Steven P. *The Age of Evangelicalism: America's Born-Again Years.* New York: Oxford University Press, 2014.

Muñoz, Vincent Phillip. *Religious Liberty and the American Supreme Court: The Essential Cases and Documents.* Updated ed. Lanham, MD: Rowman & Littlefield, 2013.

Numbers, Ronald L. *The Creationists.* New York: Alfred A. Knopf, 1992.

Williams, Daniel K. *Defenders of the Unborn: The Pro-Life Movement Before Roe v. Wade.* New York: Oxford University Press, 2016.

Williams, Daniel K. *God's Own Party: The Making of the Christian Right.* New York: Oxford University Press, 2010.

Chapter 14

Immigration, Religious Diversity, and the Culture Wars

Classic secularization theory once held that traditional religious belief would not survive in the modern world. As late as the 1960s, scholars such as the anthropologist Anthony F. C. Wallace contended that "the evolutionary future of religion is extinction" and that "belief in supernatural powers is doomed to die out, all over the world." The belief was that supernaturalism would become marginal and irrelevant as naturalist thought spread. Yet the late twentieth century dealt a severe blow to classic secularization theory, as the world saw global revitalization of traditionalist faith among Muslims, Hindus, Catholics, Protestants, and others.

Catholicism, for example, seemed locked into a modernizing shift with the changes introduced by Vatican II in the 1960s. Church officials and much of the Catholic laity, however, did not envision Vatican II as inaugurating a Catholicism tailored for modern sensibilities. In

1968, Pope Paul VI issued the landmark encyclical *Humanae vitae* ("On Human Life"). There had been much discussion in the Catholic hierarchy about liberalizing the church's traditional opposition to birth control, but Paul VI used *Humanae vitae* to reaffirm the value of life from conception to death. Specifically, the pope restated the church's belief that married couples should not use artificial means to stop the conception of children. In an era of sexual experimentation, the birth control pill, abortion rights, and fears about overpopulation, *Humanae vitae* ran against prevailing trends. Many American Catholic laypeople, even those who attended mass regularly, did not abide by the church's teaching on contraception. However, other Catholics reveled in the classic Catholic emphasis on the value of children and in the way that *Humanae vitae* set their faith apart from modern secular norms. Many other religious Americans similarly found enduring spiritual vitality in the way that their faith contrasted with dominant social trends. But that very contrast often set the stage for harsh conflict over religion in modern America.

No development was more important for Catholic traditionalism than the accession of Poland's Karol Wojtyła as Pope John Paul II in 1978. John Paul II, the first non-Italian pope in hundreds of years, became a great champion of anticommunist movements in Poland and elsewhere in Eastern Europe, as well as a powerful advocate for Catholic social traditionalism. Although many Protestants in America still had reservations about Catholics and the papacy, John Paul II charmed many Protestant conservatives. His papacy bolstered an evangelical-Catholic alliance reflected in American periodicals such as *First Things*. Founded in 1990 by the Roman Catholic convert and veteran civil rights activist Father Richard John Neuhaus, *First Things* became one of the most influential platforms for Christian and Jewish traditionalist thought in America. Neuhaus cooperated with evangelical convert Charles

Colson in the 1994 statement "Evangelicals and Catholics Together." Evangelicals and Catholics Together reflected a major diminution of anti-Catholic sentiment among American evangelicals, due in part to evangelicals' admiration for John Paul II. Traditionalist evangelicals and Catholics also often shared more in common by the 1990s than they did with liberals in their own denominations.

John Paul II visit to United States

John Paul II's connection with evangelicals was not merely a matter of shared social concerns. He also had deep familiarity with American evangelicals, having invited Billy Graham to speak in Poland and partnered with Campus Crusade for Christ missionaries in youth ministry there. John Paul's message also resonated with many American Hispanic Christians, both Catholics and Protestants. As we have seen, John Paul canonized Juan Diego as a saint in 2002 and affirmed the most important symbol of Catholicism in the Western Hemisphere, the Virgin of Guadalupe. John Paul emphasized a "new evangelization" program that sought to turn nominal Catholics in Latin America into practicing ones and to deflect Pentecostals' recruiting efforts among

Hispanic Catholics. During his long tenure as pope, the number of Hispanic bishops in the Catholic church grew from just eight to thirty-six. The pope employed an evangelical style of ministry too. One Hispanic minister who attended a 1987 papal mass at Los Angeles Coliseum reflected that the meeting could have been "a Billy Graham crusade."

Immigrants to the United States had always been indispensable to the vitality of the Catholic Church, and that remained the case in the post-1965 period. The American Catholic Church saw an extraordinary decline in mass attendance, the number of nuns, and a slower reduction in the number of priests. Immigration, especially from Latin America, was essential to some parishes, which became dominated by Hispanics and worshipers not born in America. As we have seen, Middle Eastern immigrants represented a host not only of new Muslims in America but also of Catholic and Orthodox Christians. Many Vietnamese people also immigrated to the United States in the 1970s as a result of the communist take-over of their home nation. These immigrants often settled in cities such as San Jose, California, Houston, or the Dallas-Fort Worth area. Vietnamese immigrants were disproportionately Buddhist or Catholic by background.

Vietnamese Buddhists founded temples in American cities, especially in California and Texas. Vietnamese Buddhist nun Thich Dam Luu helped to establish the Perfect

Buddhist temple in Port Arthur, Texas

Wikimedia Commons, Public Domain

Harmony Temple in San Jose in 1990, which offered adult education courses in Buddhist ritual and philosophy, as well as Vietnamese language classes. Catholics also nurtured parishes catering to Vietnamese immigrants and their children. In 2011, the two thousand-seat Vietnamese Martyrs Catholic Church opened in Arlington, Texas (between

Dallas and Fort Worth), in a former Food Lion grocery store. It was the largest Vietnamese Catholic parish in the United States, and the church honored a group of martyrs from nineteenth-century Vietnam who had been canonized as saints by John Paul II.

Although immigrants helped to bolster the number and diversity of American Catholics in the decades since 1965, these fresh adherents could not compensate entirely for the terrible struggles the church was enduring. Native-born and immigrant Catholics alike were affected by the Catholic sexual abuse scandal, which became a crippling global crisis following revelations in the Boston archdiocese in 2002. Pulitzer Prize–winning coverage by the *Boston Globe* newspaper made the city's sex abuse scandal national news. Catholics demanded accountability from church leaders as thousands of accusations of abuse and cover-ups mounted around the globe. Countless Catholic laypeople became disaffected or left the church altogether.

Protestants had their own scandals too. The crimes and dalliances of televangelists such as Jimmy Swaggart and Jim Bakker made for sensational media storylines in the 1980s. Likewise, in 2006 the charismatic megachurch pastor Ted Haggard, who was also president of the National Association of Evangelicals, fell into disrepute when it came to light that he had engaged the services of a male prostitute. The fact that Haggard had publicly advocated against gay marriage in Colorado added to the hypocritical aspect of the episode. The apparently vital piety of figures such as Swaggart and Haggard made them ripe for media scandal when their sins came to light. The Southern Baptist Convention also faced a series of charges about sexual abuse in its churches, culminating in a *Houston Chronicle* exposé in 2019 that documented the experiences of more than seven hundred victims over a twenty-year period.

Immigration changed the character of American Protestantism too. In a way, the change for Protestants due to mass immigration was more stark, as American Catholicism had been an immigrant-driven faith since the nineteenth century. The changes to US immigration law in 1965 represented the hinge of change; Protestant churches afterward showed major signs of infusions of adherents from around the globe. As with Catholics, Hispanics represented the most prominent immigrant group among Protestants. From Los Angeles to Boston, churches saw substantial growth in Latino Protestants. In Los Angeles County alone, the number of Hispanic Protestant churches rose from 227 to 687 between 1971 and 1986. The growth was disproportionately reflected in Pentecostal churches, especially denominations such as the Assemblies of God (AG) and the Apostolic Assemblies of the Faith in Christ Jesus, a Hispanic-led Pentecostal denomination that traces its origins to the 1906 Azusa Street revival.

Latino Pentecostal Church in Silver Spring, Maryland

Although the hippie-led "Jesus movement" of the 1960s and '70s received more media attention, the growth of Pentecostalism among Hispanics during the same era brought equally monumental changes to American Protestantism. Some Pentecostals made inroads into the gang cultures of New York and Los Angeles. The best-known instance of this trend was the conversion of New York Puerto Rican gang leader Nicky Cruz, whose relationship with evangelist David Wilkerson was depicted in the bestselling 1962 book *The Cross and the Switchblade* and in the 1970 movie of the same name. Cruz founded an evangelistic ministry with special emphasis on reaching gang members. One of Cruz's most influential converts was Sonny Arguinzoni, also a Puerto Rican New Yorker, who established Victory Outreach/Alcance Victoria in Los Angeles. Arguinzoni set up an international network of drug rehab centers, rescue shelters, and hundreds of churches affiliated with Victory Outreach.

By the 1980s, Hispanic Pentecostalism had become a major force on the American Protestant scene, especially in denominations such as the AG. Perhaps the most influential Hispanic Protestant leader of the late twentieth century was AG pastor Jesse Miranda. Miranda grew up in Albuquerque, New Mexico, as the son of Mexican mill worker. His family developed a deep attachment to the AG when his mother experienced physical healing at an AG service. Miranda went on to receive a doctorate from Fuller Seminary and became the most visible Hispanic leader in the AG. In 1985 he gave a keynote address at an AG national convention, the first Latino speaker to do so. He served as the district superintendent of the AG's Pacific Latin American District and founded Alianza de Ministerios Evangélicos Nacionales (AMEN), the leading Hispanic evangelical advocacy organization of the era. In 2006 AMEN merged with the National Hispanic Christian Leadership Conference (NHCLC), headed by Miranda's protégé Samuel Rodriguez. Miranda and Rodriguez became sought-after Hispanic Christian leaders in media and political circles, with presidents from Ronald Reagan to Donald Trump consulting them on Hispanic-related issues. Although Hispanic evangelicals' relationship with President Trump was strained by differences over immigration policy, Rodriguez delivered a prayer at Trump's inauguration in 2017.

As immigration quietly changed Catholic and Protestant churches, political controversies garnered the most headlines about American religion. Jerry Falwell stepped down as the head of the Moral Majority in 1987 and the group disbanded in 1989. Yet American Christians' fraught relationship with political power continued to be a major issue. The 1988 presidential campaign saw starkly opposed versions of Christians in presidential politics with the candidacies of Jesse Jackson (Democrat) and Pat Robertson (Republican).

Robertson was the host of *The 700 Club*. His show combined conservative political news with charismatic Christian ministry, including prayers for healing and "words of knowledge" about people's specific afflictions. Robertson's charismatic convictions created tension with other Christian right leaders, including Jerry Falwell. Still, his huge media platform made Robertson a formidable primary candidate. Robertson insisted that Christians needed to be politically assertive. He aspired to not just advise the Republican establishment but to take control of it, and he scored a surprising second-place finish in the bellwether Iowa caucuses. Ultimately, he was overwhelmed by the GOP establishment's choice, Vice President George H. W. Bush. Bush was a moderate Episcopalian and no evangelical, but as the South Carolina primary loomed, Bush affirmed that Jesus was his "personal savior." Such catering to the Christian right had become necessary for Republican candidates by 1988, and it helped carry George H. W. Bush to the presidency.

The African American civil rights leader Jesse Jackson ran for the Democratic presidential nomination in 1984 and 1988. Jackson worked with Martin Luther King in the later years of King's life. In 1971 Jackson founded Operation PUSH (People United to Save Humanity), a civil rights organization focused on economic justice and opportunity. Jackson sought to revitalize a Democratic coalition defending the rights of the poor and ethnic minorities. Similar to the

Christian right's commitment to the GOP, black Protestants tended overwhelmingly to support Democrats by the 1970s. Jackson had little chance of securing the Democratic nomination himself. However, his performance, including eleven primary or caucus wins in 1988, paved the way for Barack Obama, a product of the progressive black church in Chicago. Obama successfully ran for president twenty years after Jackson's 1988 campaign.

On the GOP side of the aisle, the closing of the Moral Majority and the failure of Robertson's candidacy hardly signaled a decline of conservative Christian activism. The 1988 campaign showed Robertson that he had the makings of a national political network. He tasked the young operative Ralph Reed with turning that network into an enduring organization, which became the Christian Coalition. Reed brought political sophistication and a certain ruthlessness that the Christian right had lacked until 1990 when the Christian Coalition opened. Reed helped white conservatives maximize their political advantages, focusing on issues such as late-term and partial-birth abortions and openly gay servicemen in the military. Reed hoped that through an emphasis on such issues, which a broad range of Americans opposed, the Christian Coalition could build bridges to conservative Americans who might not be practicing evangelicals.

Christian conservatives also rallied around the cause of religious liberty in reaction to court decisions such as *Edwards v. Aguillard*, which seemed to curtail Christians' roles in the public sphere. For a time, there was an overwhelming bipartisan consensus in favor of protecting religious liberty, illustrated in the nearly unanimous congressional passage of the Democratic-sponsored Religious Freedom Restoration Act (1993). That act was inspired by the Supreme Court decision of *Employment Division v. Smith* (1990), which denied legal protections to Native Americans fired from their jobs for the ritual use of the psychoactive drug peyote. After 1993, the most prominent religious liberty claims typically focused on Christians' rights.

One of the most important institutional reflections of the fight for religious liberty was the Alliance Defense Fund (later the Alliance Defending Freedom), a legal advocacy group founded in 1993 by evangelical stalwarts such as Bill Bright of Campus Crusade for Christ and James Dobson of Focus on the Family. Dobson had earlier founded the influential Family Research Council, whose president Gary Bauer made his own short-lived run for president in 2000. The Christian Coalition, Alliance Defending Freedom, and Family Research Council joined with more broadly conservative groups such as the Heritage Foundation to bolster Christian conservative lobbying, campaign advocacy, and legal work.

Popular forms of evangelical faith became more culturally pervasive in the 1990s too. Concerns about the family and Christian masculinity shaped Promise Keepers, a series of stadium rallies for Christian men. Promise Keepers was the brainchild of University of Colorado football coach Bill McCartney, whose formerly dismal team had won the national championship in 1990. McCartney parlayed his newfound fame into a platform for Promise Keepers. Although he came out of a Catholic background, McCartney had experienced conversion though Campus Crusade for Christ, and in 1988 he began attending a Vineyard Church, one of the denominations produced by the Jesus movement of the 1960s. Having struggled with alcohol abuse and having committed marital infidelity, the repentant McCartney felt that God was leading him to start a mass movement of Christian husbands who would keep their promises to God, their wives, and their kids.

Promise Keeper rallies in cavernous stadiums featured emotional appeals by pastors from a range of churches and ethnic backgrounds. They called on attendees to reassert themselves, with God's power, as the "servant leaders" of their homes, and say no to the temptations of affairs, alcohol, and workaholism. The ethnic diversity of Promise Keepers stood in contrast to the largely white leadership of the Christian right, but Promise Keepers still had political overtones. McCartney touted his support for the pro-life cause and for traditional heterosexual marriage. The latter was a response to some states, including

McCartney's Colorado, beginning to attempt to liberalize marriage laws by the early 1990s in order to include gay and lesbian couples.

Evangelical influence on popular culture was also reflected in Christian literature. Christian novels and books of pop theology had been staples of American culture from *Uncle Tom's Cabin* before the Civil War to Hal Lindsey's *The Late Great Planet Earth*, one of the most popular books of the 1970s. Lindsey had also illustrated the American reading public's appetite for end-times books, a desire that Tim LaHaye and Jerry Jenkins exploited in the wildly popular *Left Behind* series of the 1990s and 2000s. LaHaye was a longtime Christian right leader who worked with Jenkins to spin a compelling tale of the end-times "rapture" of true Christians from earth and the rise of the Antichrist. The novels focused on the unbelievers left behind when Christians were taken in the rapture. The series had done well already before the terrorist attacks of September 11, 2001, but the attacks helped set off a publishing bonanza about the last days, and *Left Behind* was the chief beneficiary. The ninth book in the series appeared shortly after 9/11 and became the bestselling book of 2001.

The apocalypticism of *Left Behind* was entertaining and likely comforting to many readers. Yet a similar apocalyptic strain could have terrible consequences for Americans who saw themselves as personally living out end-times scenarios. The 1990s saw tragic confrontations between radical sects and the federal government, who identified the sects as threats to public safety. In 1992, the Federal Bureau of Alcohol, Tobacco, and Firearms (ATF) engaged in a shootout with the family of Christian Identity survivalist Randy Weaver. Weaver had embraced the Christian Identity teachings of white supremacy, anti-Semitism, and apocalyptic fundamentalism, along with its belief that the American government was under the control of a shadowy Zionist Occupation Government. The fight led to the deaths of a federal agent, Weaver's wife, and his teenage son.

David Koresh's Branch Davidian sect of Seventh-day Adventists likewise ran afoul of federal authorities, with horrible results. The Branch

Davidians had existed as a separate sect since the 1930s, but the charismatic Koresh took control of it in the 1980s. Koresh convinced his followers that they were participating in events described in the book of Revelation. Koresh forecast that the people of God would have soon have to war àgainst the power of Antichrist. It was through this lens that the Branch Davidians interpreted the aggression of the ATF, which raided their Mount Carmel compound in central Texas in 1993. The ATF justified the raid by citing reports that Koresh was storing assault weapons and sexually preying on children. Yet the ATF attack fed right into Koresh's apocalyptic scenarios, and four agents were killed in the raid.

This led to a seven-week siege that captured the attention of the nation. In the end, the FBI sought to end the siege with another attack on the compound. The Mount Carmel facility caught fire—the reasons for the conflagration are debated—and Koresh and more than a hundred followers, including a number of children, perished in the flames. Critics insisted that the ATF and FBI's tactics virtually guaranteed the siege's deadly conclusion. The attacks on Weaver and on the Branch Davidians spurred more sectarian conspiracy theories, especially as the internet became a breeding ground for unusual religious and political views in the mid-1990s. The Weaver and Branch Davidian tragedies were also among the grievances that Timothy McVeigh cited to explain his terrorist bombing of an Oklahoma City federal building in 1995.

Additionally, strange combinations of New Age thought, utopianism, and apocalypticism led to two of the worst episodes of religiously based mass suicide and killings in American history: Jim Jones's People's Temple and the Heaven's Gate sect. Jones's People's Temple began in Indianapolis as an offshoot of the Disciples of Christ but soon became consumed with what Jones called Apostolic Socialism. In the mid-1960s, he and more than a hundred of his followers relocated to a California commune. Jones made increasingly extravagant claims about himself, saying he could raise the dead. As Jones's ministry came under increased scrutiny, he took his followers—now almost a thousand people—to Guyana in South America, where they built a settlement called Jonestown. The move to Guyana set in motion Jones's final doomsday scenario. In 1978, members of an investigating American delegation, including a congressman and several journalists, were attacked and shot by Jones's henchmen. Jones then instructed his followers to drink cyanide-laced Flavor Aid, and those who would not voluntarily take it were apparently poisoned. More than nine hundred people died, including many children.

An assortment of New Age thought, belief in extraterrestrials, and biblical apocalypse also informed the Heaven's Gate cult, founded by Marshall Applewhite and Bonnie Lu Nettles. The two leaders believed they were experiencing scenarios forecast in the book of Revelation. When Nettles died in 1985, Applewhite soldiered on with their end-times message. The group, which had at times attracted hundreds of members, practiced radical communal living. Applewhite taught that God was preparing his people to leave their physical bodies behind on earth and enter the kingdom. Demonic spirits were deceiving world leaders and encouraging people to live a bourgeois lifestyle, he said. Applewhite interpreted the 1995 Hale-Bopp comet as a divine signal for the commune members, who were then living in Rancho Santa Fe, California, to make the decisive break with their bodies. At his behest, the group ingested a deadly combination of alcohol and medicine. Thirty-nine commune members, including Applewhite, died.

The enduring vitality of traditional faith, along with the prominence of secularism in elite cultural circles, made for explosive encounters that escalated during the 1990s. Secular liberals, typically Democrats, and religious conservatives, typically Republicans, jousted regularly on the battleground of politics. Not that these political-religious camps were the only options. There were many traditionalist Christian African Americans who reliably voted for Democrats, and there were secular Republicans who cared little for the conservative Christians in the

GOP. Still, activists and the media often framed the great political wars of the 1990s as Republican Christians versus Democratic secularists. Conservative writer Pat Buchanan, a Catholic, depicted the clash in memorable terms at the 1992 GOP convention. "There is a religious war going [on] in this country," he declared. "It is a cultural war, as critical to the kind of nation we shall be as the Cold War itself. For this war is for the soul of America."

For critics such as Buchanan, 1992 Democratic nominee Bill Clinton was aligned with the forces of secular humanism. Clinton was all the more dangerous, white conservatives believed, because he had a background in southern Christian culture. Growing up as a Baptist in Arkansas, Clinton knew the language of faith and was comfortable speaking about his own beliefs. Yet he and his wife Hillary Rodham Clinton, who was deeply influenced by her Methodist upbringing, affirmed legalized abortion and the rights of gays and lesbians. Clinton defeated George H. W. Bush in the 1992 election and went on to craft the "don't ask, don't tell" policy that made a way for practicing homosexuals to serve quietly in the military. President Clinton also repeatedly vetoed laws banning partial-birth abortion, a controversial and rare procedure used in late-term pregnancies.

The controversies over Clinton's presidency came to a head when congressional Republicans impeached and sought to remove Clinton for perjury and other offenses related to his affair with White House intern Monica Lewinsky. The press had tended to overlook evidence of earlier indiscretions by presidents such as Franklin Roosevelt and John Kennedy. Clinton faced a twenty-four-hour cable news cycle and rage about his presidency from Christian conservatives. The president made his situation worse by lying about the affair to the American people. Independent counsel Kenneth Starr, an evangelical, produced a detailed report about Clinton's escapades with Lewinsky and the president's efforts to evade responsibility. The House of Representatives impeached Clinton, but in 1999 the Senate failed to remove him. Key GOP leaders including House Speaker Newt Gingrich, who was engaged in an affair too, ended up resigning during the controversy, and Republicans seemed to gain little from their impeachment crusade.

The Clinton-Lewinsky scandal was also one of a series of high-profile controversies in which Americans struggled to find an adequate sexual ethic to replace older conventions jettisoned in the sexual revolutions of the 1960s. Mainstream cultural outlets glorified sexual liberation but seemed uncertain about when, if ever, to classify consensual sexual behavior as immoral.

The 2000 election became a referendum on Clinton, who remained surprisingly popular in spite of the scandal. The contest pitted Vice President Al Gore of Tennessee against Texas governor George W. Bush. Gore, like Clinton, came from a Southern Baptist background. His wife Tipper Gore briefly sided with Christian conservatives in the 1980s when she founded the Parents Music Resource Center, which sought to make parents aware of profane lyrics in some of America's most popular music. Gore chose Connecticut senator Joe Lieberman as his running mate. Lieberman was a devout Modern Orthodox Jew who spoke openly about his faith and was the first Jew to run on a major party presidential ticket in American history. Al Gore's faith had been in flux for most of his adult life, ever since he had enrolled briefly at Vanderbilt Divinity School in the early 1970s. There he began cultivating a religiously themed environmentalism, which became his preeminent concern after his career in politics ended.

Christian conservatives had not coalesced around a political champion since the end of Reagan's presidency, and they had been cool toward George H. W. Bush and the 1996 Republican candidate, Kansas senator Bob Dole. In 2000, Gary Bauer of the Family Research Council made a brief run but failed to recreate Pat Robertson's success in the 1988 primaries. Religious conservatives came to rally around George W. Bush in 2000, who, unlike his father, was comfortable talking about his relationship with Jesus. Bush had experienced conversion in 1984 after years of partying and alcohol abuse. In a 1999 debate, Bush explained that Jesus was his favorite philosopher in history because Jesus had changed his heart. Bush won the allegiance of Christian conservatives, who helped him defeat Gore in one of the narrowest presidential victories in American history.

Taking cues from evangelical professor and journalist Marvin Olasky, Bush as president emphasized "compassionate conservatism" and government partnerships with faith-based charitable organizations. But domestic issues would not define George W. Bush's presidency. The threat of jihadist terrorism and war in the Middle East would be his signature concerns following the terrorist attacks in New York and Washington, DC, on September 11, 2001. Those attacks made the fear of Islamic terrorists one of the defining issues in early twenty-first-century American religion.

WORKS CITED
AND FURTHER READING

Brettell, Caroline B., and Deborah Reed-Danahay. *Civic Engagements: The Citizenship Practices of Indian & Vietnamese Immigrants*. Stanford, CA: Stanford University Press, 2012.

Downen, Robert, Lise Olsen, and John Tedesco. "Abuse of Faith." *Houston Chronicle*, February 10, 2019. https://www.houstonchronicle.com/news/investigations/article/Southern-Baptist-sexual-abuse-spreads-as-leaders-13588038.php.

Finke, Roger, and Rodney Stark. *Acts of Faith: Explaining the Human Side of Religion*. Berkeley: University of California Press, 2000.

Gormley, Ken. *The Death of American Virtue: Clinton vs. Starr*. New York: Crown, 2010.

Harvey, Paul, and Philip Goff, eds. *The Columbia Documentary History of Religion in America Since 1945*. New York: Columbia University Press, 2005.

Hertzke, Allen D. *Echoes of Discontent: Jesse Jackson, Pat Robertson, and the Resurgence of Populism*. Washington, DC: CQ Press, 1993.

Jenkins, Philip. *Mystics and Messiahs: Cults and New Religions in American History.* New York: Oxford University Press, 2000.

Knopf, Christina M. "Al Gore's Rational Faith and Unreasonable Religion." In *What Democrats Talk About When They Talk About God*, 93–113. Edited by David Weiss. Lanham, MD: Rowman & Littlefield, 2010.

Miller, Steven P. *The Age of Evangelicalism: America's Born-Again Years.* New York: Oxford University Press, 2014.

Weigel, George. *Witness to Hope: The Biography of Pope John Paul II.* Updated ed. New York: Harper Perennial, 2004.

Wright, Stuart A. *Armageddon in Waco: Critical Perspectives on the Branch Davidian Conflict.* Chicago: University of Chicago Press, 1995.

epilogue

AMERICAN RELIGION IN THE TWENTY-FIRST CENTURY

Built in 1766, St. Paul's Chapel of Trinity Church, New York City, stands across from the site of the 2001 attacks that destroyed the World Trade Center towers. The colonial-era structure miraculously survived the attacks almost unscathed. It became a quiet refuge of prayer, reflection, and rest for first responders and relief workers in the days after the attacks. Two centuries earlier, St. Paul's had been the site of a worship service attended by George Washington on the day he became the first US president in 1789. The chapel thus reflected the enduring presence of faith and its vitality amid violence, from our nation's earliest days to the travails of the culture war and controversy following 9/11. For most religious Americans, faith has remained a source of daily comfort and hope, even as public debates over religion grow more rancorous and sometimes menacing.

Yet the 9/11 attacks reframed American debates about religion and sharpened the concerns of many Americans about jihadist terrorism. America and Europe had dealt with Muslim-inspired terror for decades, including a 1993 bombing at the World Trade Center that killed six people. The previous worst terrorist attack in American history, the 1995 bombing of the Murrah Federal Building in Oklahoma City, was perpetrated by native-born white antigovernment extremists. The horrific scale of 9/11 transformed Americans' views of Muslims and of terrorism. Jerry Falwell and Pat Robertson speculated on *The 700 Club* shortly after the attacks that they represented the judgment of God on America for its indulgence of "abortionists," "gays," and "Christ-haters." The aging Billy Graham also addressed a national prayer service in the days following 9/11, but President Bush offered the most enduring interpretation of the war on terror. Anticipating the looming American invasion of Afghanistan and later of Iraq, Bush told a joint session of Congress that "freedom and fear, justice and cruelty, have always been at war, and we know that God is not neutral between them."

Library of Congress, Prints & Photographs Division, HABS NY, 31-NEYO, 2–22

Interior of St. Paul's Chapel, New York City

As Falwell and Robertson became more marginal in the 2000s, Billy Graham's son Franklin emerged as a key evangelical Republican insider. He had prayed at President Bush's inauguration in 2001 and insisted upon concluding the prayer with "in Jesus' name." Graham became even better-known after 9/11 when he opined that Islam was an "evil and wicked religion." The evangelical community divided over how to talk about Islam. Some, such as President Bush and missionaries working among Muslims, pled with leaders like Franklin Graham not to denigrate all of the world's one billion Muslims as jihadists. On the American home front, though, evangelical leaders kept up the verbal attacks on Islam and its founder. To the dismay of some Southern Baptist missionaries, prominent Florida Baptist pastor Jerry Vines in 2002 averred that the Prophet Muhammad had been a "demon-possessed pedophile."

By the time of Donald Trump's candidacy in 2016, Franklin Graham had become one of a small number of white evangelical and prosperity gospel leaders who appeared regularly on the Fox News Channel, the key pro-Republican cable news outlet. Partly through the influence of Fox News, "evangelicals" became increasingly seen as white religious Republicans. In spite of differences with many evangelicals over Muslims, President Bush and his adviser Karl Rove had made evangelical mobilization a foundation of their successful 2004 reelection campaign. For the most part, the GOP could count on white evangelical support for their presidential candidates, even when they nominated Mormon Mitt Romney in 2012 and thrice-married Donald Trump in 2016. Christian Republican insiders such as Franklin Graham convinced self-identifying white evangelicals that abortion, homosexual marriage, religious liberty, and the status of the Supreme Court overrode any concerns that they might have about individual Republican candidates. Hispanics, including Hispanic evangelicals, were more divided in their political allegiances, in spite of Samuel Rodriguez's prayer at Donald Trump's 2017 inauguration.

In the early twenty-first century, African American Christians continued their strong attachment to the Democratic Party and liberal politics, even though many African American churches and pastors harbored reservations about Democratic priorities such as legal recognition of gay marriage. The civil rights movement remained relatively decentralized in the 2000s, with no figure emerging in the role once held by Martin Luther King in the 1960s and briefly claimed by Jesse Jackson in the 1980s. In politics, Bill Clinton and especially Barack Obama, who was elected in 2008 and 2012, served as rallying points for members of black churches who carried on the civil rights legacy. Obama was heavily influenced by Chicago's Trinity United Church of Christ and its pastor, the Rev. Jeremiah Wright, though the president resigned his membership at the church in 2008 due to controversial statements that Wright made about God damning America for its racial sins. Obama had attended the church for almost twenty years, and he experienced Christian conversion there. As he recalled in his autobiography, as a young man he set aside his previous skepticism in order to "walk down the aisle of Trinity United Church of Christ one day and be baptized . . . kneeling beneath that cross on the South Side of Chicago, I felt God's spirit beckoning me." Despite Obama's election, the black church has continued at times to attract white contempt and even outbreaks of vandalism and violence, including the Charleston church shooting in 2015.

In academia, Cornel West emerged as among the most accomplished Christian advocates for racial equality. The son of a Baptist minister from Oklahoma, West in 1980 became the first African American to receive a philosophy PhD from Princeton. West held appointments at Harvard, Princeton, and Union Theological Seminary, and he wrote that Christianity resonated with African Americans' enslaved ancestors because the faith was "first and foremost a theodicy, a triumphant account of good over evil." Jesus boldly identified with the "lowly and downtrodden," West noted, and so the Christian faith held existential appeal for poor, marginalized, and oppressed people.

West likewise described the Rev. William Barber II, a North Carolina Disciples of Christ pastor, as "the closest person we have to Martin Luther King Jr. in our midst." Barber, who described himself as a "theologically conservative liberal evangelical biblicist," became one of America's most prominent religious leaders calling for living wages, health care reform, and other initiatives related to the poor and minorities. Barber gave a rousing address at the 2016 Democratic National Convention. Alluding to Donald Trump, Barber declared that "when some want to harden and stop the heart of our democracy, we are being called like our foremothers and fathers to be the moral defibrillator of our time. We must shock this nation with the power of love." Barber's endorsement of Hillary Clinton for president illustrated the enduring commitment of black clergy and churches to the Democratic Party. Just as some white Christian conservatives expressed doubts about Republican leaders' sincerity regarding social conservatism, some African American Christians worried that Democrats only paid lip service to their concerns. Yet many in the black church felt like the Republican Party was not a realistic alternative, especially when it was headed by Donald Trump.

In addition to terrorism and Islam, the most fraught religiously themed issue since 2001 was gay marriage. Key media and academic outlets had heralded sexual freedom and jettisoned the exclusivity of monogamous heterosexual marriage since the 1960s. More than a dozen states still had laws against homosexual acts, or "sodomy," until the Supreme Court decision of *Lawrence v. Texas* (2003) struck down those laws as invasions of privacy. Around the same time, courts began recognizing the unions of homosexual couples. The political tide on gay marriage turned quickly. As late as Barack Obama's first election to the presidency, there was broad bipartisan opposition to recognizing gay marriages, and Obama himself professed to be opposed to legalizing gay marriages per se. By the early 2010s, however, supporting gay marriage had become a signature issue for Democrats. The Supreme Court struck down federal and state laws against gay marriage, culminating in the decision of *Obergefell v. Hodges* (2015). Catholic and evangelical critics argued in response that the legalization of gay marriage undermined the historic purpose of the family. Catholic scholar Ryan Anderson wrote that the court in *Obergefell* falsely concluded "that marriage is an essentially genderless institution," and then it discovered a right to that new vision of marriage in the US Constitution.

Mainline denominations wrestled over performing gay weddings and ordaining homosexual clergy. One of the first women ordained as a priest in the American Episcopal Church in 1977, Ellen Barrett, was a lesbian. In 2003, the Episcopal diocese of New Hampshire elected the practicing homosexual Gene Robinson as a bishop. The US Episcopal Church went on to formally open any ministry position to gays and lesbians and to develop a liturgy to bless homosexual partnerships. These moves shook the worldwide Anglican communion, of which the US Episcopal Church is a part. American and Canadian openness to gay clergy and weddings generated resistance in the fast-growing Anglican churches of sub-Saharan Africa, and among Anglican conservatives in the United States. The Anglican Church in North America (ACNA) emerged as a traditionalist alternative to the Episcopal Church in 2009. ACNA's dioceses and congregations aligned with conservative Anglicans in Africa and South America. Not only did ACNA demonstrate the turmoil in mainline denominations over homosexuality; it also illustrated the growing global connections of Christian traditionalists, especially in denominations with international networks such as the Anglican Church.

The number of religiously unaffiliated Americans grew in the initial decades of the twenty-first century, and as countless news articles noted, increasing numbers of Americans identified as having "no religion," registering more than 20 percent in some polls. The media often called this group the "nones." Scholars debated what the nones actually meant by saying they have "no religion," however. To cite just one statistical oddity, small but significant numbers of nones actually attended church regularly. Perhaps they disliked the term *religion* or were uncertain about their denominational affiliation, so they told pollsters they did not have a religion. Although media reports sometimes portrayed "nones" as atheists, doing so was a mistake. Nones commonly affirmed belief in God (or at least a higher power), the afterlife, and other spiritual realities. The number of self-identified atheists remained steady, at about 3 or 4 percent of Americans.

Popular skeptics also launched new attacks on religion itself. Published critiques of Christianity and the Bible in America date back at least to Thomas Paine's *Age of Reason* (1794). The 2000s saw sensational tirades against Christianity and Islam, launched by writers collectively labeled the "New Atheists." They cast faith in the supernatural as unwarranted, damaging, and delusional. The British-born writer Christopher Hitchens was arguably the most prominent of the New Atheists. In his manifesto *God Is Not Great* (2007), Hitchens asserted that religion "wholly misrepresents the origins of man and the cosmos," that it is rooted in sexual repression, and that it is based in "wish-thinking." The New Atheists' prominence faded after Hitchens's death in 2011. Americans have long stood out as a distinctively religious-minded people as compared to the native-born people of Britain and Western Europe. However, the work of the New Atheists helped give American unbelief greater salience. The New Atheists seemingly made it more socially acceptable to profess no belief in religion.

As the New Atheists garnered media coverage, as well as consternation from traditional believers, a number of mainline denominations kept suffering staggering losses of adherents. Even the evangelical Southern Baptist Convention entered a season of slow decline. There were powerful reasons to believe that American religion in its traditional forms could be poised to follow the religious collapse among western Europeans since the 1950s.

Yet signs of religious vitality remained pervasive too. In general, Pentecostal and charismatic denominations were the fastest-growing in America, fueled by increases in immigrant populations. The Catholic Church likewise was able to mitigate some losses in adherents because of an influx of immigrants, especially from Mexico and Central America. The Assemblies of God saw declining numbers of white adherents from 2001 to 2015, but Hispanics made up for those losses as the denomination approached a "majority-minority" composition. The Church of God (Cleveland, Tennessee) likewise saw major Hispanic growth, with the percentage of Hispanic members rising from 10 to 28 percent between 2007 and 2014. The traditionally African American Church of God in Christ also saw its number of Latinos approach 10 percent of the denomination.

The eclectic spiritual experience of Florida GOP senator Marco Rubio was, perhaps, increasingly typical of American Hispanics. Rubio's Cuban family was traditionally Catholic, but they affiliated for a time with the Mormons. Then Rubio and his wife spent some years attending an evangelical church in Miami, even though Rubio himself reaffirmed his commitment to the Catholic Church. By 2016, Rubio seemed like both a Catholic and an evangelical, and he appealed to voters from both constituencies in his unsuccessful presidential campaign.

Wikimedia Commons, Public Domain

A Spanish-speaking Oneness Pentecostal congregation worshiping at La Iglesia Pentecostal La Senda Antigua, Richmond, Virginia

Maybe the most distinctive religious movements in America by the 2010s were the dynamic ministries *led* by immigrant pastors and missionaries. Hispanic Pentecostal churches were the most common immigrant-led congregations. African Pentecostals, who had a dominant presence in nations such as Nigeria, Kenya, and Ghana, established a more visible role on the American religious landscape since about 1990, and African-born Catholics, evangelicals, and Pentecostals became clergy and frequent attendees of many churches affiliated with historic American denominations. Independent African denominations, especially Pentecostal ones, also established a significant presence in America. Nigerian churches such as the Redeemed Christian Church of God, the Mountain of Fire and Miracles Ministries, and the Winners' Chapel (or Living Faith Church Worldwide) have founded congregations in American cities since 2000.

Our Lady of Vietnam Church

The Redeemed Christian Church of God (RCCG) became especially conspicuous, not least because of its eight-hundred-acre camp and North American headquarters in Floyd, Texas, an exurb of Dallas. According to RCCG North America, most large- and medium-sized cities in America had a RCCG parish by the 2010s, including in towns from Phenix City, Alabama, to Eau Claire, Wisconsin. Such churches often struggled to recruit non-African members, and they did not enjoy the dominant role in the United States that they played in Africa or in Europe, where African Pentecostal congregations were among the largest churches in cities from London to Kiev. Nevertheless, such immigrant-led churches undergirded the social connections and spiritual lives of many recent immigrants to America. These kinds of churches often made little news, unless related to scandal, but they took on an increasingly central role in American religious practice. Churches like the RCCG may be a part of making American Protestantism more diverse in the future than it has been in the past. Continuing patterns of Christian immigration, as well as the immigration of followers of other religions, seem likely to contribute a major impulse of religious vitality as older segments of American Christianity stagnate and decline.

Hispanic, African, and other nonwhite Pentecostals provide a different outlook on what it means to be "evangelical" in America today. These groups are conversionist and intensely supernatural in focus, but they do not have the same political trappings of many white evangelicals in America. At the very least, immigrants' political concerns are not so neatly tied up with the Republican Party as are many white evangelicals'. Franklin Graham and other well-connected GOP activists supplied a ready-made narrative of white evangelical dependence upon the Republican Party. This remained the case even when the party was headed by Donald Trump, whose personal characteristics seemed to contradict evangelical ideals such as marital faithfulness. The fact that 81 percent of self-identifying white evangelical voters supported Trump in the 2016 election gave critics reason to question whether "evangelical" had become a fundamentally political and ethnic category rather than a spiritual one.

Among white evangelicals, political and culture war concerns may not dominate "lived religion" in the ways suggested by media coverage of the culture wars. Most Christians, as well as people of other faiths, do not see their faith as primarily political, even if their beliefs about marriage, abortion, and religious liberty have inescapably political implications. For such people, faith is about the pursuit of God, the search for assurance of grace, the study of sacred scriptures, raising godly families, and the extension of kindness to one's neighbor. Those sources of religious vitality have, undeniably, produced or overlapped with rhetorical rage and political combativeness and occasional outright violence, giving critics ample opportunity to attack American believers' sincerity. Nevertheless, the intensity of American religious zeal shows little sign of waning. In the coming decades, we should expect Americans of differing faiths and of no faith in particular to continue clashing with one another over culture, belief, and the exercise of religion in all its forms.

WORKS CITED
AND FURTHER READING

Adogame, Afe. "The Redeemed Christian Church of God: African Pentecostalism." In *Global Religious Movements Across Borders: Sacred Service*, 35–60. Edited by Stephen M. Cherry and Helen Rose Ebaugh. Burlington, VT: Ashgate, 2014.

Anderson, Ryan T. "Marriage, the Court, and the Future." *Harvard Journal of Law and Public Policy* 40, no. 2 (2017): 361–416.

Bedford, Tori. "Rev. William Barber on DNC Speech, Morality, and the Future of Civil Rights in America." *WGBH News*, Aug. 1, 2016.

Hitchens, Christopher. *God Is Not Great: How Religion Poisons Everything*. New York: Twelve Books, 2007.

Hout, Michael, and Tom W. Smith. "Fewer Americans Affiliate with Organized Religions, Belief and Practice Unchanged." National Opinion Research Center (NORC), March 10, 2015.

Kidd, Thomas S. *American Christians and Islam: Evangelical Culture and Muslims from the Colonial Period to the Age of Terrorism*. Princeton, NJ: Princeton University Press, 2009.

———. *Who Is an Evangelical? The History of a Movement in Crisis*. New Haven, CT: Yale University Press, 2019.

Kruse, Michael. "Marco Rubio's Crisis of Faith." *Politico Magazine*, January 22, 2016. https://www.politico.com/magazine/story/2016/01/marco -rubios-crisis-of-faith-213553.

Lincoln, Bruce. *Holy Terrors: Thinking about Religion Since 9/11*. 2nd ed. Chicago: University of Chicago Press, 2006.

Obama, Barack. *The Audacity of Hope: Thoughts on Reclaiming the American Dream*. New York: Crown, 2006.

Sánchez-Walsh, Arlene. *Pentecostals in America*. New York: Columbia University Press, 2018.

West, Cornel. *Prophesy Deliverance! An Afro-American Revolutionary Christianity*. Anniv. ed. Louisville, KY: Westminster John Knox, 2002.

Index

Abbott, Lyman, 190
Abington School District v. Schempp
(1963), 239–40
abolitionists, 58–59, 78, 116,
125–28, 131–37, 141–42, 230,
245
and the Civil War, 143
criticism of, 135–36
abortion, 243, 246, 249–51, 253–54,
269, 276, 281, 286–87, 294
Abrams, Minnie, 192–93
Abyssinian Baptist Church, 199
Act Concerning Religion (1649), 22,
59
Adams, John, 80–81, 93
Adams, John Quincy, 132
African Americans, 144–45, 179–80,
182–83, 191–92, 197, 208–9,
213, 229–37, 250, 275–76, 280
and African colonization, 73, 133
and the American Revolution, 56,
58–59
churches of, 65, 71–74, 113–18,
132, 146–47, 152, 164–66, 190,
199, 213–14, 223, 287–88
in the Civil War, 141, 143–44, 146

evangelization of, 34, 39–40, 43,
73, 76, 136
and the Great Migration, 164–66,
191
African Baptist Missionary Society,
103
African Methodist Episcopal
Church, 10, 65, 111–12, 126,
134, 146, 182, 191, 232
African Methodist Episcopal Zion
Church, 134
Agassiz, Louis, 171
alcohol, 47, 78, 103, 108–9, 180–81,
277, 280, 282
Ali, Muhammad, 235
Alianza de Ministerios Evangélicos
Nacionales, 274
Allen, John, 54–55
Allen, Richard, 65, 73, 111
Allen, W. B., 144
Alliance Defending Freedom, 277
American Baptist Churches, 146, 241
American Baptist Home Mission
Society, 158–59
American Bible Society, 93–94,
99–100, 106–7, 194

American Board of Commissioners
for Foreign Missions, 92, 94,
98–104, 195–96
American Civil Liberties Union, 212,
239, 264–65
American Colonization Society, 133
American Missionary Association,
146, 160
American Revolution, 9–10, 51–68,
72–73, 103, 130–31, 172
American Sunday School Union, 107,
124
American Temperance Society,
108–9
American Tract Society, 106
American Unitarian Association, 81
Amish, 189
Anabaptists, 29, 189, 202
Anderson, Lucretia, 114
Andover Theological Seminary,
99–100, 102, 107
Andrew, James, 134–35
angels, 34, 42, 44, 87, 214
Anglican Church in North America,
the, 290
Anglicans, 22, 23–24, 27–28, 32–34,
39, 52–52, 56, 60–62, 290
anti-Catholicism, 46–48, 51–52, 96,
138–39, 196–98, 219, 250
anti-Saloon League, 180
anti-Semitism, 154, 198–99, 278
antinomianism, 25, 43
anxious bench, 78, 117, 125
apocalypticism, 34, 83–85, 112, 117,
161, 278–80
Apostolic Assemblies of the Faith in
Christ Jesus, 273
Applewhite, Marshall, 280
Arguinzoni, Sonny, 274
Asbury, Francis, 65

Assemblies of God, 163, 166,
191–92, 196, 217, 258, 273–74,
291
atheists, 57, 172, 211–13, 219, 239,
242, 290–91
Auschwitz, 204
*Awful Disclosures by Maria Monk of
the Hotel Dieu Nunnery* (1836),
96
Azusa Street revival, 163–65, 176,
192, 222–23, 243, 273
Backus, Isaac, 44–45
Bakker, Jim, 272
Balfour Declaration, 190, 198
baptism, 26–27, 45, 76, 102–3, 117,
158
of the Holy Spirit, 163, 165–66,
176, 192, 243
Baptist Triennial Convention, 103,
106, 135–36
Baptists, 25, 27, 33, 54, 70, 81, 84,
93, 95, 107, 111–12, 118, 126,
128, 142, 144, 146–47, 165, 174,
192, 195, 199, 208, 210, 213–14,
216, 222–23, 238–39, 241, 243,
248, 250–52, 256, 258, 261,
281–82, 288
and civil rights, 229, 231–35
and disestablishment, 59–63
and the First Great Awakening, 32,
39, 43–46
and the Second Great Awakening,
71–76
and slavery, 126, 131, 133, 135–36
*See also specific Baptist
denominations*
Barber, William, II, 288–89
Barnard, Thomas, 48
Barrett, Ellen, 289–90
Barrows, John Henry, 166–67

Index

Barth, Karl, 201, 224

Bauer, Gary, 277, 282

Bean, Joseph, 42

Beecher, Lyman, 94–96, 108, 139

Bellah, Robert, 218

Benedict XVI, Pope, 220

Bennett, Dennis, 243

Bethel Bible College, 165

Beveridge, Alfred, 188

Bible Institute of Los Angeles, 179

Bible, 24, 35, 42, 45, 64, 83, 86–87,
    132, 178, 182, 185, 190, 225–26,
    233, 235, 246, 256, 262, 264, 294
  and creationism, 170–71, 263–64
  criticism of, 80–81, 170, 172–78,
    183, 189, 214, 218, 222, 239–40
  and debates over slavery, 128, 133,
    141–42
  and inerrancy, 173, 178, 222–24
  the King James Version of, 58, 159,
    237
  and political rhetoric, 54–55, 61,
    130, 143–44, 207, 235
  proliferation of, 93, 106–7, 194,
    196
  and slave religion, 114–15, 118, 127

Billups, Charles, 233

Billy the Kid, 150

Biola University, 179

Black, Hugo, 238–39

black liberation theology, 236–37,
    241

Blackwell, Antoinette Brown, 175–76

Blessitt, Arthur, 243–44

Bob Jones University, 252–53, 265

Book of Discipline, Methodist, 105

Book of Mormon, 87

Bonaparte, Napoleon, 71

Boston Common, 225

Boston Tea Party, 51

Boxer Rebellion, 194

Brainerd, David, 98–99

Branch Davidians, 278–79

Brandeis, Louis, 198

Briggs, Charles A., 174–75

Bright, Bill, 277

Brown, John, 131, 140–43

Brown vs. Board of Education (1954),
    234

Brownson, Orestes, 96

Brusi, Thaddeus Amat y, 138

Bryan, William Jennings, 185, 188,
    248, 264

Buck, Pearl S., 195

Buckley, William F., 212

Buchanan, Pat, 281

Buddhist Mission of North America,
    157

Buddhists, 157, 166, 202–3, 259, 271

Budenz, Louis, 212

Burchard, J. L., 160

Burned-Over District, 86

Burns, Anthony, 117

Burroughs, Nannie Helen, 182–83

Bush, George H. W., 275, 281–82

Bush, George W., 227, 282–83,
    286–87

Bushnell, Horace, 145

California gold rush, 121, 139, 157

Calvary Chapel, 244–45

Calvin, John, 24

Calvinism, 24, 35, 37–39, 73, 76–77,
    79–80, 141–42, 258

Campbell, Alexander, 83

Campus Crusade for Christ, 270, 277

Cane Ridge Revival, 70, 75–76

Capone, Al, 181

Carey, William, 103

Carroll, John, 95

Carter, Jimmy, 248–50, 252–53

Cary, Lott, 103
Catholic Worker, 201
Catholic Worker movement,
    200–201
Catholics, 28, 45, 55, 64, 92, 95–97,
    119–25, 137–39, 162, 171, 177–78,
    186, 190–91, 197–98, 200–201,
    209–211, 214–15, 219–20,
    237–40, 245, 250, 252, 255–56,
    259, 265, 268–72, 281, 289
    African Americans and, 118–19
    and colonial North America,
        17–21, 36, 46–48, 51
    and communism, 207–8, 212–13
    conflict between, 151–53, 269
    and immigrant communities,
        215–16, 236, 260, 270–71,
        291–92
    and sexual abuse scandals, 220,
        272
    and slavery, 133, 136–37
Cayuses, 101–2
Chak, Fung, 158
Chaldean Catholics, 260–61
Chambers, Whittaker, 212
Channing, William Ellery, 81, 132,
charismatic movement, 243–45, 262,
    272, 275, 279, 291
Charles II, 30
Chávez, César, 237
Cherokee Phoenix, 100
Cherokees, 99–100, 104,
Chickasaws, 99
children, 10, 26–27, 39–40, 45, 74,
    107–8, 161, 196–97, 259, 263,
    265, 269
Chilean revival, 192–93
Chinese Exclusion Act, 157–58
Choctaws, 99
Christian Broadcasting Network, 254

Christian Church (Disciples of
    Christ), 83, 279, 288
Christian Coalition, the, 276–77
Christian Identity movement,
    278–79
Christian and Missionary Alliance,
    190, 192
Christian Missions in Many Lands,
    196
Christian perfection, 78–79
Christian realism, 201
Christianity Today, 223–24, 250
Church of God in Christ, 147,
    165–66, 190–92, 223, 233, 258,
    292
Church of God (Cleveland, Tennes-
    see), 291–92
Church of the Nazarene, 78
Churches of Christ, 75–76, 83, 105,
    190
Chauncy, Charles, 79
"city on a hill," 24
civil religion, 189, 203, 210–13,
    214–15, 217–19, 238–40, 242
civil rights movement, 213–14,
    229–37, 245, 269, 275, 287
Civil War, the, 74, 114, 116, 125,
    130–31, 142–47, 163
Clay, Henry, 133
Clinton, Bill, 281–82, 287
Clinton, Hillary Rodham, 281, 288
Coke, Thomas, 65
Colburn, Mary, 160
Cold War, the, 201, 207–8, 210–13,
    225, 254
colonization, 16–29, 36, 67–68, 71,
    100–101, 188–89, 194
Colson, Charles, 248, 269–70
Columbus, Christopher, 14–15
Cone, James, 236–37, 241

Index

Committee for the Spanish Speaking, 215

Communist Party, the, 211–12

communists, 194, 198–99, 201, 207–8, 211–13, 219, 226, 245, 271

Compromise of 1850, 137

Confucianism, 157

Congregation of the Holy Cross, 107

Congregationalists, 33, 36, 44, 52, 59, 83, 94–95, 99, 102, 137, 146–47, 176, 179, 181, 183, 190, 216,

Congressional Medal of Honor, 190

Connecticut Missionary Society, 99

Connor, Bull, 233

Constitution of the United States, 57, 61, 63, 71, 127, 211, 240, 256–57, 289

and the Eighteenth Amendment, 180

and the Fifteenth Amendment, 230

and the First Amendment, 61, 63, 89, 238–40, 264

and the Fourteenth Amendment, 175, 230

and the Thirteenth Amendment, 230

Continental Congress, the, 52, 57

Cook, Charles, 74

Cooperative Baptist Fellowship, 252

Cox, Harvey, 241

Creeks, 99

Criswell, W. A., 234, 250–51,

Cromwell, Oliver, 53

Crowder, Thomas, 135

Cruz, Nicky, 274

Cumberland Presbyterian Church, 176

D-Day invasion, 203

Dabney, Robert L., 175

Daly, Mary, 241

Darby, John Nelson, 85–86

Dark Day, the, 64–66

Darrow, Clarence, 185

Darwin, Charles, 170

Darwinism, 171–72, 174

Daughters of Charity of St. Vincent de Paul, 121

Davenport, James, 41

Davies, Samuel, 47

Dawkins, Richard, 242

Day, Dorothy, 200–201

death of God theology, 241–42

Declaration of Independence, 52, 57–58, 131

deists, 52, 80, 172, 241

Delaware Indians, 9–10, 47

Dennett, Daniel, 242

Democratic Party, the, 138, 185, 197–98, 248, 275–76, 280–83, 287–89

denominationalism, 146–47

and the First Great Awakening, 43–46

and the Second Great Awakening, 76, 78, 82–86

Department of the Interior, 160

Desiring God, 258

Diego, Juan, 17–18, 270

dispensationalism, 85–86

Dobson, James, 277

Dole, Bob, 282

Dominicans, 17

Douglass, Frederick, 116, 127–28, 132, 143

Drexel, Katherine, 159

Du Bois, W. E. B., 179

Dutch Reformed Church, 28–29, 36, 209

Dwight, Timothy, 92

Eastern Orthodox Christians, 156, 260, 271

Edwards, Jonathan, 36–38, 40, 42, 46, 58, 79, 86, 98, 102, 225

Edwards, Sarah, 42–43

Edwards v. Aguillard, 264, 276

Eisenhower, Dwight, 203, 210, 217–18, 227

Eliot, John, 14, 99

Elliot, Jim, 196

Elizabeth I, 21

Elkhorn Association of Baptists, 76

Elmore, Grace Brown, 145

Emancipation Proclamation, 143

Emerson, Ralph Waldo, 81–82

Emmons, Nathanael, 102

Employment Division v. Smith (1990), 276

Engel v. Vitale (1962), 238–40

England, John, 133

English Baptist Missionary Society, 103

Enlightenment, the, 60

Episcopalians, 106, 199, 216, 243, 257, 275, 289–90

Epperson v. Arkansas, 263–64

Equal Rights Amendment, 249, 253–56

Evangelical Lutheran Church in America, 124, 216, 257

evangelicals, 32–33, 35, 40–41, 44, 52, 76, 83, 93, 114–16, 125–26, 130, 140, 163–64, 172, 178–80, 190, 192–94, 196, 208–10, 215, 221–26, 243–45, 257–58, 262–66, 269–70, 292

and political activism, 226–27, 239–40, 242–43, 246, 248–55, 275–78, 280–83, 286–87, 289, 294–95

"Evangelicals and Catholics Together" (1994), 269–70

Everson v. Board of Education (1947), 238–39

evolutionary theory, 170–72, 174, 185–86, 263

Executive Order 9066, 202

Falwell, Jerry, Sr., 243, 251–54, 256, 275, 286

Family Research Council, 277, 282

Federal Bureau of Alcohol, Tobacco, and Firearms, 278–79

Federal Bureau of Investigation, 279

Federal Council of Churches, 191, 222

Federalist Papers, 106

Federalists, 63

Female Society for Missionary Purposes, 102

feminist theology, 241

Finney, Charles, 77–79, 107, 117, 127

First Great Awakening, 32–46, 59–60, 79, 207, 226, 258

First Things, 269

Flushing Remonstrance, 29

Focus on the Family, 277

Ford, Gerald, 249

Ford, Henry, 199

Fox News Channel, 287

Francis I, Pope, 19

Franciscans, 18–19, 30, 67, 119

Frank, J. H., 180

Franklin, Aretha, 192

Franklin, Benjamin, 39, 48, 52, 80, 92, 172

Franklin, C. L., 192

Franklin, William, 48

Freewill Baptists, 73, 77

Frelinghuysen, Theodorus, 36

Fuller, Charles, 223–24

Fuller, Daniel, 224
fundamentalists, 125, 178–80, 189–90, 216, 221, 239–40, 252–55, 264–65, 278
Fundamentals, The (1920), 179, 184
fur trade, 20
Galagina (Elias Boudinot), 99–100, 104
Gallup polling, 249
Gam, Jee, 159
Gandhi, Mohandas, 195, 214
Garrison, William Lloyd, 127, 132
gay marriage, 272, 278, 287, 289, 294
General Synod of Lutheran Churches, 124
George, David, 73, 111, 133
German Reformed Church, 125
Ghost Dance, 161
Gilruth, James, 95
Gingrich, Newt, 281–82
Gladden, Washington, 183
Glorious Revolution, the, 29, 46
Gnadenhütten massacre, the, 9–10
Gore, Al, 282–83
Gospel Coalition, the, 258
gospel music, 191–92, 245
Graham, Billy, 86, 164, 199, 207–8, 210, 219, 221–22, 223–27, 234, 242, 248, 252–54, 270–71, 286
Graham, Franklin, 286–87, 294
Grant, Ulysses, 159, 164
Gray, Asa, 171
Great Depression, the, 199–202, 208, 231
Gregory XVI, Pope, 133
Haggard, Ted, 272
Hale-Bopp comet, 280
Halfway Covenant, 26–27
Hamer, Fannie Lou, 213
Hamilton, Alexander, 51–52

Hampton Institute, 146
Harvard University, 22, 35–36, 52, 107, 171, 179, 195, 209, 241, 250, 288
Haselby, Sam, 93
Hasseltine, Ann, 102–3
Haynes, Lemuel, 58, 125, 131,
Hearst, William Randolph, 226
heaven, 14, 43, 76, 116, 190, 236
Heaven's Gate, 279–80
hell, 24, 37–38, 76, 97, 117–18, 158, 231, 262
Henry, Carl, 223–24
Henry, Patrick, 54–55, 62,
Herberg, Will, 218, 259
Heritage Foundation, 252, 277
Hiacoomes, 14
Higginson, Thomas Wentworth, 141
Hindus, 166, 195, 259, 268
Hitchens, Christopher, 291
Hite, Elizabeth Ross, 118–19
Hitschler, Cynthia, 20
Hocking, William, 195
Hodge, Charles, 108, 172–73
Holbrook, Robert, 251
Holiness movement, 78–79, 108, 147, 162–66, 186
Holocaust, the, 154–55, 198, 204
Holy Fairs, 74
Holy Spirit, the, 25, 33, 35, 37–45, 73–74, 79, 81, 95, 160, 173, 176, 243–45
Home School Legal Defense Association, 265
homeschooling, 265–66
homosexuality, 124, 272, 276, 281, 286, 289–90
Hoover, Herbert, 198
Hoover, Willis, 192
Hope, Bob, 242

Hopkins, Samuel, 43
Hosier, Harry, 65, 73
House Committeeon Un-American
    Activities, 211
Howe, Julia Ward, 143
Hughes, John, 121
Huguenots, 28,
Humanae vitae (1968), 269
Hunt, H. L., 179
Hurons, 20;
Hutchinson, Anne, 25–26,
Iglesia Metodista Pentecostal, 192
immigration, 24, 67, 95, 120–24,
    138, 140, 150–67, 180, 189,
    197, 215, 220, 258–61, 271–74,
    292–94
Immigration Act of 1965, 158
Inglis, Charles, 56
Institute for Creation Research, 264
Interdenominational Mexican
    Council of Christian Churches
    (Pentecostal), 163
Internal Revenue Service, 253
International Church of the Four-
    square Gospel, 177, 191, 244
International Jew, The, 199
Intolerable Acts, 51
Iran-Iraq War, 261
Iranian revolution, 259
Ireland, James, 60
Ireland, John, 177
Iroquois, 20
Israel, 154, 190, 198
Jackson, Andrew, 100, 104
Jackson, Jesse, 275–76, 287
Jackson, J. H., 232
Jackson, Mahalia, 192
James, William, 209
Jamestown colony, 21–22
Japanese internment, 202–3

Jay, John, 106
Jefferson, Mildred, 250
Jefferson, Thomas, 52, 57, 59–62, 71,
    80–82, 89, 107, 128, 172, 238
Jehovah's Witnesses, 189, 202
Jemison, T. J., 231–33
Jenkins, Jerry, 278
Jesuits, 20–21, 28–29, 36, 102,
    121–22, 241
Jesus Christ, 22, 35, 37, 43, 56–57,
    73, 79–81, 87, 94–95, 112,
    115–17, 125, 128, 143–44, 160,
    164, 173–74, 177–79, 181, 184,
    194, 207–8, 213–14, 224–25,
    234, 242, 246, 255, 275, 282,
    286, 288
Jesus movement, 243–245, 273, 277
Jesus Seminar, 173
Jewish Theological Seminary,
    155–56, 198
Jews, 64, 67, 139–40, 154–56, 175,
    189, 197–99, 204, 211, 214,
    217–18, 220, 238–39, 242, 252,
    259, 269
    in colonial North America, 25,
    28–29
    Orthodox, 154–55, 198, 217, 259,
    282
    Reform, 155, 198, 217
    and revivalism, 97–98
jihadist terrorism, 10, 259, 283,
    285–86, 289
Jim Crow, 230–36
Jones, Absalom, 65
Jones, E. Stanley, 195
Jones, Evan, 104
Jones, Bob, Jr., 252–53, 265
Judeo-Christian tradition. *See* civil
    religion
Judson, Adoniram, 102–3

Kansas-Nebraska Act, 141
Kapiolani, Chiefess, 101
Kellogg, John Harvey, 85
Kennedy, John F., 24, 219, 281
Kenyon, E. W., 208–9
Khomeini, Ayatollah, 259
King, Martin Luther, Jr., 182,
    213–14, 229–33, 235–36, 239,
    242, 275, 287–88
King Philip (Metacom), 14
King Phillip's War, 14, 27
Kingsley, Bathsheba, 43
Koop, C. Everett, 251–52, 254
Koresh, David, 278–79
Know-Nothings, 138
Ku Klux Klan, 197–98, 230–31,
    233–35
Kuan Ti, 157
LaHaye, Tim, 278
Lakotas, 161
Lamy, Jean Baptiste, 121, 138
Lankford, Sarah, 79
Las Casas, Bartolomé de, 17
Lathrop, Mary, 44
Lawrence v. Texas (2003), 289
Laymen's Foreign Missions Inquiry,
    195
Lazarus, Emma, 154
Le Jau, Francis, 34
League of Nations, 191
Lee, Ann, 65–66
Lee, Jarena, 78
Lee, Robert E., 141
Leeser, Isaac, 97–98
Lemon v. Kurtzman (1981), 240
Leo XIII, Pope, 171
Lewinsky, Monica, 281
Liberator, The, 127
Lieberman, Joe, 282
Lincoln, Abraham, 130, 142–44

Lincoln, Mary Todd, 142
Lindsell, Harold, 224
Lindsey, Hal, 278
Livermore, Harriet, 78
Locke, John, 53, 57, 60–61
López, Abundio and Rosa, 176
Lord, Benjamin, 44
Lord's Supper, the, 24, 26–27, 33,
    124–25, 152
Louisbourg campaign, 46
Louisiana Baptist Association, 71
Louisiana Purchase, 70, 94
Luce, Henry, 226
Luther, Martin, 17
Lutheran Church—Missouri Synod,
    124, 216
Lutherans, 29, 34, 67, 124, 151, 174,
    186, 197, 200, 216, 243
Luu, Thich Dam, 271
Lynchburg Christian Academy, 253
lynching, 88, 112, 230–31
Macartney, Clarence, 196
Machen, J. Gresham, 184–85, 221
Madison, James, 60–64
mainline Protestantism, 83, 146,
    186, 191, 207, 209, 211, 213,
    216, 221–22, 239, 243, 246, 254,
    256–58, 262, 289–91
Malcolm X, 235–36
manifest destiny, 119–21
March on Washington, 235
Maronites, 260
Marsh v. Chambers (1983), 240
Mason, Charles H., 165, 190
Mason, George, 61
Massachusetts Missionary Society, 99
Matthews, J. B., 211
Mayflower Compact, 23
McCarthy, Joseph, 211
McCartney, Bill, 277

McCormack, John, 219
McCosh, James, 171–72
McCoy, Isaac, 103–4
McGready, James, 74
McIntire, Carl, 240
McKinley, William, 188
McPherson, Aimee Semple, 177, 191,
    244
McVeigh, Timothy, 279
Mecca, 236
megachurches, 261–62, 272
Melville, Herman, 101
Mennonites, 189
Mercersburg theology, 125
Methodists, 64–65, 70, 72–77, 78, 81,
    83, 93, 95, 111, 118, 126, 146–47,
    163, 188, 211–12, 216, 250
  and the civil rights movement,
    232, 234
  and slavery, 131, 134–35
Methodist Missionary Society, 105
Mexican-American War, 95, 119–21
Mexican Revolution, 162
Michaux, Lightfoot Solomon, 208–9
Micmacs, 16
millenarianism, 66, 83–86, 145
Miller, William, 84–85, 117
Mills, Samuel, 93
Miracle Sunday, 233
Miranda, Jesse, 274
missionaries, 139, 286
  African American, 100–101, 103,
    105
  Anglican, 34, 38–40, 52, 72
  Baptist, 32, 102–6, 135–36, 158,
    193, 286–87
  Catholic, 17–20, 27, 36, 67, 102–3,
    150–51, 159
  Congregationalist, 38, 93, 98–99,
    102, 159

criticism of, 101, 105–6
  Methodist, 64–65, 105, 109, 158,
    160, 192–95
  Native American, 104
  Pentecostal, 191–93, 292–93
  Presbyterian, 32–33, 158, 184, 194
  Puritan, 13, 99
  Quaker, 29
missions
  domestic, 98–100, 103–5, 106–9,
    146, 158–62, 274
  foreign, 100–103, 157, 192–96, 270
modernists, 125, 155, 166–67,
    173–75, 178–80, 183–86,
    189–91, 195–96, 211–12, 214,
    221–22, 238–39, 241, 280
Mohawks, 20
Mohegans, 56
Mohler, Albert, 258
Montgomery bus boycott, 214, 231–32
Moody, Anne, 235
Moody Bible Institute, 163–64
Moody, Dwight, 86, 163–64
Moon, Lottie, 193
Moore, Raymond and Dorothy, 265
Moral Majority, 243, 246, 251–53,
    275–76
Moravians, 9–10,
Mormons, 86–89, 101, 255, 287, 292
Morris, Henry, 263–64
Mott, John R., 194
Mountain of Fire and Miracles
    Ministries, 293
Muhammad, 287
Muhammad, Elijah, 235–36
Muhammad, Wali Fard, 235
Murray, Madalyn, 239
Muslims, 16, 166, 235–36, 259–61,
    268, 271, 285–87, 289
Narragansetts, 44

Index

Nation of Islam, 235–36

National Association for the Advancement of Colored People, 232

National Association of Evangelicals, 222–23, 250, 252, 272

National Baptist Convention, 147, 182, 223, 231–33

National Black Evangelical Association, 223

National Council of Churches, 222

National Day of Prayer, 210

National Hispanic Christian Leadership Conference, 274

National Right to Life Committee, 250

National Training School for Women and Girls, 182

Native Americans, 15–16, 36, 39, 47–48, 56, 150, 276

   conflict between colonists and, 13, 22, 27, 46–48

   displacement of, 70, 100, 103–4, 137

   evangelization of, 13–14, 17–19, 34, 44, 67, 98–100, 103–4, 159–61

   See also specific tribes

nativism, 138, 157–58, 196–97, 286–87

Nazis, 201–2, 204

Neff, Lawrence, 234

Neolin, 47

neoorthodoxy, 201

Nettles, Bonnie Lu, 280

Neuhaus, Richard John, 269–70

Nevin, John Williamson, 125

New Age thought, 279–80

New Atheists, the, 291

New Divinity, the, 58, 98–99, 102

New Thought, 208–10, 216

Niebuhr, Reinhold, 182, 201–2, 204, 212, 222, 248

Niles, Samuel, 44

Nixon, Richard, 199, 219, 242, 248–49, 252

nones, 290

Noriega, José de la Guerra y, 121

Norman, Larry, 245–46

Notre Dame, University of, 107, 171, 212, 243

nuclear weapons, 202–4, 207

Obama, Barack, 276, 287–88

Obergefell v. Hodges (2015), 289

Occom, Samson, 56

Ockenga, Harold John, 222–24, 226

O'Connor, Sandra Day, 254

Oklahoma City bombing, 279, 286

Olasky, Marvin, 283

Olazábal, Francisco, 162–63

O'Neill, Tip, 219

Operation PUSH, 275

Orsi, Robert, 153

Orthodox Presbyterian Church, 184–85, 221

Ortiz, Ramón, 119–20

Osages, 99

Osborn, Sarah, 43

Osteen, Joel and Victoria, 262

Ottawa Indians, 103

Oxnam, G. Bromley, 211–12

Ozman, Agnes, 165

pacifism, 189, 202

Padilla de Armas, Encarnación, 215–16

Paine, Thomas, 54–55, 57, 142, 172, 291

Palmer, Phoebe, 78, 108

Parents Music Resource Center, 282

Parham, Charles Fox, 165

Parker, Theodore, 141
Parks, Rosa, 231–32
Paul, the apostle, 13
Paul II, Pope John, 18, 269–70, 272
Paul VI, Pope, 269
Payne, Daniel Alexander, 146
Peale, Norman Vincent, 209
Pearl Harbor, 202
Penitentes, 138–39
Penn, William, 30
Pentecostal Church of God, 216
Pentecostals, 147, 162–66, 176–77,
    186, 189–93, 196, 215–16,
    222–23, 226, 243–46, 253,
    257–58, 261–62, 291–92
  and immigrant communities,
    163–64, 167, 176, 257–58, 260,
    270–71, 272–74, 292–95
People's Temple, 279–80
Pepperell, William, 46
Pequot War, 13
Pew, J. Howard, 179
Philadelphia Baptist Association, 45
Pierce v. Society of Sisters (1925), 197
Pilgrims. *See* Separatists (Pilgrims)
Piper, John, 258
Pius X, Pope, 178
Pius XII, Pope, 171
Plymouth Brethren, 196
Pocahontas, 21
Polish National Catholic Church, 153
Pontiac's Rebellion, 47
Pontifical Biblical Commission, 171
Popé, 18–19
poverty, 40, 94, 180–82, 196,
    199–200, 262
Poverty Point, 15
Powell, Adam Clayton, Sr., 199
Powell, Adam Clayton, Jr., 199
Powhatan Indians, 21

Prayer Meeting Revival, the, 140
Presbyterian Church in America, 258
Presbyterian Church (USA), 221, 257
Presbyterians, 33, 35, 52, 95, 108,
    140, 166, 171–72, 174–76, 178,
    184–86, 196, 216, 221, 243, 251
  and the First Great Awakening, 32,
    36, 39
  and the Second Great Awakening,
    74–77
  and slavery, 131, 134, 146
Presley, Elvis, 192
Primitive Baptists, 105–6
Princeton Theological Seminary, 108,
    124, 171–72, 184, 221
Princeton University, 22, 38, 101,
    171, 184, 288
Progressive National Baptist Conven-
    tion, 233
prohibition, 180–81
Promise Keepers, 277
prosperity gospel, 209, 262, 287
Protestant Interest, the, 46–48
Protestant Reformation, 17, 21,
    23–24
Protocols of the Elders of Zion, The
    (1905), 199
public education, 107, 185, 197,
    237–40, 263. *See also* religious
    education
Pueblo Indians, 18–19
Puritans, 23–28, 53, 80, 92, 141
Quakers, 26, 28–29, 33, 43, 45, 82,
    175, 189, 202, 212
Quebec Act, 51–52
radio, 192, 208–210, 214, 222–23,
    225
Rale, Sebastien, 36
Rauschenbusch, Walter, 181–83
Re-Thinking Missions (1932), 195–96

Reagan, Ronald, 24, 252–54, 263, 274
Reconstruction, 164, 230
Red Cross, the, 196
Redeemed Christian Church of God, 293–94
Reed, Ralph, 276
Rehnquist, William, 264
religious conversion, 17, 20–21, 32–36, 44, 72–78, 84, 95, 101, 103–5, 117–18, 125, 130, 140, 158–60, 162–63, 212, 226, 229, 242, 248, 271, 277, 282, 288
religious decline, 26–27, 33–35, 72, 220, 257, 271, 291
religious education, 35–36, 96–97, 99, 100, 107, 150–51, 155–56, 159, 163–65, 174–75, 179, 182–83, 197–98, 211, 221, 223–24, 237–38, 253, 264–66, 271
Religious Freedom Restoration Act (1993), 276
Religious liberty, 22–27, 29–30, 59–64, 89, 172, 197, 220, 276–77, 287, 294
Religious persecution and violence, 9–10, 29, 36, 46–48, 60, 71, 88, 96, 120–21, 123–25, 138, 161, 202
Religious practices
ancestor worship, 16
celibacy, 66
convulsions, 75–76
fasting, 57
glossolalia, 163, 165–66, 192, 222–23, 243–45
interpreting signs, 36, 64–66, 83–85, 190
music, 114–16, 143, 145, 152, 160, 191–92, 245, 262

prayer, 42–44, 46, 48, 57, 73, 77, 114, 160, 214, 230, 238, 240, 246, 254, 263–64, 286
preaching, 35–39, 40–42, 64–65, 71–79, 95, 97, 114, 164, 214, 225, 244
repentance, 29, 38, 97
trances, dreams, and visions 42–44, 112, 118, 192
séances, 142
veneration of relics, 56
religious print, 38–39, 106, 278
Republican Party, the, 138, 208, 219, 226–27, 240, 242, 248–49, 252–54, 266, 275–76, 280–83, 287, 289, 292, 294
Revista Católica, 121
Reynolds v. United States (1879), 89, 238
Rice, John R., 222
Robertson, Pat, 254, 275–76, 282, 286
Robinson, Gene, 290
Robinson, Jo Ann, 232
Rockefeller, John D., 195
Rodriguez, Samuel, 274, 287
Roe v. Wade (1973), 243, 246, 250, 252, 254, 266
Rolfe, John, 21
Romanticism, 137, 145
Romney, Mitt, 287
Roosevelt, Eleanor, 200
Roosevelt, Franklin, 281
Rose, Ernestine, 175
Round Valley Indian Reservation, 159–60
Rove, Karl, 287
Rowlandson, Mary, 14
Sabbath, 30, 63, 139–40, 160
Salem witchcraft controversy, 28

Salvation Army, the, 180, 200
Sandy Creek Baptist Church, 45
Sankey, Ira, 163–64
Santa Maria Institute, 151
Scalia, Antonin, 264
Schaeffer, Francis, 246, 251–52
Schaff, Philip, 125
Schechter, Solomon, 155, 198
Schlafly, Phyllis, 255–56
Schleiermacher, Friedrich, 173–74
Schmucker, Samuel, 124
Schuller, Robert, 216
Scofield Reference Bible, 86
Scopes, John, 185, 264
Scopes Trial, 178–79, 185, 221, 263
Scottish Covenanters, 28
Sears, Milton, 213
Second Great Awakening, 70–90, 94,
    98, 117, 226, 245
secularists, 211–12, 218, 240–42,
    251, 266, 280–81
secularization theory, 268
Segale, Blandina, 150–52
Segale, Justina, 151
segregation, 113, 117, 231–35, 253
Seixas, Moses, 64
Seneca Falls convention, 175
Senzaki, Nyogen, 202
separation of church and state. *See*
    religious liberty.
Separate Baptists, 44–46, 59–60
Separatists (Pilgrims), 23
September 11, 2011, 10, 259, 278,
    283, 285–86
Sequoya, 100
Serra, Junipero, 19,
Seton, Elizabeth Ann, 95, 150, 159
settlement houses, 151
700 Club, The, 275, 286
Seven Years' War, 46–48, 51–52;

Seventh-Day Adventists, 85, 140,
    189, 197, 202, 278–79
Seymour, William J., 165
Shaftsbury Baptist Association, 73
Shakers, 65–66, 83
Shea, George Beverly, 164
Sheen, Fulton J., 210, 212
Sheldon, Charles, 181
Sherman, Roger, 52
Sherman, William T., 144
Shintoism, 157
Sierra Leone, 73
Sikhs, 10, 157–58
Simpson, A. B., 190, 192
Sisters of the Blessed Sacrament for
    Indians and Colored People, 159
Sisters of Charity, 95, 150
Sisters of Charity of Nazareth, 96
Sisters of Loretto, 96
Sitting Bull, 161
slavery, 58–59, 111–19, 130–37,
    140–42
    Christian support of, 34, 40, 74,
       111–12, 114, 126–28, 131–37
    and hush harbors, 114, 116–17,
       126–27
    of Indians, 17, 20, 136
    and Islam, 16
    and traditional African religion,
       16, 28, 119
Smith, Alfred E., 197–98, 219
Smith, Arthur, 194
Smith, Chuck, 244
Smith, Daniel, 93
Smith, Joseph, 86–88
social gospel movement, 164,
    180–84, 189, 211
Society for the Propagation of the
    Gospel in Foreign Parts (SPG),
    34, 52

Society of St. Vincent de Paul, 200
Sola Scriptura, 93
Southern Baptist Convention, 106,
   136, 146–47, 174, 186, 193, 196,
   214, 216, 221, 234, 249–52,
   261–62, 286–87, 291
   conservative resurgence within the,
   256–58
   sexual abuse scandals within the,
   272
Southern Christian Leadership
   Conference, 232
Speer, Robert, 194
Stanton, Elizabeth Cady, 176
Stamp Act, the, 53–54
Starr, Kenneth, 281
Stead, William, 181
Stearns, Shubal, 45
Stewart, John, 105
Stewart, Lyman, 179
Stockbridge Indians, 38
Stockton, Betsey, 100–101
Stoddard, Solomon, 36
Stone, Barton, 75, 83
Stowe, Harriet Beecher, 96, 131, 137,
   278
Strauss, David, 173
Stringfellow, Thornton, 128, 133
Student Volunteer Movement, 194,
suburbanization, 215–18, 226, 261
Sulpicians, 96–97
Sumner, Charles, 132
Sunday, Billy, 190
Sunday schools, 107, 200, 249
Supreme Court, the, 63, 89, 100,
   106, 197–98, 219, 238–40, 250,
   254, 263–64, 276, 287, 289
Swaggart, Jimmy, 272
Taoists, 157
Tastheghetehee, 104

Tekakwitha, Catherine, 20–21
televangelists, 272
television, 208, 210, 214, 225, 233,
   254, 262, 272, 275, 281, 286–87
temperance, 94, 108–9, 137, 160, 245
Tennent, Gilbert, 36, 41–42
Tharpe, Rosetta, 191–92
Thurman, Howard, 213–14, 236
Time (magazine), 226, 242
Tolton, Augustus, 118
Town of Greece v. Galloway (2014), 240
Toy, Crawford, 174–75
transcendentalists, 82, 96
Truman, Harry, 207
Trump, Donald, 210, 274, 287–89, 294
Tufts University, 242
Turner, Nat, 112–13, 125–28,
   131–32, 143
Union Theological Seminary, 174–75,
   201, 212, 222, 236, 288
Unitarian Universalist Association, 81
Unitarians, 80–82, 93, 107, 132, 141,
   171, 214, 239
United Church of Christ (UCC), 83
United Farm Workers, 237
United Methodist Church, 221,
   254–55, 257, 262
United Nations, 191
universalists, 79, 81, 183
urbanization, 108, 180, 230, 241
Vahanian, Gabriel, 241
Vatican II, 219–20, 268–69
Verot, Augustin, 136
Vesey, Denmark, 10, 111–12, 143, 146
Victory Outreach, 274
Vines, Jerry, 287
Vineyard churches, 244–45, 277
Virgin Mary, the, 153
Our Lady of Guadalupe, 17–18, 122,
   162, 237, 270

Virginia Declaration of Rights, 57, 61
Walker, David, 126–27
Walla Wallas, 101–2
Wallace, Anthony F. C., 268
Wampanoag Indians, 13–14
Waorani Indians, 196
War of 1812, 103
War on Terror, 261, 286
Ward, Harry F., 212
Warren, Rick, 261
Washington, Booker T., 116
Washington, George, 63–64, 285
Weaver, Randy, 278–79
Webb, Mary, 102
Weld, Theodore Dwight, 127
Wells, Ida B., 230–31
Wesley, Charles, 64–65
Wesley, John, 39, 64–65, 72, 134, 225
Wesleyan Church, 78, 134
West, Cornel, 288
Westminster Confession of Faith, 76
Weyrich, Paul, 252–53
Wheatley, Phillis, 40, 125
Whig Party, 138
White, Ellen, 85
white supremacists, 112–13, 230–31, 278
Whitefield, George, 38–42, 46, 56, 163, 207–8, 225
Whitman, Marcus and Narcissa, 101–2
Whitman, Walt, 82
Wiesel, Elie, 204
Wilhelm II, 190
Wilkerson, David, 274
Wilkinson, Jemima, 65–66
Willard, Frances, 180
William and Mary (monarchs), 27
Williams, Roger, 25–26,
Willis, Joseph, 71–73

Willke, John, 250
Wilson, Woodrow, 189–91
Wimber, John, 244–45
Winners' Chapel, 293
Winthrop, John, 24, 26, 203
Wise, Rabbi Isaac Mayer, 198
Woosley, Louisa, 176
Worcester, Samuel, 100
Worcester v. Georgia (1832), 100
World Vision, 196
World War I, 154, 164, 189–91, 198
World War II, 156, 165, 198, 201–4, 231
World's Columbian Exposition, 181
World's Parliament of Religions, 166, 178, 181
women, 25–26, 29, 40, 42–44, 137, 142, 154, 162–63, 191–92, 213, 215, 250
    and church leadership, 65–66, 78–79, 116–17, 176–77, 254, 256, 289–90
    and the Civil War, 137, 143, 145
    and missions, 100–103, 150–51, 158–60, 192–93
    and social reform, 108–9, 180, 182–83, 230–32, 235
    political rights of, 175–76, 254–56
    traditionalist Christian teaching on, 42, 241, 255–57
Women's Christian Temperance Union, 180
Women's Political Council of Montgomery, 232
Woodmason, Charles, 32–33, 46, 53
Wounded Knee massacre, 161
Wright, J. Elwin, 223
Wright, Jeremiah, 287–88
Wyandots, 105
Wycliffe Bible Translators, 196

Yale University, 22, 35–36, 92, 145, 212
York, Alvin, 190
Young, Brigham, 88–89
Young Men's Buddhist Association, 157
Young Men's Christian Association, 157–58

Young Women's Christian Association, 200
Youth for Christ, 225
Yukis, 160
Zahm, John, 171, 177
Zionism, 190, 198